# Prologue

Picture the scene. It's a cold and wet November in 1993 and two young men are stood in the cramped and smoky manager's office of Tokyo Joe's, a nightclub in Preston. It's six o'clock in the evening, and they each take a pair of extremely baggy jeans and an ill-fitting Day-glo shirt out of their Head sports bag.

*They make their way towards the dancefloor, where a grumpy and overweight DJ is introducing them as the star attraction at the Tuesday-afternoon under-18s disco. Hidden behind the DJ booth, the young men take a quick peek at their audience. It's predominantly made up of thirteen-year-old schoolgirls, some of whom have dragged their boyfriends along. The intrepid performers step out on to a sticky dancefloor and spend the next three and a half minutes miming to their one and only single, while dancing as best they can in shirts and jeans made for men twice their size. For the entire performance, the assembled schoolgirls let out ear-splitting screams, while their boyfriends offer a slightly different response: they hurl ice cubes and ashtrays – and, when they've run out of them, start spitting at the two young men.*

Exhausted from the effort of dodging such missiles while lip-synching, the two retreat to the manager's office to get changed. One of them turns to the other, and says,

*'Why the hell do we do these things?'*

'Look on the bright side,' the other one replies. 'It's one for the book.'

*Well, those two young men were us – Ant and Dec.*
*And this is that book.*

*Before we go any further, we should explain one thing: when you see words in italics, that's me, Ant.*

**And when you see them in bold, that's me, Dec.**

*So that's Ant – italics.*

**And Dec – bold.**

*Got it? Good.*

*This year, 2009, is the twentieth year the two of us have spent working together and, for the last two decades, whenever something embarrassing happens, whenever something we're proud of happens, whenever something pinch-yourself-unbelievable happens, we turn to each other and say, 'One for the book.'*

**Whether it was attempting to do the Junior Great North Run in Newcastle dressed as Teenage Mutant Ninja Turtles, swinging punches at each other in a Torremolinos hotel lift, trying to talk our way out of singing a cappella in Indonesia, chastising John Lydon in the middle of an Australian rainforest, or pretending not to be drunk in front of Victoria Beckham and Eva Longoria, sometimes it seems like we've been saying 'One for the book' on a daily basis. In fact, we realized we'd said it so much, it was about time we actually wrote that book – so here it is.**

# Chapter 1

I lay on the sofa, and I just kept thinking the same thing:

'It could have been me.

It should have been me.

I should have been the *Geordie Racer.*'

What am I talking about? Well, picture, if you will, a little fella called Declan Donnelly. You're thinking about how I look *now*, aren't you? But I mean a smaller Declan Donnelly. Nope, smaller than that. That's better. Think of a child who was desperate to be an actor. Well, in 1987, that was me, and that was when I went for my very first audition – for a children's drama called *Geordie Racer.* It was part of the BBC schools programme *Look and Read*, which, as those of you who grew up in the eighties will recall, featured a strange floating figure called Wordy. If you didn't grow up in the eighties, you'll have no idea what I'm talking about – look it up on the internet. Not now though, you've only just started the book – honestly, what's the matter with you?

The hero of *Geordie Racer* was Spuggy Hilton. Apparently, 'Spuggy' is short for 'sparrow', and young Spuggy kept pigeons. I know, sparrows, pigeons, it's not exactly *The Bourne Ultimatum*, but what can I say? It was the eighties – a time when stories were basic, tastes were simple and pigeons were at the heart of an entire drama.

At the audition, I got down to the last two, which meant the *Geordie Racer* would be me, or . . . someone else. Then I got the phone call every actor dreads – the phone call telling me the other lad had got the part. I can't remember his name now, I never met him, but if he's reading this, well done for being a better pigeon-fancier than me.

Not getting *Geordie Racer* broke my little heart, I don't mind

3

telling you. I cried for days – yes, days. You know what actors are like – and if you don't, let me tell you: neurotic, insecure and self-obsessed. In short, I was born for it.

Although, looking back, I think it was destiny I didn't get the part of the kid who kept pigeons.

*Yeah, because every actor should experience rejection.*

No, because I'm terrified of birds – I don't know what I was thinking; to this day I still can't go near the ostriches during the Bushtucker Trials on *I'm a Celebrity . . . Get Me out of Here!* God knows how I would have managed to spend days on end surrounded by pigeons as a mere child.

After that crushing rejection, I made a momentous decision: that was it – I was going to retire from acting. I was eleven.

Then, something happened, something that changed my mind and enticed me back into the world of showbusiness. I got a letter. As you can imagine, it was exciting enough just to get a letter at that age – no one really writes to kids, after all. And this was no ordinary letter; it was from Sue Weeks, the producer of *Geordie Racer*. She wrote that, even though I hadn't got the part, she thought I had something, that I could make it as an actor and that I should stick at it. She said I should try again if another part came up. That letter made a huge difference, someone had shown faith in me, and I made my second momentous decision: I was coming out of retirement. I was still eleven.

*He may have been sensitive enough to have his heart broken by rejection, but Dec's story fails to mention one thing – he's a complete and utter show-off, and always has been, which is why he was desperate to have the part. When it came to performing, I, on the other hand, wasn't always so keen, and that's because I like to think I'm a much more balanced individual. I'm probably not, but I like to think I am. Don't get me wrong, I still performed as a child and, by the age of eleven, I had a complete set of impressions and jokes that went down a storm with the whole audience . . . of my mates . . . in the playground. Despite that, when it came to showing off in front of people I'd never met, things weren't so easy. I was a bit like an old car – I needed a bit of a push to get going.*

*That push came from my drama teacher, Lynne Spencer. Obviously she was Mrs Spencer at the time, but you can use teachers' first names once you've left school, can't you?*

*I used to love drama lessons, and Lynne constantly encouraged me, praised me, and then put me up for an audition without telling me. It was my first ever audition, and I beat one other kid to get the part.*

**I knew it –** *you* **were the** *Geordie Racer* **. . .**

*No, I wasn't the* Geordie Racer.

*My audition was for the BBC kids' show* Why Don't You?, *although I don't think Lynne actually said, 'Why Don't You . . . audition for . . . Why Don't You?' That would've been silly and confusing. The producers went round schools all over Newcastle looking for kids to cast over the summer holidays, and so, when they arrived at my school, Rutherford Comprehensive, I decided to go for it. Or, to be more precise, Lynne decided I should go for it. As I stepped on to the stage in the assembly hall, I felt nervous, but at the same time I thought it was just a bit of a laugh, it wasn't going to lead to anything. Plus, there were other people on the stage, so it wasn't like everyone was looking at just me.*

*For the audition, we had to improvise a scene for the producers, and the theme they gave us was transport.*

*Reading this, you're probably thinking, 'Transport, eh? I wonder what the young Ant McPartlin did with that – was he the captain of a ship, perhaps? A racing driver maybe? Or even an airline pilot?*

*Guess again.*

*I was a drunk.*

*What's a drunk got to do with transport? You might well ask, but that was the genius of my performance: I was a drunk on a bus.*

*Much to my surprise, I got the part. I'm not sure if the producers were drunk as well, but they gave me the job on* Why Don't You?, *and suddenly my career was on its way.*

*Along with the other kids in* Why Don't You?, *I spent the summer filming on a double-decker bus, although I never once got to pretend to be drunk on that bus, which seemed a shame after my audition. But it was brilliant: I learnt lines, I performed to camera, and I felt like I'd well and truly arrived, which – being on a bus that constantly moved around – I often had.*

*I was convinced I'd found my calling; I would perform for the rest of my life. Then, one earth-shattering event changed all of that. I went back to school.*

*On* Why Don't You?, *I'd often been the butt of the jokes, and had been portrayed as a bit of an idiot, and that didn't help when I was back in class. The other kids were jealous, and they teased me. A lot. They'd call me a knob, or an idiot, or say they'd 'seen me acting like a tit on the telly'. To be honest, it put me off the idea of performing. It's that thing that's happened to us all at one time or another in our schooldays: you get teased for something – it could be a stupid question you ask a teacher or a pair of trousers you're wearing – and you grow to hate that thing, it makes you want to make sure you never do it again. Well, that was how I felt about performing. So I stopped going for auditions.*

Meanwhile, I was doing slightly more low-key gigs although, by this point, it has to be said, I was a hugely experienced performer. I had a CV that included dancing on stage at the Tyneside Irish Centre, singing on stage at the Tyneside Irish Centre and even telling jokes on stage at the Tyneside Irish Centre. I don't know if I've mentioned it, but my parents ran the Tyneside Irish Centre.

In fact, while I'm here, why don't I give you a bit of autobiographical information about the Donnelly family? After all, if you can't be autobiographical in an autobiography, where can you be?

My mam and dad, Anne and Alphonsus, came to Newcastle from Ireland in 1958. My dad's always been known as Fonsey, a bit like the character, Fonzie, in *Happy Days*, although he doesn't wear a leather jacket and hang out in American diners, it's just an abbreviation. I've got six – yes, *six* – brothers and sisters, and I'm the youngest. From the oldest down, they are Patricia, who was born in the Mid-Ulster Hospital, Magherafelt, Northern Ireland in 1961, then Eamonn, Martin, Dermott, Moyra and Camalia who, like me, were all born in Newcastle. Even though she's the next up, there's still five years between Camalia and me, which means I really am the baby of the family. We grew up in a council house in Cruddas Park in the west end of Newcastle, which had three bedrooms, and you don't need to be a property expert or a maths genius to work out that three bedrooms and nine people equals a bit of a squeeze. The four boys were in two sets of bunk beds in one room, the three girls were in another, and my mam and dad had the third room – it was just like *The Waltons*, but in Newcastle.

I had different relationships with each of my brothers and sisters: growing up, I annoyed them all in very different ways. As the eldest, Patricia was like a second mam to me, and she would always baby-sit. Eamonn took me to my first football match and, though Martin moved away to work as a joiner when I was quite young, he's someone I've had a great relationship with since I've got older. Dermott was away training to be a priest, so I'd only really see him in school holidays, when we'd have a real laugh together. Later on, when I was about fourteen, I did briefly consider following in his footsteps, and the footsteps of my Godfather, Father O'Connell, and becoming a priest. Then I got the bus home from school one day and it was full of lasses from the local girls' school, Sacred Heart. I knew right there and then that the priesthood wasn't for me. Anyway, back to the family – I'm assured it's just a coincidence that two of my three brothers left home when I was young, but I've got my suspicions. With Moyra and Camalia, I was the stereotypical younger brother, hanging around, annoying them when they had friends round and generally being a pain in the neck – it's in the contract when you're the youngest, isn't it?

You'd often find the Donnelly clan at the Tyneside Irish Centre on a Saturday night and so, as I say, that was where I had my earliest performing experiences. I'd usually get up on stage and do a bit of breakdancing – it was the obvious artistic choice for a kid from Newcastle in an Irish Club. I'd do my turn and then go round with an ashtray, which would get filled up with loose change. Yes, the customers of the Irish Centre would all pay good money to keep me off that stage.

Fortunately, with so many brothers and sisters; I always had a readymade audience at home. My family would always encourage me, saying, 'Do that dance again,' 'Sing that song,' or 'Watch out for the coffee table.' You know that old cliché about the youngest in a big family having to shout the loudest to get everyone's attention, being willing to do anything to get noticed and just wanting people to look at them? Well, I'd say that just about summed me up as a child. The showing off's starting to make sense now, isn't it?

That desire to perform made me a bit different from the other children, or, as they're known in the North-east, bairns. Growing up on a council estate in the west end of Newcastle in the eighties, it wasn't normal for kids to try and hog the limelight, not unless you count playing football or jumping ramps on your BMX.

There was a real sense of community in Cruddas Park. My uncle Frank and auntie Mary lived just around the corner, two doors down from us, with all my cousins. One of them, Ciaran, who's a couple of years younger than me, was my best mate. He was the perfect friend – generous, a good laugh and, best of all, a couple of inches shorter than me. I still see him at family gatherings now, but we don't get together as often as I'd like to. Maybe we should get a couple of BMXs and hit the streets for old times' sake. Back then, there were kids constantly playing on the streets, and people would always be looking out for the bairns. Obviously I've got my rose-coloured spectacles on here, but I promise I'll take them off soon. When we were kids, the summers seemed longer, there was always a game of British Bulldog or Headers and Volleys going on, and Cruddas Park was a great place to grow up. I honestly wouldn't have changed a single thing about it. Which is just as well because, unless I invent a time machine, I won't be able to.

*Although I didn't have an Irish Centre, or an ashtray full of loose change, there are similarities in our childhoods – for a start, I also grew up in the west end of Newcastle, within about a mile or two of where Dec grew up. I spent the first couple of years of my life in a flat in Westerhope with my mam Christine and dad Raymond and, when I was two, my little sister Sarha (pronounced Sarah) came along. We needed more space, so we moved into a three-bedroom council house on a cul-de-sac in Fenham. My nanna and granda, Kitty and Willy, who were my mam's parents, lived opposite us, and me and Sarha would always go to their house after school for a cup of milky coffee and, if we were lucky, a Tunnock's tea cake. We were only allowed one, because, as any child knows, 'any more would have spoiled our tea'. Nanna Kitty was Irish. She was a Liverpool fan, thanks to her Irish roots, but she loved Newcastle United too, and I used to love watching the football with her. As for Granda, when I was growing up, we used to play in his garage and garden all the time, and he was, without a doubt, the most honest, kind and genuine man I've ever met. One of my biggest regrets is that my granda never lived to see how things have turned out for me. Him and my nanna were great with me and Sarha – what is it about grandparents that means they never, ever lose their temper with their grand-children? My nanna and granda never, ever had a cross word for me and our Sarha.*

*When I was eight, my parents separated. I was old enough to know it was on the cards, and my mam and dad tried to work things out, but in the end my dad moved out and I didn't see him for a few years. He later had a daughter, Emma, with a woman called Maxine and, although Emma is technically my half sister, Sarha and me class her as our sister and we all see a lot of each other. In 1985, two years after my parents split, my mam met the man who's now her husband, Davey Woodhall. I liked Davey straight away, because he made my mam happy, and that was the only thing that mattered to me. He also treated me like an adult – he never asked me to call him Dad; he was always 'Davey' to me. When him and my mam met, Davey already had a daughter, Nicola, who's four years older than me, and a son, Robbie, who's four years my junior. Are you keeping up? There'll be questions at the end.*

*Like Dec, I've got really fond memories of my childhood. After my dad left, my granda became like a father figure to me, and I loved growing up in Fenham. There was a real sense of community there too, and that gives me and Dec one other thing in common – the ability to sound like we're eighty years old when we talk about our youth. In the summer, we'd go to my auntie's caravan in Amble, which was about thirty miles away, with my grandparents, and everything just seemed so simple and happy. In case you're wondering, me and Dec are sharing the rose-coloured spectacles.*

*I had the same four best mates for most of my childhood – Ginger (real name Craig Jobling); Athey, aka Paul Athey; Goody, who's Paul Goodwin; and Boppa, or Stephen Robson to his family, the teachers, or anyone else who was telling him off. (Just to make things confusing, Athey also had ginger hair, but two people nicknamed Ginger would have been too much.) I was very fortunate to have such great friends, and also to be the only one without a nickname. These days, I see Ginger occasionally, and I'm still really close to the other three. We used to hang around at the chippy in Fenham, because it was an equal distance from where we all lived, and because everything it sold was either deep-fried or fizzy – two very important qualities for any growing lad.*

*One thing me and all my mates had in common was very strong mothers. Most of us came from single-parent families, and the mams ruled the roost. If there was trouble at school, they went down there to sort it out, and a lot of them would work two or three jobs. I was really close to my mam, growing up. We had a fantastic relationship, and I'm proud to say we still do.*

*I've got so many happy memories of my childhood, although I did start early on the rocky road to romance. My first kiss was with a girl called Gillian, who lived at the top of my street. I must have been about ten, and me and Gillian were 'playing out', a phrase you don't hear so much these days, but a pastime that was a big hit in the seventies and eighties. It basically means going out into the street and playing games. When we'd finished playing out, Gillian asked me in to hers for a glass of juice.*

**Oh yeah, the old 'glass of juice' line, eh?**

*We went up to her room and she sort of stuck her lips on mine. Despite my tender years, I instantly felt very grown up, and I also assumed that, because we'd had a snog, Gillian was now my girlfriend – and the best thing about that was that I could brag to my mates about it. Imagine my shock, a few days later, when I heard Gillian had been snogging other boys too. I wasn't particularly heartbroken, just confused. Fortunately, Athey, who was the first person I'd told about me and Gillian, cleared it up for me.*

*'Did you ever ask her to be your girlfriend?'*

*'No.'*

*'Then she's not your girlfriend and she can kiss who she likes.'*

*Gillian had played me like a violin and, between her and Athey, I learnt some serious life lessons that day.*

As for me, I made the big leap from the Irish Centre to the telly thanks to the local paper. My dad has always read the *Evening Chronicle*, and I'd often look at the Newcastle United news in it. One night, as I sat on my BMX beanbag, I noticed something very interesting – an article that said the BBC were going to shoot a new children's drama in Newcastle. After some encouragement from my mam and my sister Camalia, I did what any confident, precocious twelve-year-old would do in that situation – I rang them and asked for an audition. I can still remember taking the big cream phone out of the hallway and into the living room to make the call. Strangely, the woman at the BBC, who'd obviously had the life bothered out of her all day by kids who'd seen the article, hadn't heard of Declan Donnelly, the famous kid who nearly got *Geordie Racer*, so I had to act as my own agent. But I cut a very good deal with myself – I took 15 per cent of my own earnings.

The BBC woman told me to write to the producer and send a photo. Again, my mam and Camalia were really supportive and helped me. I can't remember exactly what I said in that letter, but I'm pretty sure it included the words 'Irish Centre', 'dancing' and 'ashtray'.

I got a letter back from the BBC a few weeks later. Basically, it said, 'Don't call us, we'll call you.' It sounded to me like they were trying to palm me off and, I don't mind telling you, I considered retiring again.

Then, a few days later, there was a phone call informing me I had an audition – the programme was called *Byker Grove* – and I was to go to the BBC in Newcastle the following week.

They sent me a few pages of script through the post to learn, and I went along to the audition. At the end of it, after I'd recited those carefully learnt words in front of a hastily assembled video camera, they said they'd like me to come back on Saturday for the shortlist day, where I'd be reading again – this time for the part of Winston.

*I can't picture you as Winston – you'll always be Duncan to me . . .*

The shortlist day turned out to be a full drama workshop. It was horrendous. I was incredibly nervous, and it all felt a bit pretentious and actor-y to me – plus, I was one of the youngest there, which didn't help. I might've been a natural show-off, but that didn't mean I enjoyed pretending to be a tiny acorn growing into a huge oak tree. It seemed more like *Gardeners' World* than *Byker Grove*. By the end of it, I was practically wearing a cravat and calling everyone 'luvvee'.

I got home and just lay on the sofa, thinking about how awful it had been, convinced I was never going to get the part and that I'd been an idiot all along to think I would.

The phone rang later that evening. It was the producer, and he said, unfortunately, they weren't going to offer me the part of Winston. I knew it. I was just about to inform him not to consider me for any future opportunities in showbusiness as I would be retiring forthwith, when he asked if I would be interested in playing the part of Duncan.

I immediately said yes, in a voice that was supposed to sound cool, calm and collected but came out squeaky, high-pitched and over-excited. My family were thrilled too. As far as we knew, none of the Donnellys had been on telly before, and they were all very proud of me.

Right there and then I started a glamorous new life, a life where I, Declan Donnelly, pretended to be someone called Duncan for a few hours every week. This was the break I'd been waiting for since *Geordie Racer*: I was on the first rung of the acting ladder, and it meant I got to do what I did best – show off – and this time for a living.

But Duncan needed one more thing to really make his part come alive, something that wouldn't arrive till series two. Something, or rather someone, called PJ.

*For those of you without an encyclopaedic knowledge of* Byker Grove, *my character, PJ, was a maverick, this kid was a rebel, and it was often said that the Grove was never the same after PJ arrived.*

## Who said that?

*Me, mainly.*

*Thanks to Lynne Spencer, the teacher who'd encouraged me to audition for* Why Don't You?, *I'd had an audition for the second series of* Byker Grove. *Even though I'd decided I wasn't keen on performing after* Why Don't You?, *Lynne had given me yet another push. The audition was at school, and I had a plan – turn up, do the audition, not get the part and forget about the whole thing. My plan was, however, foiled, when the producers sent a letter to my house asking to see me again. The idea of another audition put all sorts of questions in my head: Would I have the courage to go through with it? Would I still get teased at school? And did they even have a drunken bloke on a bus in* Byker Grove?

*The second audition was held at an old stately home called the Mitre, in Benwell, where* Byker Grove *was filmed, so I thought I could get away with not turning up – because it wasn't at school, Lynne wouldn't be there, so I could just say I was sick, or the dog had eaten my letter, or something else equally mature. I hid the letter from my mam and only told my mate Ginger about it, and that's when fate intervened. Or rather Ginger did, because he was the one who let my mam know what I'd done.*

*My mam went mad, and rang the producers to tell them I'd definitely* be at the audition. She took me down there herself and, when we arrived, she was brilliant, she said, 'Right, now it's up to you. If you want to do it, do it. If you don't like the experience, that's fine, but at least give yourself a chance.'

So I did the audition, in a little darkened room at the Mitre, and I remember thinking, 'This place isn't even in Byker. They're crafty, these TV people.'

I'd learnt two pieces of script – one as PJ, and one as a different character and, of course, I always had a drunk up my sleeve – not literally, but you know what I mean. And, just like the audition for Why Don't You?, I was nervous, but unlike the audition for Why Don't You?, I was also terrified. This was a whole different kettle of fish to the auditions I'd faced at school.

Even now, when we watch kids audition for Britain's Got Talent, it takes me and Dec back to our first auditions, because we know exactly what they are going through. Although if, by some strange twist of fate, Simon Cowell had been at the Mitre that day, I'm not sure I'd have made it – but we'll come to The Prince Of Darkness later in the book.

I got through the audition without any major disasters, went home and, later that day, the producer rang the house and offered me the part of a character called Robert.

I was over the moon. I'd gone from feeling fairly lukewarm about it all to being ecstatic. I'd seen the first series of Byker Grove, so I knew it was a much bigger deal than Why Don't You? It was a proper acting job, with long-term prospects, so I thought it would be worth putting up with any hassle I might get at school. When I got the news, me, my mam and Sarha indulged in the traditional celebration of running round the sofa and screaming.

Then the phone rang again. I thought, 'That'll probably be Steven Spielberg, he's heard about Why Don't You? and now Byker Grove, he's probably about to cast me as the new Indiana Jones or something.' To my surprise, it wasn't Steven Spielberg, it was the producer of Byker Grove. They'd changed their mind – they didn't want to offer me the part of Robert, after all. My heart sank, until he said they'd like to offer me the part of PJ – PJ the DJ. I thought, 'PJ the DJ? That sounds cheesy,' but of course I took it and, as soon as I put the phone down, I did what any other twelve-year-old would have done in that situation: three more laps of the sofa.

I think the way we got into *Byker Grove* also tells you something about our different personalities. I know what you're thinking, but don't worry, we're not about to get all deep and psychological, this is just a quick observation.

I jumped straight in and couldn't wait to get going, and that's what I'm like with people – I'm happy to talk to almost anyone, being what's technically known as a complete show-off.

*I, on the other hand, took my time to decide acting was for me, I wasn't sure at first, and I suppose that does reflect my personality. Even now, I never jump straight into things – except swimming pools – I always reserve judgement and take my time. If you don't believe me, it took me twenty minutes just to come up with that sentence.*

*I think there's a lesson there for everyone reading this book – if you ever bump into us two, talk to Dec, he's much better with new people than I am.*

We had our parts, and we were ready to go. Just to refresh your memory, and our memories for that matter, *Byker Grove* was a weekly kids' drama on BBC1 set in a youth club in, well, Byker, which is a real area in the east end of Newcastle. Most of the characters were aged between twelve and sixteen, and the series ran from 1989 to 2006, although, obviously, the actors changed, otherwise you'd have had a load of people in their thirties going to a youth club, and that would definitely have damaged the show's credibility.

So, it's the late eighties, we've got our first proper acting jobs, and nothing was going to stop us making a go of our new careers.

*Well, nothing except a complete lack of any genuine acting experience . . .*

# Chapter 2

*I turned up on my first day at* Byker Grove *absolutely terrified, and I noticed there was a pattern emerging here:*

*Audition for* Why Don't You? *– nervous.*
*Audition for* Byker Grove *– scared.*
*First day at* Byker Grove *– absolutely terrified.*

*Between you and me, I was starting to think it might be some sort of allergic reaction to performing. I considered having a stiff drink to steady my nerves, but then I realized I was thirteen years old, so I took a deep breath and headed into the Mitre.*

*I walked into a big room where all the cast were and immediately felt intimidated. There were teenage actors everywhere, all laughing, swapping stories and generally having a great time. Most of them had been together for series one, so they'd already formed friendships, whereas the only relationship I had with them was based on watching them on the telly on a Tuesday afternoon. And even then I sometimes used to watch* Children's Ward *on ITV instead . . .*

**How could you?**

*I know, I'm sorry.*
*They really were a daunting bunch – they were all mates and, in my eyes, they were famous.*

**Oh yeah, having been in series one of** *Byker Grove* **together, we were** *huge* **celebrities – it was like a Geordie** *Ocean's Eleven.*

*Lyndyann Barrass, aka Spuggie, was there – I'll never forget that shock of red hair. There was Sally McQuillan, who played Donna; she was* the Queen Bee. Jill Halfpenny, who went on to bigger and better things, was also in the room. Like I say, I found them all very intimidating. The weirdest thing of all was that, for the entire day, we didn't do any filming. I didn't know it when I arrived, but the whole thing was designed as an ice-breaker to welcome the new kids, and with me, well, let's just say there was a lot of ice to break – a pickaxe would have come in handy.

We all sat in a big circle with Dee Wood, one of the chaperones, and played word-association games. I didn't have a clue what was going on. The only word I could associate with the whole thing was 'cringiness'. After that, we moved on to a game that they all knew and I didn't, called, 'I went to the shops and I bought . . .', where you had to recite a shopping list. Or something. I was so confused, I nearly popped out to Tesco when it was my turn.

Of course, this was the first time me and Dec met. People often ask us about that first meeting, and you probably think it was this magical moment where we instantly connected, immediately hit it off and then started finishing each other's . . .

. . . sentences.

But it wasn't . . .

. . . like that at all.

That first day was terrible. It couldn't have been scarier if I'd been walking into the Royal Shakespeare Company as the new Hamlet.

As you can imagine, I felt like a complete stranger on the edge of the group. And there was a good reason for that: I was a complete stranger on the edge of the group.

**I just thought you were a grumpy bugger.**
**In fact, I still think you're a grumpy bugger.**

Pretty soon we were all talking to each other – you know what kids are like, they'll talk to anyone, especially when adults force them to. The first *thing I noticed about Dec was how small and young-looking he was, and we quickly got chatting about a subject we both had in common, something that's caused us tears, pain and no end of misery over the years: following Newcastle United. We also bonded over the fact that we were both from the west end – a lot of the other kids on* Byker Grove *were from other parts of the North-east, whereas we lived fairly close to each other.*

*I must say that, on the whole, everyone was really nice to me. I must say that because some of them might be reading this . . .*

*But, as I said, there wasn't a magical moment where Dec and me bonded and decided to spend the rest of our lives together.*

**You make us sound like a married couple.**

*Don't be ridiculous, married couples spend every waking minute together, always know what the other one's thinking and constantly bicker with each other.*

**No they don't.**

*Yes they do.*

**No they don't. Look, what did we say? Not in the book . . .**

*Okay, okay.*

*As well as the kids who'd been in series one, there were also professionals, grown-up actors. People like 'Little' Billy Fane, who played Geoff, the youth leader in charge of the Grove.*

*Thanks to a long career in local theatre and panto, plus some TV work, Billy was a household name in the North-east. Our parents knew who he was, and the two of us certainly looked up to him.*

*Although, back then, we looked up to most people – we were even smaller than we are now . . .*

Byker Grove **was a very well-run production, very professional, and a lot of that was down to Matthew Robinson, the producer.**

To us, he was the godfather of the whole thing. Don't get me wrong, he didn't put a horse's head in PJ's bed or anything, but you knew he was definitely in charge. He directed the first six episodes and a lot of the following series, and he always had a bit of an aura about him. For a start; he'd come up from London or, to give it its proper title in Geordie, 'that London', or if you're over eighteen, 'that bloody London'. He'd worked on EastEnders, during the golden era of Den, Angie and, of course, Ethel's little Willy, and that immediately impressed everyone.

*And, let's be honest, impressing people with a little Willy isn't easy . . .*

When Matthew started on *Byker Grove,* he made a major announcement: no stage-school kids. Because he'd worked on EastEnders, whenever he made a major announcement it was followed by the sound of drums going duff, doof, duff, dufff, duff d-d-d-d-doof. That was the EastEnders theme tune, by the way, which isn't easy to type. Matthew was adamant that he wanted children from real, working-class backgrounds like ours, and that was really admirable.

*Matthew taught me, Dec and the rest of the cast so much, including how to actually act, which, looking back, is kind of vital when you're making a drama. He also taught us how to use pauses . . . which . . . was . . . great.*
    *See? I've still got it.*
    *Pacing yourself was really important, because when you first get a group of kids reading a script together, it all sounds like this:*
    *'HeyPJfancygoingtothegrovetoseeSpuggieandhaveawaterfightbeforewe-gototheshopsintown?'*

He also taught us how to work together as actors, and how to get the mood of a scene right. And when you have huge storylines, like going to the shops in town, or going to the shops near the Grove, that kind of stuff is crucial. It's got to be done with gravitas, with impact and with emphasis – in all the right places.

Imagine the bit in *Empire Strikes Back* when Darth Vader tells Luke Skywalker he's his dad – it was like that, but with shops.

*Matthew had the patience of a saint – and he needed it, working with a bunch of hyperactive kids who'd never really done any acting before. He also lived and breathed Byker Grove, and he really took to Newcastle as a city. After about a year there, he could even speak some of the language. He would also be careful not to go on about London – sorry, 'that London' – all the time.*

The most important and valuable thing Matthew taught us, though, was professionalism. He treated us all like adults and made sure we understood that, when you were filming, you were at work, and time was money. We might have been kids, but we were getting paid, and there was a word for what we were doing. It was called a job, and he made sure none of us forgot that.

*That's something that Dec and I have tried to maintain throughout our career: wherever we've worked and whatever we've done, we've always tried to be professional. Whether we've succeeded is another matter, but we're always trying. And I know the people we work with now agree with that. We often overhear them saying that we're both really, really trying . . .*

I also think that attitude has helped us two as a double act. If I'd been through *Byker Grove* and Ant hadn't, or vice versa, our partnership would have been very different.

The main reason for that is that we probably would never have met. Trust me, I've been doing this a long time now, and one of the hardest things in showbusiness is to form a double act with someone you've never met – in fact, it's almost impossible.

*We owe Matthew and Byker Grove a huge debt and, these days, whenever we get complimented on our professionalism, we both think about Matthew and the whole Byker team, and how we've got them to thank for that.*

*We don't thank them out loud, obviously, we prefer to sit back and take all the credit ourselves, but we think it, and that's the important thing.*

Seriously, though, we do want to say a big thank-you to every single person we worked with on *Byker Grove*. They laid the foundations for the rest of our career, and everything we learnt from them still helps us to this day.

# Chapter 3

At the end of the first series, Matthew told me that the role of Duncan was going to get bigger and, naturally, I couldn't wait to find out what kind of heavyweight storylines I'd be tackling. After all, I was a professional actor now, and I was desperate to show what I could do. I was waiting to discover what my first big, emotionally demanding story would be – and then, at last, all was revealed: I was going to be addicted to arcade games.

Not even fruit machines, arcade games. Duncan was supposed to be sensible, he'd often be the voice of reason, but this storyline showed how even the most level-headed lad could be sucked into the murky world of arcade-game addiction. It wasn't exactly gritty social drama, but I suppose it beat the water fights I'd been confined to in series one.

In order to successfully convey my addiction, I had to go to the Metro Centre, a huge shopping centre in Gateshead, and play the driving game *Chase HQ* in one of the arcades there. I say 'play', but actually I'd just stand there, with a camera pointed at me, while I *pretended* to be chasing a criminal in a black Porsche 928. I didn't even get to play for real. I was bored stiff. I was actually jealous of the kids who were just there for a day at the arcades. Meanwhile, the grumpy bugger had scored a big juicy storyline right from the start.

*I was setting up a pirate radio station. Just to be clear, that's not a radio station for pirates – it wasn't called Shiver Me Timbers FM, it was an illegal radio station.*

I couldn't believe it. I'd spent series one earning my stripes – a day at the Grove here, a trip to the fair there, and this new kid was straight into pirate radio. It was a much cooler story than anything I'd been involved in, and it showed what an edgy, risk-taking kind of guy this PJ really was. Part of me thought, 'That's great, Ant's got a big story, I'm really chuffed for him,' but the other 99 per cent of me thought, 'That's awful, Ant's got a big story, I think I hate him.'

In the end, Duncan was saved from the jaws of those evil arcades, and Declan was saved from the jaws of boredom. Geoff came and found him and persuaded him to go back to the Grove, putting a friendly arm round his shoulders and saying, 'Come on, Duncan, lad, let's get you home.' That was one of his many catchphrases, along with, 'Come on, PJ, lad, let's get you home,' and of course, 'Come on, Spuggie, lass, let's get you home.' That was Geoff all over – he was always there to save you when you did something stupid, like pretending to play arcade games for hours on end. Although he could be strict too. There was one episode where all the lads went up to the attic in the Grove for a party, and he said, 'No funny business, mind, or yous'll all be down quicker than the first pint on a Friday night.' It was one of the finest lines in the history of TV drama.

The pirate-radio storyline was when PJ and Duncan had their first scenes together. The characters met when Duncan and the lads turned up at a radio station to record an advert for a jumble sale at the Grove. The 'script' they'd put together was pretty dull, but PJ the DJ turned it into . . .

*'Bargain's bestsellers in bric-a-brac down at Byker Grove, I–I don't believe it! Yes, they're giving them away, well, almost – at the big, big Byker Grove bonanza – sale starts at two o'clock, so bowl on down to Byker Grove!'*

*With that kind of verbal dexterity, it's no wonder I became a rapper in later life.*

*At the time, PJ was dressed in the coolest clothes around – Troop trainers, a cap and an 8-Ball jacket. I was wearing other stuff too, they wouldn't have let anyone on kids TV dressed in nothing but trainers, a cap and a jacket – I would've got done for indecent exposure. But you get the picture.*

From then on, the characters became friends and, pretty quickly, so did me and Ant.

*I suppose in a way that was the start of our double act, although, even then, we didn't know that PJ and Duncan would end up going together like bacon and eggs, bangers and mash, or fish and chips.*

All right, they get the point; you're making me hungry . . .

*There was one defining moment that kickstarted our friendship properly, and it was all due to a deadly combination of Fred Flintstone and Newcastle United. I sent Dec a Christmas card in December of 1990 that said, 'Have a Yabba-Dabba-Doo Christmas' – I know, I know, but it was part of a multipack, okay? And I was only fifteen. Inside, it just said, 'Happy Christmas, mate – have a good one. PS Fancy going to the Swindon match on Boxing Day?' We went to the game, and it was the first time we'd socialized outside of* Byker Grove *gatherings. Boxing Day 1990 was our first date.*

Newcastle drew 1–1 with Swindon, thanks to a goal from Mickey Quinn. Before the match, we enjoyed the same pre-match routine as most teenage lads in Newcastle – meet at Grey's Monument in the centre of town at one o'clock on a Saturday afternoon, walk round the clothes shops on High Bridge looking at stuff we couldn't afford, go to Greggs the Bakers for a pasty, then get inside the ground, at the Gallowgate end, nice and early, so we could get a good spot. And then, at five to three, when all the big blokes came out of The Strawberry, a pub near the ground, lose our spot and get thrown about the terraces.

*Back on* Byker Grove*, a pattern quickly emerged. PJ and Duncan, along with their mates on the show – Fraser, played by John Jefferson; Lee, portrayed by Rory Gibson; Speedy, aka Steven Bradley; and Craig Reilly, who was Winston – provided light relief to the main stories. While the girls would deal with issues like teenage pregnancy or child abuse, we'd be involved in trying to work out if the Grove was haunted.*

24

Which, by the way, it wasn't – it was Paget the gypsy all along. That plot typified the relationship between PJ and Duncan. PJ was a maverick – he liked pranks and harebrained schemes – while Duncan was more level-headed. PJ wanted to break into the Grove and spend the night in there ghost-hunting, while Duncan suggested picking the locks. He was like the logistics man, definitely PJ's partner in crime, but much calmer. In another early episode, Duncan discovered a 'listening device' and planted it in the girls' toilets. He was a proper little James Bond, only without the flash cars. Or the girls. Or the licence to kill. It was more a licence to listen to girls and pick locks, really.

*When we weren't chasing ghosts, or gypsies posing as ghosts, we were involved in yet more gritty social drama, like putting on a magic show when PJ decided to raise money for Robert's physiotherapy. Dec sawed a girl in half – not for real, obviously, he did it via the gift of magic.*

*In the same magic show I rode a unicycle – don't ask me what's magical about that, because I don't know. All I do know is that it meant going to a church hall in Jesmond – a posh part of Newcastle – every Wednesday night and hanging around with a bunch of people from the circus who wore tie-dye clothes, had dreadlocks and were all juggling while smoking roll-ups. They were multi-skilled; I'll give them that. I was in my hoodie and baseball cap, listening to loads of rap music at the time, and I would have given my right arm to saw someone in half, if you know what I mean.*

*As well as the acting itself, which as you've gathered, was pretty high-octane stuff, there were so many other reasons to enjoy* Byker Grove *– the buzz of being on set, the joy of getting sent scripts but, more than any of that, there was something that gave us both a huge amount of pleasure and satisfaction.*

## Time off school.

*The more scenes we were in, the more time off we had. There were rules about how many days a week you were allowed to miss – I think the maximum was three – and it was brilliant.*

*Just stop now and imagine that you're thirteen years old and you can miss three days a week of school.*

*Nothing could have made us happier. Well, maybe five days a week off school, but there was no need to be greedy.*

Obviously, there was a tutor at *Byker Grove*, and by law we had to do three and a half hours' schoolwork every day on set. The tutor would liaise with your teachers, get your course work and blah blah blah, who are we kidding?

We got time off school.

We tried our damndest to do as little schoolwork as possible, although we did both manage to get an excellent education in one subject – playing pool. There was a table in the actors' green room at the Mitre, so we'd take the chance to play whenever we had a spare ten minutes between scenes.

*Realistically, we couldn't have done a lot of homework on set because we'd be out and about so much for filming, and that had its downsides. Doing scenes in the west end of Newcastle, for example, wasn't always easy. In fact, it was never easy. If you were shooting on the street, you'd often get kids hurling abuse at you. They'd use the kind of shocking, foul and disgusting language that, up until then, we'd only ever heard coming out of each other's mouths. One of their favourite tricks was to wait until the director shouted 'Action!' and then shout 'Wankers!' at the top of their voice.*

*It would always be left to some poor runner or work-experience girl to go over and politely ask them to be quiet. They'd always say, 'Aye, no problem, pet, no problem,' and then, of course, the minute the director shouted 'Action!' again, they'd start yelling 'Wankers!' again.*

*Looking back, it's actually quite funny but, back then, it was . . . actually, it was quite funny back then too – but it wasn't the only disruption we had to deal with.*

*Me and Dec were filming a scene next to a block of flats one day, and you wouldn't believe some of the things people threw out of their windows at us – potatoes, eggs, tomatoes: there was almost enough for a full English some days. I nearly asked them to chuck down a bottle of ketchup and a couple of rashers of bacon. I always assumed the reason they threw that stuff was a combination of boredom and perhaps a bit of jealousy – to them, it might have looked like we had the most glamorous job in the world and were earning a fortune. The reality, though, was more like we were missing a few lessons at school and getting a bit of extra pocket money.*

Without a doubt, the worst day's filming I ever had to do was when Duncan got mixed up in a cult. I'll never forget it.

The cult was called Psychandrics, and they brainwashed Duncan. I'm not quite sure *how* they did it, but there was a girl he fancied, and it was the old story: boy meets girl, boy likes girl, boy joins extreme religious cult to impress girl. We've all done it, haven't we?

He got really into it though. He was usually quite sensible but, every now and then, Duncan could be a damn fool – especially if there was a girl involved. We had to film these scenes at Grey's Monument, which is right in the middle of Newcastle city centre and, for reasons that still escape me to this day, I had to do this while wearing what looked like a pair of pyjamas.

*P-jays and Duncan!*

Apparently, nothing says 'cult' like a pair of pyjamas. I don't know what it was with me and pyjamas. A few weeks earlier, in a school swimming lesson, I'd retrieved a brick from the deep end wearing a pair – it seemed like the only thing I didn't do in pyjamas was go to sleep. It was as if the producers had sat down and had a meeting where the theme was 'Making Dec look as stupid as possible', and they hit the jackpot with this one.

*Of course, when I heard Dec would be filming in the middle of town in a natty pyjama-style outfit, I did what any mate would do – got straight down there to have a proper laugh at him.*

As if this wasn't enough, the director didn't want to tell the general public we were filming so, in between takes, when the cameras weren't there, I just looked like a boy in pyjamas standing on his own in the middle of Newcastle.

They say the only things that are certain in life are death and taxes, but I can add another one to that list, which is 'If you're wearing pyjamas in the middle of town, you're guaranteed to bump into someone you know.'

And I did. I saw several people who knew my mam and dad, and they'd stop for a chat, a chat which usually went something like this:

'Are you Fonsey and Anne's littl'un?
    'Yes.'
    'Are you still in that TV show?'
    'It's funny you should say that actually, I'm filming it right now.'
    'Is that why you're wearing them pyjamas?'
    'Yes.'
    'Well, tell your mam I said hello.'
    'Will do. 'Bye.'

*To be fair, it was sometimes possible to have a laugh when you got recognized in town. When we used to meet up at the Monument on Saturday afternoons and go to the football together, we were so famous that sometimes as many as two people would come up to us and say, 'You're thingy and thingy from Thingy Grove, aren't you?'*

*And if one of us was waiting for the other, then . . .*

*Hang on, that's not right, what I really mean is, when I'd be waiting for Dec – which, incidentally, I've spent half my life doing . . . Why are you always late?*

Ah, there's a good reason for that. It means I never wait for anyone . . . shall we talk about this later?

*Okay, I'll wait till you're ready to talk about it. Typical.*

*When I'd be waiting for Dec in town, people would come up and say, 'You're thingy from Byker Grove. You're not filming now, are you?', and I realized I could have a laugh with it, so I'd say, 'Yeah, I am actually, could you keep walking?', and they'd say, 'Sorry, sorry,' and walk off, ducking down to avoid this invisible camera. It meant no one ever stopped to talk to you.*

Well, not unless you had your pyjamas on . . .

The worst kind of attention came from lads the same age as us. These lads often had a lovely way with language, calling you 'poof', 'wanker' *and* 'tit'. You'd get it from lads in town, on the bus, or at the end of your street – they weren't fussy.

To be honest, I didn't blame them, you'd have been the same. No thirteen-year-old is going to go up to a child actor, pat them on the back and say, 'Well done, Declan, I really enjoyed your gritty portrayal of arcade addiction, darling!'

*As we got more and more airtime, we'd get recognized more often. It all became a bit like that bloke down my local supermarket who talks to the shopping trolleys – a bit weird and a bit scary.*

*At first, just being looked at in the street felt a bit odd. It was all new to us – you don't get lessons at school on how to react when you're being stared at. Although, even if you did, we would have missed them, 'cos we'd have been busy at* Byker Grove.

*It could be hard to deal with. Just stop for a moment and imagine what you were like at thirteen. If you were anything like most teenagers, you were probably awkward, self-conscious and uncomfortable – and that's if you were one of the more well-adjusted kids. Most teenagers that age didn't like their own family looking at them, never mind having their peers pointing and laughing at 'that poof off the telly'.*

Of course, the staring did have one big advantage: girls. If girls were looking at you, you'd be thinking, 'Wicked, I wonder if they fancy me?', even though they were probably thinking, 'Look, it's that poof off the telly.'

*If it was lads doing the staring, you always thought the same thing – 'Oh no, this could end up in a fight,' and, as a child actor, fighting was never going to be one of your strengths.*

*If those lads had wanted me to* pretend *to have a fight with them, great, I was their man – acting hard wouldn't be a problem. But a real fight? No thank you. So you'd keep your head down and concentrate on playing the part of a terrified child actor who was determined to avoid a fight. Over the years, it was a role we both became very good at.*

*Being recognized is a weird thing, though. Even now, when one of us is on our own, people say, 'Look, it's Ant and Dec,' and you think, 'Well, not really, it's just me.'*

That's a second lesson, if you do ever see us out and about. Just to refresh your memory: the first lesson was talk to me, not Ant, I'm better with new people. The second one is, don't say, 'Look, it's Ant and Dec.' I know you may not know which one's which, but at least say, 'Look, there's one of Ant and Dec.' It'll make us really happy, *and* we'll know you've read this book.

At *Byker Grove*, Matthew made sure we had someone to turn to in case the weight of fame as an international celebrity on children's telly became too much. The night before the first ever episode went out, he rang me up with a warning.

He said now that I was on telly I was going to get a little bit of fame; he said it wouldn't be easy and it was important to keep both feet on the ground. I immediately took my feet off the sofa and made sure both of them were firmly on the ground. Suddenly, my mind was racing – how would I keep both my feet on the ground when I went to bed? He was right: this wasn't going to be easy.

After Matthew had patiently explained the concept of metaphors, he told me I should get an agent. He sent me to see someone who he knew and trusted, Dave Holly. Dave was the biggest agent in the North-east and, over the years, he had looked after household names like Robson Green and Jimmy Nail.

Dave worked out of a small office on the upper floors of the Tyne Theatre and Opera House. I remember going to see him for the first time. I clambered my way up several sets of stairs to his office, the walls of which were covered in black-and-white photos of various men and women. I was immediately curious – how did he find the time to be a theatrical agent *and* a keen amateur photographer? He later told me they were all his clients – the actors and actresses on his books.

He was a big man with a neat swathe – I love that word – of black hair and the wheezy chuckle of a heavy smoker. He was a really lovely bloke. I signed a twelve-month contract with him and agreed that he would take 10 per cent of my earnings. That meant Dave's income was due to shoot up by something in the region of £65 a year, although he did a very good job of hiding his excitement.

*Matthew had the same chat on the phone with me when I started – and I was very aware that nobody in my family had ever done anything like that before.*

*Acting, I mean, not talking to people on the phone, they'd done plenty of that. An agent sounded like a good idea. I contacted Dave straight away, but I heard nothing until the end of the second series.*

*I discovered much later on that he'd found my performance in my first episode 'awful'. To Dave, clearly everything was black and white and, to be fair to him, I was quite awkward on screen to start with. By the end of the series, I'd improved enough for Dave to take me on and try and put me right where I belonged – on his wall, in a little picture frame.*

I think *Byker Grove* also gave us both a newfound sense of maturity – suddenly you had a job, and it wasn't a paper round, so you had to take it seriously. No offence to any paperboys reading this: you guys do a great job.

*In fact, I was one of you for a while. In between* Why Don't You? *and* Byker Grove, *I had a paper round. Like any out-of-work actor, I needed to make ends meet between gigs and, like any eleven-year-old, I needed money for sweets. I delivered for the corner shop at the top of my street, and worked every morning before and after school, for a whopping weekly wage of £6.10. I'm not embarrassed to admit I was the world's worst paperboy. The shop would give you a laminated card that listed the houses you were delivering to, and the paper they wanted, and you had to check it every single morning, because people's choices changed from day to day. The only trouble was I kept posting the laminated card through the letterboxes by accident, which meant I had to knock on the door, wake up the residents and sheepishly ask for it back. Needless to say, that career didn't last long, and once I realized the paper round wasn't going to work out, I knew I had to take acting seriously.*

As I say, we both treated acting like a job from the start – and our families were a huge part of this. When I started on the show, I sat down with my mam and dad and they said, 'We'll support you whatever you do but, ultimately, you've got to make your own decisions.' They gave me a lot of responsibility, which I appreciated and took seriously. We were both treated like adults at an early age, but in very different ways.

*My mam had two jobs, so if she was still at work, I would make dinner for Sarha, tidy up, or just generally help around the house. I had responsibilities at home from very early on, and that meant I was mature enough to try and deal with all the changes that came with being in* Byker Grove. *It also meant I did a mean Spaghetti Bolognese . . .*

He still does.

*More of my culinary adventures – and Dec's inability to cook even beans on toast – later in the book.*

That's some tease, isn't it? Go on, admit it, you're thinking, 'Beans on toast? I can't wait for that story.'

Well, you'll have to wait; we're on *Byker Grove* for now. We both relished our newfound responsibilities, but also managed to have a laugh. One of the best things about being in the cast was the premieres; they were a celebration of finishing another series and months of hard work. The producers would put on a screening at the Civic Centre in Newcastle for the cast and crew, then we'd all have a bit of a 'do' afterwards. Imagine a

Leicester Square film premiere – the red carpet, the press, the glamour. Now imagine the opposite of that, and you've got our premieres.

*They were great nights. All the girls would put on make-up, get their hair done and stick some high heels on, and the lads, well, it would always be the same – go to town, buy a new shirt from Topman and then cover yourself with aftershave, even though you hadn't started shaving yet. They should call it 'Before Shave'.*

*Matthew would say a few words before they showed the first episode, and then we'd sit back and watch ourselves on the big screen. I never liked watching myself in* Byker Grove, *though, and for my first few episodes, I think most of the viewers felt the same. I was never a big one for making the family watch it at home either.*

**Me neither.**

*The novelty of one of the family being on telly wore off pretty quickly anyway. People had lives to lead – my mam had to go to work, and Sarha had friends to play with and homework to do. My sister was a really dedicated student, especially on Tuesdays, at 5.05 – she'd always make sure she did her homework then, which, coincidentally, was exactly when* Byker Grove *was on.*

**My mam was the same – the minute** *Byker Grove* **started she'd go and put the dinner on – you could set your watch by her.**

# Chapter 4

Inevitably, we grew close to our fellow actors, and a lot of the cast formed relationships. At that age, there are a lot of hormones flying around, so there'd always be someone who was constantly giggling, flirting and fluttering their eyelashes. And it was usually Ant.

*All in all, there were quite a lot of intercast shenanigans. I'm sure it's the same on most soaps. Matthew told us that Ethel's little Willy had an affair with Den and Angie's Roly once . . .*

*I went out with Jill Halfpenny, who played Nicola Dobson. Jill later went to be on* EastEnders, Coronation Street *and* Strictly Come Dancing. *Even on* Byker Grove *it was clear to everyone that she was a very good actress. For a start, she convinced people she found me attractive, which is still probably the most impressive performance of her career.*

*Jill and I fancied each other from the moment we met, but I was rubbish at reading the signs. You know what you're like at that age – terrible at picking up on those subtle hints, such as, 'Ant, Jill fancies you.' She once asked me what I was doing on Saturday; I told her I was going to see Newcastle play Grimsby.*

*She said she'd love to come, and if you knew how bad Newcastle were back then, well, you'd know that she either fancied me or had a screw loose – some people would say they go hand in hand. I still didn't quite get it.*

*We were a couple for exactly a week – and we spent the most of that week talking on the phone but not seeing each other, even though we were officially 'seeing each other'. At the end of that week, we went on our only real date – to see* Dances With Wolves. *Even when I see Jill now, she swears it was* The Commitments, *but I know it was* Dances With Wolves *and, trust me, a three-hour western is not the ideal film for a first date – not unless you're taking a cowgirl to the cinema. If you're reading this and you've got a first date coming up, do not, I repeat, do* not *go and see* Dances With Wolves. *You'd probably have trouble finding a cinema showing a western from 1990 anyway but, if you do, avoid it like the plague.*

*While we're on the subject, I've got a few bones to pick with Kevin Costner – no one, not one person, danced with a wolf in that film; it should have been called 'Riding On Horses', but I'm getting sidetracked. After the film, we had a little kiss at the metro station and, the next day, Jill rang me and said she didn't think it was going anywhere, and that spelt the end of our week-long, one-date whirlwind romance. I don't know if it was my fault, or if Costner was to blame but, at the time, I was gutted. Jill was very mature about it, though. We had to work together the next week, and it could have been awkward, but she made it easy, and I got over the whole thing fairly quickly.*

*Within a few months I was going out with Jill's onscreen younger sister. Her character name was Debbie, and she was played by Nicola Bell.*

**It sounds like something from** Jeremy Kyle, **doesn't it? 'Help! I can't stop dating sisters from** Byker Grove.'

*Apparently, according to the cast gossip, or Dec, as it was otherwise known, Nicola had fancied me for a while. We got talking at a party one night, and Nicola looked really pretty, and I think that was when we had our first kiss. Miraculously, unlike the previous effort, the kiss didn't lead to me being dumped the next day. Nicola was my first love, and our relationship really blossomed, helped by the fact we didn't see a single Kevin bloody Costner film the whole time we were together. It was great having a romance with someone you saw on set every day – and Nicola was certainly a lot better looking than Keith the cameraman, who was lovely, but just not my type.*

*It was going really well, and everyone was really happy for us – until our characters started going out with each other on the show. And then the unthinkable happened – there was a scene where we had to kiss. I know what you're thinking 'Kiss your own girlfriend? What next, wear your own clothes? Eat your own lunch?'*

**The whole thing was hilarious . . .**

35

*You might think I'm overreacting, but stop for a moment and imagine yourself as a teenager kissing your first boyfriend or girlfriend, and then imagine that being televised. See? I had sleepless nights for weeks before we filmed it. I was worried people would question my technique, or that they would tease me.*

*When the day came, the cast and crew ribbed us all morning. It was the last thing to be filmed before lunch. I assume that, if it was done after lunch, they were worried about people being sick. We both anxiously sat on set, cringing whenever the director called out 'Action!' When he finally did, the kiss was fine. We had to do a couple of takes, though, and each time the director yelled 'Cut!', we immediately stopped kissing and giggled nervously, which was daft, considering we were going out with each other anyway. Like so many things in life, the anticipation was much worse than the event itself.*

Ant's first date may have been *Dances With Wolves*, but I went for something a bit shorter that was horse-less and wolf-less. It was *Three Men and a Little Lady*, the disappointing sequel to *Three Men and a Baby*. My companion was a girl called Lynne. I'd met Lynne a few years earlier, at primary school. She was in the year above and widely regarded to be 'the best-looking girl in the school', and I can still remember asking her out. I got her phone number, rang her up, and after mumbling, 'Is Lynne there?' to her mam, she came on the phone.

'Hi, Lynne, it's Dec. Would you like to go to the pictures?'
  'Yeah, okay then.'
  'Great, 'bye.'
  'Bye.'

I put the phone down and punched the air with delight. I was over the moon, and then, after a couple of seconds, realized I hadn't made any arrangements – I suppose I've never been any good at the finer details in life. I rang her back, and we agreed we'd go on Saturday. She was my first proper girlfriend, and we went out for a couple of months. I'd go round when she was babysitting her nieces, and we'd watch videos like *Ghost* and *Dirty Dancing*. Basically, if it had Patrick Swayze in, we watched it. I don't really remember how our relationship finished – maybe there weren't any Swayze films left to see, and the magic just went.

After my romance with Lynne, I looked further afield for love, unlike Ant. I wasn't the kind of bloke who was happy to go out with someone just because they were in *Byker Grove*, I had my eyes on bigger things – *Grange Hill*. In 1990, on my second year on *Byker Grove*, the cast of the two biggest children's dramas . . . on a weekday . . . afternoon . . . on BBC1 went head to head in a charity football match in Newcastle for Children in Need. I noticed a girl who I had only ever seen on the telly, and I tried to impress her with my dribbling. I quickly realized that it wasn't working, so I wiped my chin and played football instead. That girl was Clare Buckfield, who played Natasha Stevens in *Grange Hill*, and I fancied her at first sight – I'm a real romantic like that, I've always believed in fancying at first sight.

Understandably, she didn't really take any notice of me but, the following year, we went down to London for the return fixture of *Byker Grove* versus *Grange Hill*. After the game, we all went to the bar together, and the two of us got chatting. She said all the right things – 'How's the arcade-game addiction? When are you next on pirate radio?', that kind of stuff – and we hit it off straight away. We all went on to another pub, and John Jefferson, who played Fraser, chatted up Clare's sister, Julie, and in the process got her address. That's right, not her phone number, her address. When the time came to leave, Clare told me to get her address from John, and that was how we stayed in touch. The telephone *had* been invented, I hasten to add, it was just addresses that were given out that night. Don't ask me why.

I got home the next day, and decided to write Clare a letter. The only paper I had was *Byker Grove* notepaper, so I wrote it on that – classy or what? I can't remember what I said in that letter, but after an agonizing two-day wait, she wrote back to me – I don't think it was on *Grange Hill*-headed notepaper, but I didn't mind too much. In the letter, Clare gave me her phone number, so we could stop acting like it was the 1920s and have an actual conversation, and that was the start of our relationship. We'd visit each other whenever we could – she'd come up on the coach with her sister, or I'd go down to London, and every day we'd write to each other. I'd spray my aftershave on the letters I sent, and she'd spray her perfume. It cost me a fortune in fragrance and stamps, but it was worth every penny. It all felt so romantic, and I was happy as Larry, whoever that Larry bloke is.

*Anyhow, when Dec could tear himself away from a sheet of headed notepaper and a bottle of Blue Stratos . . .*

Actually, it was Jazz.

*Whatever. When he could tear himself away, the whole cast would often go on trips together. They were supposed to help new cast members bond with the regulars and to maintain a sense of camaraderie between the actors, but the predominant theme was underage drinking. They were brilliant – Paris, Rome, New York . . . were just some of the places we wanted to visit, but we always ended up going to the log cabins at Clennell Hall, near Rothbury, which was like another world – it was a full 31 miles from Newcastle.*

The trips would usually be organized by Dee Wood, the head chaperone. I don't know if we went to log cabins because Dee's surname was Wood but, looking back, I'm just glad the trips weren't organized by the other chaperone, Dave Sewage Farm.

When you get the whole cast of a children's soap together for one night, they all want to do the same thing – sing, dance, act or, if you're very unlucky, all three. Those nights could've been called *Byker's Got Talent*, but without much talent.

When it came to the log cabins, one night in particular sticks in my mind. Me, Ant and Rory Gibson, who played Lee, had decided to do something together, but we couldn't think of an act; we just had no idea what to do in front of an audience.

*To be honest, it's a problem me and Dec still face on a weekly basis . . .*

*The girls would always be singing – if you could call it that – 'I will always love you', and that kind of thing, but we wanted to do something different. The big problem was that neither me, Dec or Rory were great singers.*

*I was really into The Doors at the time and, suddenly, inspiration struck. The Doors were four American hippies in their twenties with long hair and leather trousers.*

*We were three teenage lads from Newcastle with gelled spiky hair and tracksuit bottoms. The similarities were uncanny.*

We looked and sounded nothing like them, but we weren't going to let a little thing like that hold us back – yes, tonight, Matthew, we were going to be The Doors.

Then we realized that we did have something in common with The Doors, something that was going to evoke the spirit of the sixties and help our performance no end.

*Dec was wearing a beaded necklace.*

I loved a beaded necklace in those days and wore one all the time. If we were lucky, people might actually think we *were* The Doors. As long as they didn't have any eyes, or ears . . .

We decided to mime to 'Light My Fire', which, let me tell you, in a log cabin, was a risky choice. If any of the audience had taken it too literally, the whole place could've gone up. I told Ant to check where the fire exits were before we took to the stage.

*Due to being the biggest Doors fan and the proud owner of their Greatest Hits CD, I took the part of Jim Morrison, while Dec and Rory used a cunning combination of tennis rackets and that beaded necklace to represent the rest of the band.*

*Before we went on, we'd had a band meeting and decided we needed a big finish. We were determined to do something that, in the true spirit of Jim Morrison, would have the girls in the audience screaming and fainting so, at the end of the song, we all tore our tops off. As soon as we did it, every girl in the place started screaming her head off.*

*I can still hear them now:*

*'Please, please, put your tops back on.'*

Of course, we were only teenagers, our bodies hadn't really developed then, it would take another few years before we'd be real men, with hairy chests and, of course, fully formed beer bellies.

*Those trips away were fantastic. The boys would be in one cabin and the girls in another, and I would sneak out to the girls' cabin at night to see Nicola for a quick snog. Those stolen kisses were exhilarating, they were forbidden and, best of all, they weren't on telly.*

That wasn't the only time art – well, *Byker Grove* – imitated life. There'd be regular parties at the other cast members' houses, and whoever's house you went to, you could guarantee one thing: their parents were away.

The whole cast would turn up and, at times, it felt just like an episode of *Byker Grove*.

*Although off screen, I never started a pirate radio station.*

And I never joined a religious cult.

Which was a shame – that beaded necklace would've gone a treat with a nice pair of pyjamas.

# Chapter 5

*Around late 1991 and at the beginning of 1992, our agent, Dave Holly, started getting requests for personal appearances at various roadshows.*

*Not for him — I mean, he was a lovely bloke, but he'd never been in Byker Grove and no one at those roadshows would have known who he was. No, the requests were for me and Dec. PJ and Duncan were becoming more and more popular and, by this point, the fanmail was coming in by the sackload. Hardly any of it was for us, the sacks weren't that big and they weren't always full, but we got a few letters and photos from girls, and it was a real thrill.*

The requests for these personal appearances would often be for roadshows based around teen magazines.

One of the first ones me and Ant did was the *Fast Forward* Fun Day. It was put on by the BBC kids' magazine *Fast Forward*, and it was a day of fun. You probably could have gathered that from the title, but I just wanted to make sure. It featured some of the biggest stars from the world of children's TV, and I think we must have done a few interviews with the magazine beforehand. You know what those magazine features were like in the early nineties: favourite colour, favourite pop star, favourite member of the *Baywatch* cast, that kind of thing.

And, since you ask, my favourite was the stunner with the big chest.

*David Hasselhoff?*

That's the one.

We'd turn up at these roadshows, along with other members of the cast. Whoever was hosting would say, 'It's the cast of *Byker Grove*,' we'd all shuffle onstage, give the crowd a wave, maybe get asked a question or two, and young girls would scream. We'd always think two things – 'This is great' and 'I must bring some earplugs next time.' It was a bit like when *EastEnders* or *Coronation Street* wins an award and the whole cast wanders on to the stage and just stands there, not quite sure what to do with themselves.

There'd be metal barriers to keep the fans from storming the stage or, more likely, escaping from the venue and, after much waving, we'd go over to the barriers, have pictures taken with fans of the show and sign autographs. Of course, by now I was very experienced when it came to this sort of thing – I'd spend hours every week practising my poses in the mirror, and I'd been perfecting my autograph since the age of six. Now all I had to do was sign a copy of *Fast Forward*, rather than my maths exercise book.

A lot of the time the girls would also ask me to get Ant's autograph for them too. This was because – and there's no easy way to say this – they thought he looked miserable and they were scared of asking him themselves.

*I must admit, I've got one of those faces. I do look miserable if I'm not smiling, and I was always a bit apprehensive at those things. I understood the girls wanted us to sign stuff, but if they didn't shout 'Ant' or 'PJ', then I wouldn't go over.*

Treat 'em mean, keep 'em keen, eh?

*More like, 'Treat 'em mean, because I'm scared of this whole thing and feeling really nervous.'*

That's not as good, as a catchphrase, is it? It doesn't even rhyme . . .

*The point is, I'd always wait to be asked when it came to autographs, I didn't know how it worked, and I didn't want to look big-headed.*
*I know exactly what you're thinking: I've always looked big-headed.*

*Well, it's not my fault, I was born with this forehead and I'm stuck with it.*

One of the biggest events in the early nineties roadshow calendar was the *Mizz* magazine roadshow in Birmingham. Yes, you read that right, the *Mizz* magazine roadshow. I don't think we need to tell you we were getting pretty big-time by then.

After a brief rehearsal to get our waving right before the doors opened for the audience, we got chatting to Tim Vincent. Tim had quite a similar background to the two of us, he was in the ITV kids' drama *Children's Ward*, and we had so many questions for him. Did they do a lot of work on location? What was the schedule like? And, most importantly, could me and Ant have his autograph?

I also asked Tim if *Children's Ward* was on that week, and he said it wasn't, because of the Budget. He obviously meant the Chancellor of the Exchequer's Budget – ITV were broadcasting it, so they'd cancelled children's programmes for the day.

*But I hadn't quite got to grips with that, I thought he was talking about the budget for* Children's Ward. *In my mind, that was the one that really mattered, not some stupid announcement that would only affect the entire British economy. So I said to Tim, 'That's weird, just missing out an episode in the middle of the series 'cos there isn't enough money in the budget. You'd think they'd just do one less episode at the end – or plan their finances better.'*

*Tim looked at me like I was a complete idiot, which of course I was.*

I immediately stepped in and explained the complex political repercussions of the Budget to Ant.

I think my exact words were 'That posh bloke with the red suitcase means *Children's Ward* isn't on this week.'

*My face turned crimson, and Tim just walked off. That was the first time I'd felt really embarrassed in front of someone else 'off the telly'. But it wouldn't be the last . . .*

In spite of Ant's Tim Vincent faux pas, the two of us had become best mates by now, and there was no doubt that helped with our performances on *Byker Grove*. We spent all our time at work together, we'd meet at the weekends and go to football matches, we were both experiencing the beginnings of fame and we had become really close. I suppose you could say we were method actors – in the same way Robert De Niro drove a taxi round New York to prepare for *Taxi Driver*, we became best mates in real life and then best mates on screen.

*I was starting to think that the scriptwriters didn't have much faith in my acting abilities. My girlfriend off screen was now my girlfriend on screen, my best mate off screen was now my best mate on screen. I was half expecting them to write a storyline where I had an embarrassing chat about the budget with someone from* Children's Ward*.*

*They were definitely starting to give me and Dec more to do, though. We even had a story where PJ and Duncan tried to go underage drinking, which involved them going round various pubs in Newcastle and not getting served. For our characters, it was a rite of passage that typified the issues facing young lads but, for us, it was three days hanging round in pubs. We loved it. Even though it was a fairly small storyline, we'd been doing extensive research into that area for years.*

By this point, we'd been acting for a couple of years and, the more experienced we got, the more inquisitive we became about how things worked. We were much more interested in what happened on the production side and what the producer and the director were doing every day.

We were starting to approach acting as a long-term career. We still had no idea where it was going to lead, but there was one thing we realized around that time: we both had a dream. We hoped that, one day, we could get that golden opportunity, that big break, the one thing the two of us wanted more than anything else: a part in *Spender*.

*Spender was a BBC1 drama set in Newcastle that was created, written by, produced and starred (phew!) Jimmy Nail. Local actors like Jimmy, Tim Healy and Kevin Whately were a huge inspiration to us. Robson Green was another one and, back then, it was a real thrill for us when he got a big part in Casualty. Those actors had 'made it' and, as far as we were concerned, they couldn't have done better if they'd been cast as the new Batman.*

For the record, I would pay good money to see Jimmy Nail as Batman, but it's probably too late for the big man now. To jump from where we were, to the level they were at, seemed almost impossible. We thought the best we could hope for was a good run in *Byker Grove*, and then, if we were really lucky, a role in *Spender* as third motorcycle thug from the left.

*Without even realizing it, I suppose me and Dec were already mentally preparing for life away from Byker Grove and possibly for life as a double act. We were really starting to enjoy performing together, and this became obvious to us one night at the BBC Club, the staff bar at BBC Newcastle.*

*Due to phenomenal public demand, we'd retired our Doors tribute act after just one gig, so we had to come up with a new act, and we got up and did a rendition of an old soul song called 'Me and Mrs Jones'.*

*The idea came from Dec, and this takes us on to something you should all know about the man sitting next to me: he has the musical taste of a ninety-year-old. His iPod is full of albums like* Now That's What I Call the 1940s *and* The Best Chamber Music Album in the World . . . Ever. *When it comes to music, he's got one very simple rule: if it was written after England won the World Cup, it's too modern.*

*Old man Donnelly here played me this song and, to be fair, I really liked it. It's all about a bloke who's having an affair with Mrs Jones and how the two of them meet up in secret. Looking back, it seems a strange choice – not just because it was released before we were born, but because it wasn't a duet, which meant the whole thing turned into a bit of a threesome – me, Dec and Mrs Jones.*

When we got on stage and started singing, the audience seemed to find it very funny, so we began to ham it up further and play the whole thing for laughs. At least, that's our story, and we're sticking to it.

*Dec's right, though, we deliberately did the whole song very tongue in cheek, which wasn't easy. You try singing with your tongue in cheek, it's almost impossible.*

*Have a go. See? Chances are you've covered this page in spit and, if you're on the bus, you're probably getting some pretty strange looks right now.*

*But by the end of our performance, most of the audience was in fits of laughter at us trying to get through this song together.*

I suppose that was the first time we really performed as a double act. It was also the first time we'd made an audience laugh and, standing on the stage, looking at the audience's faces, I thought, 'I didn't realize I had that in me, I liked doing that.'

*What's more, we still had our tops on, which was good news for everyone.*

We were having the time of our lives – showing off to girls, having a laugh and, at the same time, we were earning a living. We thought we'd cracked the holy trinity of job, money and girls, and it felt good. By now, school was a bit like MC Hammer's career – a thing of the past – and *Byker Grove* was a full-time job, which meant, for the first time, we both had a few quid in our pockets.

I saved up all my wages to get my first car – I was so keen that I had my first driving lesson on my seventeenth birthday. I went to that lesson with the two things that were vital to my driving ambitions – my provisional licence and a cushion to sit on.

I eventually passed, at my third attempt, and spent £950 on an MG Metro Turbo. It was metallic blue with red go-faster stripes and red seatbelts. Yes, even as a teenager, I oozed class. The only thing that was missing was a pair of furry dice and stickers on the windscreen saying 'ANT' and 'DEC'.

*Obviously, we've both got them in our cars now – that's one of the perks of being on the telly.'*

You know what it's like when you first pass your test – you go *everywhere* by car. If I could've driven from the living room to the toilet in that car, I would have. When my mam needed a pint of milk from the shop at the end of the road, I'd have the keys in the ignition before she could say 'semi-skimmed'.

*I wasn't quite so good as Dec with my wages. I didn't have the foresight and business acumen to invest in an MG Metro Turbo – and even if I had, I didn't have a driving licence, so it wouldn't have been much use.*

*At first, when I started earning money, I was too young to have a cash card. My mam didn't think it was a good idea to keep my wages in a shoebox under my bed – she was clever like that – so she gave me her card for an account she never used. The good thing was I could get my hands on my money whenever I liked, so I'd just take out £30, £40 or £50 at a time and buy trainers, clothes, CDs, petrol for Dec's car, that kind of thing. In those days, you could get a pair of trainers, a couple of albums and a McDonald's for . . . well, about £100. It's pretty much the same as now really.*

*I'm not that old, you know . . .*

*The trouble was I never really paid attention to how much money was in that account. I wasn't ridiculously frivolous, but I wasn't shy of spending it either.*

*The other trouble was that all the statements got sent to my mam and, eventually, my spending caught up with me. One morning, my mam burst into my room, with a statement in her hand, and it wasn't long before there was a statement coming out of her mouth.*

*If my memory serves me correctly, it was 'Where the bloody hell has all your money gone?'*

*I had exactly £50 left out of what had been a couple of thousand pounds I'd earned over the years. I was the Nick Leeson of Byker Grove.*

*I learnt a very valuable lesson that day, a lesson any younger readers would do well to heed – make sure your money goes into your bank account, and not your mam's.*

Shouldn't that be 'Be responsible and don't squander your money'?

*Oh yeah, that as well, yeah.*

*All in all, I learnt a lot from that spending and, in a way, I was glad it happened.*

I wasn't – I had to lend him £100 for Christmas presents.

That's what being a teenager is all about, isn't it? Wasting your money, hanging around with your mates and, of course, drinking.

My first real experience of drinking came at a family party when I was sixteen. It was a christening, and it was a very special day. I was so thrilled by a new addition to the family, so overjoyed at the gift of life, that I decided to celebrate . . . by drinking loads of lager.

The problem was we had a lot of filming to do the next day, but that didn't stop me putting away three pints – yes, three whole pints. Drinking that amount at sixteen was no mean feat, especially given the added obstacle that no man actually enjoys the taste of beer when they first drink it. Despite that, I soldiered on – I've always been good with stuff like that.

*What, drinking?*

Yes.

I arrived at work the next day and to say I felt sick, dizzy, sweaty and disorientated would be the understatement of the century. Your first hangover is like your first love – you never forget it.

I tried to struggle through at work but, in the end, the producers sent me home – with suspected alcohol poisoning.

It seemed like a fancy name for a hangover, but I didn't care, I got to go home and sleep it off, and that was all that mattered.

*When I heard the words 'alcohol poisoning', right there and then I knew one thing – me and Dec were going to be friends for life . . .*

*We started spending more and more time together, and now that we were older, we started going out to concerts or, as you're contractually obliged to call them as a teenager, gigs. Our first one was the Inspiral Carpets at Newcastle Mayfair, and it was absolutely brilliant. The first hurdle of the night was always getting past the bouncers – being in a children's drama meant people looked on you as, well, a child, but it seemed like the bouncers didn't even watch* Byker Grove.

**They looked more like *Children's Ward* fans to me . . .**

*Not only did the bouncers let us in, we were always left alone at indie gigs too. There was a good reason for that: the people there didn't have a clue who we were either.*

**We also went to a fantastic Jamiroquai gig at the Newcastle Riverside. I can still picture those venues now – the air thick with the smell of cigarette smoke, old beer and stale urine . . .**

**They were really magical places.**

**We loved both those bands and, years later, our paths crossed again. Clint Boon, from the Inspiral Carpets, wrote the theme tune to *Engie Benjy* – a children's animation series that me and Ant provided the voices for.**

*And people say we're not rock 'n' roll . . .*

**We also interviewed Jay Kay (from Jamiroquai) at his house for *cd:uk*. It was a huge country mansion in Buckinghamshire, and we had a great day. We played on his quad bikes and mini motorbikes, but never got the chance to try on his giant hats – unfortunately.**

*When we weren't going to gigs, we'd go to bars in town. Whatever it took to perfect the art of alcohol poisoning, we were prepared to do it. It was harder to be anonymous in pubs though. We would often get recognized, and that nickname that followed us around for years would come out: 'those two poofs off the telly'.*

*One year, after a premiere, me, Dec, Nicola, Jill and John went into town for a few drinks and, when a few members of the cast went out together, well, you were asking for trouble.*

*You may as well have gone up to the bar and said, 'Three pints, a Bacardi and coke and, if it's not too much trouble, could you find someone who'd like to beat me up, just so I can get it out of the way early?'*

*We were walking from one bar to another and a stocky lad in his late teens came up to me and asked me to take off my trousers. I thought, 'That's quite a chat-up line,' but I said no, I was using them and I had no intention of standing in the middle of town in my underpants. He asked again – 'Give me your trousers' – and I said no again. Then, surprise, surprise, the truth came out – the trouser request had been a red herring to distract from the main point of this encounter: he wanted to punch me in the face. After having the – pardon the pun – bare-faced cheek to keep my own trousers on, well, in his opinion, I was asking for it. And he gave it to me, in the form of a black eye.*

*It didn't go down very well at home – my mam hit the roof because, as she quite rightly pointed out, I should have run away, or just done anything but get punched in the face. The make-up girls at work weren't too pleased either: I was now doing a convincing impression of a bloke who was half man, half panda, and it made their job much harder. The next time I went out in town I wore two pairs of trousers, just to be on the safe side.*

I really felt for Ant but, at the same time, I was glad the lad hadn't gone for me. Clare was with me on one of her visits from London, and we were walking a few metres behind, so the lad just got to him first. Plus, my trousers weren't as nice as Ant's.

*It has to be said, I was also capable of bringing trouble on myself on a night out, like the time we went out for Boppa's eighteenth birthday. I had a lot of scenes to do the next day, so the sensible thing to do was take it easy and have an early night. I decided to go for the other option, which was to get blind drunk. We went to the same pub we'd been going to for a couple of years and, as we were all saying 'Happy eighteenth' to Boppa, you could* see the landlord looking at us thinking, 'Happy eighteenth? Hang on, I've been serving these kids for two years . . .'

Then, towards the end of the night, not content with consuming our own body weight in lager, we decided it was time to move on to the spirits, and Boppa got a drink called 'The Top Shelf'

**Oh no.**

*Oh yes.*

*The experienced pub-goers among our readers are already ahead of me here. This drink contained every single spirit from the top shelf in the same glass – vodka, Bacardi, Baileys, whiskey – you name it, it was in that glass – and we all had to down one. Well, I say, 'had to', we didn't have to, but we were all obeying the first law of teen life: if your mates tell you to do something, you do it, no matter how stupid, reckless and hangover-inducing it might be.*

*At the end of the night, I staggered home and did what everyone does at some point in their teenage years – I threw up all over my bedroom.*

*I woke up the next morning with a puzzle to solve. How had someone managed to break into my room and hit me over the head with a hammer for eight hours solid?*

*I felt absolutely dreadful. My head was banging, and the phone was ringing. It seemed louder than usual but, frankly, so did everything. I finally answered it, and it was the production office at Byker Grove, demanding to know why I was an hour late for filming. I'd forgotten all about it. To be honest, it was a miracle I'd even remembered where I lived.*

*I jumped up, begged Sarha to help me clean my room, had a shower and got to the shoot. We were heading to location, and I got on the minibus and sat next to Dec. I thought, 'At least my best mate'll be sympathetic, he'll help me get through this and give me a shoulder to cry on.' I was wrong.*

*He just took one look at me and said . . .*

**'You absolutely stink!'**

**And he did, he stank of Baileys, and pretty soon, the whole mini bus stank of Baileys – all the way to location. And this wasn't any ordinary location.**

We were filming at the Junior Great North Run. And we were dressed as Teenage Mutant Ninja Turtles.

*I'll just repeat that, in case you thought your eyes were playing tricks on you.*

*We were filming at the Junior Great North Run.*

*And we were dressed as Teenage Mutant Ninja Turtles.*

*And I stank of Baileys.*

*I considered jumping out of the moving minibus to try and get out of it, but in the end I decided there was no choice, I'd just have to try and get through the shoot.*

We were dressed as turtles because PJ and Duncan were doing the run in fancy dress for charity, and we didn't even have proper turtle outfits, because they were supposed to look homemade. So we had to wear white boiler suits made out of paper and painted green, homemade shells on our backs and turtle masks from a joke shop. The only thing greener than those turtle outfits was Ant's face.

We put the costumes on and jumped out of the minibus into the middle of a baking-hot day and thousands of people warming up for the run.

I turned to Ant and said, 'Cowabunga dude, Turtle Power!'

*I won't repeat what I said back to him.*

# Chapter 6

'He cannot see, can he? He can't see, man!'

Not my words, but the words of my character, Duncan, immediately after his best mate, PJ, had been blinded in a horrific paintball accident.

*It was definitely the most memorable storyline we were involved in on Byker Grove and, even now, nearly twenty years on, I still get people coming up to me and mentioning it. In fact, if you're reading this and you bump into me in the future, desperate to check how I am, all I'll say is my eyes are okay, my vision is fine and I haven't been paintballing since, thanks for asking.*

*It all happened towards the end of our time on the show, and we both took it very seriously. The plot was basically that, during a paintball contest between Byker Grove and rival youth club Denton Burn, PJ took off his mask to warn his mate Noddy – played by Brett Adams – about a shot that was coming towards him, when not one, but two paintballs were fired into his eyes. How's that for bad luck? To make it even more tragic, the shots came from the two girls PJ was seeing at the same time. He was involved in a love triangle with Debbie, played by Nicola, who was still my real-life girlfriend, and Amanda, played by Gemma Graham. As a result of the accident, PJ lost his sight and his girlfriend, but his best mate Duncan vowed to help him through his ordeal.*

*The producers had a long chat with me and Dec and explained the size and importance of the storyline and how we'd need to do some research.*

*As I mentioned before, Byker Grove had a history of tackling serious issues, like teenage pregnancy or gay kisses (we weren't involved in that one by the way), and when they covered these subjects, it was always done in a very professional way.*

*Other than Dec dabbling with arcade-game addiction, this was the first time we were asked to do proper research for one of these issue stories, so we knew this wasn't your normal pirate-radio-starting, cult-joining stuff: this was a big deal.*

*We went to a school for the blind in Newcastle and spoke to some kids who'd been able to see and had then lost their sight. And what came across was that a lot of them, understandably, were quite angry and frustrated, and that was definitely something that I tried to put into my performance. Another part of our research involved meeting a mobility officer, who taught me how to use a cane and Dec how you guide a blind person. She also taught me how to sit, stand and cross the road in the way a partially sighted or blind person would. She even blindfolded me and made me cross a busy road in Newcastle, using only my sense of hearing. It was the most demanding thing we'd faced in our short careers and the story dominated that series.*

To add to the drama, Duncan ended up in the arms of Debbie, PJ's girlfriend. She was wracked with guilt after the accident, and Duncan comforted her. With kissing. It was pretty strange kissing Ant's girlfriend, but it was all in the name of acting, and now that we weren't sawing people in half or unicycling, this was the sort of challenge that came with the job, and we just had to deal with it. It was also my first screen kiss, which added to the pressure, but Ant helped to prepare me and told me what it would be like – not what it would be like kissing his girlfriend, but doing an onscreen kiss.

*It was fine for me, the three of us were all mates anyway, and I was just thankful I didn't have to do it myself. Kiss Debbie, that is, not Dec – that would have been very unpleasant. The love triangle and the blindness meant we had some seriously meaty stuff to get our teeth into, although there were still a few lighter moments within it all.*

*After he left hospital, there was a scene where PJ went home and was greeted by his mam, which obviously meant an actress was required to play the part. Now, normally, the producers would cast an experienced thespian in a demanding role like this one, but on this occasion they decided to break with tradition and cast a complete unknown, someone who'd never done any acting in her life. That someone happened to be my mam.*

*It was an odd experience having her on set. Imagine bringing your mam to work with you – I half expected her to tell the director to eat his greens or shout at the props girl for not tidying up.*

*Then again, when it came to playing the role of bringing up a grumpy teenager who looked uncannily like me, well, my mam had been playing that part for several years, so she was perfect for it.*

*In the scene, PJ's mam just had to open the door and let him in, she didn't have to say anything. After a couple of takes, it was clear something was bothering her. Just as we were about to have another go at recording the scene, she stopped.*

*'Hang on,' she said in front of the assembled crew. 'If I was PJ's mam, I'd speak to him. He's just got out of hospital, hasn't he? I'd tell him I loved him, or give him a kiss or a cuddle or something, otherwise I'm going to look heartless!'*

*I couldn't believe it. She wanted to find out her character's motivation and improvise dialogue. Although, to be fair, she was absolutely right – and the director learnt a lesson then and there that I'd learnt as a small child: don't mess with my mam.*

*Her performance was great and, shortly afterwards, she went on a one-woman-theatre tour as 'PJ's Mam'. (That last bit's not true.)*

By now, the show was into its fifth series, and PJ's blindness was the main thing going on, which meant me and Ant were given a lot of screen time. In an attempt to take PJ's mind off the accident, the lads formed a band – Grove Matrix – because, of course, as any doctor worth their salt will tell you, the best cure for blindness is forming a boy band. The band consisted of me and Ant, plus three other lads who hadn't really been our mates in the series but were obviously very musical. They were Barney, who played keyboards, Marcus, who played, er, keyboards and Frew, who just danced – he was our Bez.

We even got to record a real song, in a real recording studio. It was called 'Tonight I'm Free' and was written by Richie Wermerling, who was the lead singer of a band called Let Loose.

Nicky Graham was going to produce it. He had written and

produced tracks for Bros, and he came up to Newcastle to produce 'Tonight I'm Free' for us. There was a slight problem when we got into the studio and discovered we weren't exactly the best singers in the world, but after pushing a few buttons and twiddling a few knobs, we sounded, well, almost okay.

*We did miss one trick when it came to the band performing the track on the show. We came out to a rapturous welcome and, naturally, PJ was helped on to the stage with his white cane. Once the track started, though, he miraculously took part in the full, energetic dance routine, despite the fact he supposedly couldn't see a thing. It wasn't the most realistic moment in TV history, but I'd learnt those dance moves, and I was damned if I was going to let that go to waste.*

Things couldn't have been going any better: we'd recorded a song, we were the main characters in the show and we were even getting quite a bit of fanmail. We were so happy, we were doing cartwheels.

*Not literally, I've always had a bad back, and it just wouldn't have been sensible.*

Then, one day, we were called up to Matthew Robinson's office for a chat about the next series. I can still picture that office now – it was at the back of the Mitre, and I always thought it was very small for the executive producer, which was what Matthew was by then. We sat down, and he swung round on his swivel chair – like a Bond villain, but without the cat to stroke, or the dastardly plan to take over the world. He told us that our characters were hugely popular, and the show was getting great ratings. 'This meeting's going pretty well,' we thought. But, apparently, *Byker Grove* was being watched by too many older kids. It was getting a big audience, but it was the wrong audience. The BBC was very keen to introduce some younger characters, and lower the average age of the viewers.

*'Good idea,' we said. 'We look forward to working with them next year – we can show them the ropes, give them a few tips – it should be fun.'*

He looked at us with a pained expression and explained that PJ and Duncan wouldn't be coming back. They were too old for a show about a youth club; this was the end of the line. Matthew told us he'd argued with the BBC, he'd tried to keep us, and had even suggested a spin-off show, but the big cheeses at the Beeb had quickly spotted the shortcomings of a drama about a blind boy and his heartbroken best mate. There would be a few more scenes in this series, and then PJ and Duncan would leave the show. I was stunned at the news, and I started to feel sick.

*We were both in shock. Matthew shook our hands, wished us luck and thanked us for taking it like men, then we left his office. We walked down the corridor together, side by side and in total silence, past the production offices, which were still buzzing, full of staff and crew getting on with their jobs, oblivious to the fact that our world had been shattered.*

I clearly remember thinking about the handful of scenes we had left to shoot as we drifted down the huge sweeping staircase that had featured in the show so often – they would be the last things we'd ever do on *Byker Grove*. I was devastated. We were seventeen, and it felt like we were about to be tossed on the scrapheap. But then, just as we reached the bottom step, something happened that changed our lives for ever.

*The door of Matthew's office burst open, and he shouted after us, 'Stop, stop! Telstar Records have just been on the phone, and they want to offer you a record contract.'*

We couldn't believe it and, in fact, at first, we *didn't* believe it, we thought it was a practical joke – but he was for real.

'Tonight I'm Free' had been so popular on the show that a record company thought there was a market for what we had done and that there was a chance we could crack the Top 40.

Without that moment, and what it did for us, we wouldn't be where we are today.

*In short, it's all Telstar's fault.*

PJ and Duncan the children's drama stars were about to undergo a drastic transformation and become PJ and Duncan the pop stars.

*It would be tough, though, and we quickly discovered our pop career wasn't going to be easy – not for us, not for our families . . .*

. . . and, most of all, not for the people who had the misfortune to buy our records.

But we were on our way to pop stardom, although it would still be another year before PJ and Duncan would 'Get Ready to Rhumble' . . .

# Chapter 7

*By the autumn of 1993, we'd left* Byker Grove. *We knew Telstar wanted to release our track, but we still couldn't quite believe it, so we took out a kind of insurance policy, a Plan B, just in case we didn't end up releasing the record and becoming bigger than The Beatles.*

*Our Plan B was something that all great pop stars do at one time or another – we started a B-Tech in Performing Arts at Newcastle College. We were both still really keen on acting and we thought that, if the music didn't work out, we'd complete our B-Tech and then, with any luck, go to drama school in London, then the BAFTAs, the Oscars and Hollywood. Either that, or we'd carry on crossing our fingers for a part in* Spender *anyway.*

*Telstar Records were as good as their word, though, and they did offer us a deal. We knew they had faith in us: they were confident we would deliver and convinced we were going to become icons of the pop world.*

They were so convinced that they offered us a one-single deal. That's right, folks, a deal to release one, whole single.

We might have been at college, but we still took time out from the important student stuff, like eating Pot Noodles and watching *Countdown*, to discuss the pros and cons of becoming pop stars. In fact, we did what any sensible adults would do in that situation and had a business meeting to discuss it. I can still picture it now: it was us two, sat in a big boardroom with bottles of mineral water and baskets of fresh fruit. Oh no, sorry, that's right: we were in my Mini Metro with two cans of Fanta and a bag of Mini Cheddars.

And we had to make a decision – were we going to give it a go?

It was a pretty tough meeting, which lasted for one, maybe even two cans of Fanta.

*We'd seen other soap stars move from TV to the charts, and it could be clichéd and cheesy, and we didn't want that — after all, we had principles, we'd appeared at roadshows for Mizz <u>and</u> Fast Forward magazines, for goodness' sake.*

*But then it dawned on us we had hardly any money and no career, so we decided to give our principles the same treatment as our empty bag of Mini Cheddars — and throw them out the window.*

Telstar had noticed that acts like Will Smith and Kriss Kross had done well with hip-hop/pop crossover tracks, and they were convinced that was going to be the next big trend. They told us we could be a part of that, and we decided to take their word for it. After all, these people were seasoned music-industry professionals and they were obeying one of the first laws of pop music: 'If you want hip-hop, go to a couple of lads from council estates in the west end of Newcastle.'

*They told us that they knew the response to Grove Matrix on Byker Grove had been huge and viewers had written in asking where they could buy the single. Who knows, maybe you sitting there reading this on the train, or you in the bath or even you in your bed may even have written one of those letters. If you did, then our advice to you is simple: don't ever admit it to anyone.*

*Something Telstar recognized was that, because kids had been watching us on TV for three years, we had something of a readymade fan base, and that gave us a head start. At least that's what Telstar told us. We were still standing there saying, 'Us? A single? Really?'*

We also made a decision that would help us deal with life in the music business. We decided to treat it just like all the other acting jobs we'd had, or *Byker Grove*, as it was otherwise known. We weren't real musicians, or trained singers so, in all honesty, we felt a bit like frauds. We were slightly embarrassed by the whole thing. We figured that, if we removed ourselves from it, it meant that when people ridiculed us, they would differentiate between our pop-star personality and our real personality.

*We basically told ourselves we'd be playing the part of pop stars. Don't get me wrong, I looked very like PJ, and Dec bore an uncanny resemblance to Duncan, but it helped us to draw a line between them and us.*

The decision was made. There was only one problem: we had to be eighteen to sign the record contract, and Ant's birthday wasn't until 18 November. If you're under eighteen, you're a child in the eyes of the law (if not in the eyes of the bouncers at the Newcastle Mayfair) and, essentially, that meant you had to get your parents' permission to be a pop star.

Don't get me wrong, I don't think there was an actual contract that said, 'I the undersigned hereby give my permission for my son to go on tour and be a pop star and that. Yours sincerely, Ant's mam,' but there were legal issues, and the alternative was our parents coming on tour with us.

*My mam might have been an accomplished actress by this point, but there was no way she was coming on the road with PJ and Duncan. Besides, who would cook Sarha's tea every night?*

*So with 'Tonight I'm Free' already 'in the can', and time to kill before Ant's birthday, we decided to carry on acting. That's not a Carry On film, by the way, we actually just carried on acting.*

*Through Dee Wood of chaperone and log-cabin fame, we'd already started helping out backstage at the Tyne Theatre in Newcastle. We worked on* The King and I *and* The Little Shop of Horrors. *Dec would operate the follow spot. It must have been hard for a show-off like him to put other people in the spotlight. I used to work in the flies, high above the stage, which basically entailed dropping the scenery down when there was a scene change. It would all be attached to a rope on a kind of pulley system and, displaying the same dexterity I'd shown on my paper round, I would regularly get the rope length wrong, which meant the scenery would crash on to the stage and surprise the actors. It was another sign my future lay in performing, rather than behind the scenes. At the end of every night, we'd get a pay packet.*

*Well, by 'pay', I mean lager, and by 'packet', I mean pint glass. We got paid a pint of lager, that's what I'm trying to say.*

*But we loved it. We loved being in and around the world of theatre, we loved the camaraderie and the crack with the stage crew and we loved a drink at the end of the night.*

*They were great lads, the crew, always making jokes: 'You two idiots haven't got a hope in hell of getting in the charts,' 'There's more chance of Joan Collins playing centre forward for Newcastle United,' that kind of thing. They were hilarious, they really were.*

**By now, we'd both worked out that, whatever happened, we wanted to be involved in performing somehow. It was really all we knew, and we felt very passionate about it, which meant a normal job was no longer an option. Oh, and there was also the fact that we'd already left school and had never done a proper day's work in our lives.**

*Dee approached us one day with an exciting proposition. She asked if we'd like to be in a production of* The Wizard of Oz. *It was going to be on over the half-term holiday, and she thought that, as the two lads from* Byker Grove, *we'd really bring the audiences flocking in. Well, that and the fact there was nothing else to do during half term. So we agreed. It was only after we'd already promised to do it, that we got round to asking who was going to take which part. I can still remember that conversation with Dee:*

*'So, who are we going to be? The Tin Man?*
    *The Lion?*
    *The Scarecrow?'*

**'The Wizard himself, perhaps?'**

*'Not quite,' Dee said.*
    *'Ant's going to be the Coroner of the Munchkin City, and Dec will play the Mayor of the Munchkin City.'*
    *'The what!?'*

*We immediately regretted signing up for it. It would be humiliating. If we wanted a venueful of people to roll in the aisles laughing at us, we could just sing to them. Things were also about to get a lot worse, because before we knew which parts we were playing, I'd told Nicola to come and see the show. She was really keen and told me she was going to bring all our mates from the cast of* Byker Grove. *I calmly tried to talk her out of it – 'Please don't come, I'll do anything, I beg you' – but she told me she'd already booked the tickets and was really looking forward to it. Little did she know her boyfriend was about to go from blind breakdancer to dwarf coroner.*

*On our first night, we walked out to see two whole rows in the stalls of the* Byker Grove *cast, including Rory, John Jefferson and Lyndyann, all killing themselves laughing. Our faces were going redder and redder with embarrassment, although fortunately, thanks to our already-painted-rosy, Munchkin cheeks, no one could see that. Their hilarity reached a crescendo as we belted out our only lines:*
*'As coroner, I must aver / I thoroughly examined her / And she's not only merely dead / She's really most sincerely dead.'*

Then I'd come in with, 'Then this is a day of independence/ For all the Munchkins/And their descendants/Yes, let the joyous news be spread/The wicked old witch at last is dead.'

We then launched into a full-blooded song-and-dance routine of 'Ding Dong, the Witch is dead, which old Witch? The Wicked Witch . . .' By this point, rows F and G could hardly breathe for laughing. We weren't going to be allowed to forget this one in a hurry.

*I only wish we could have clicked our heels three times, said, 'There's no place like home,' and ended up in Kansas City, or even back up the road in Fenham would have done – I just wanted to be anywhere but the Tyne Theatre.*

*Nicola and I split up not long after that. After many heartfelt phone calls, we realized it just wasn't working out. I've spoken to her since; we're still in touch and are still good friends but, at the time, it hit both of us hard, because we were each other's first love and we'd been together for three years. We briefly dated again the following year but, again, called it a day. I don't think the amount of time I was spending away from Newcastle helped. Having said that, she might just never have got over seeing me as that dwarf coroner.*

You'd think after *The Wizard of Oz* experience we'd have learnt our lesson about performing in plays, but there were still a few more theatrical disasters to come. That autumn, Dee decided to put on a specially written pantomime. Christmas was still a few months away, but Dee always did like to get things organized early. It was called 'Strike in Pantoland' and, although we had insisted on better parts in this one, it still had – well, let's just say it had complications.

The idea behind the pantomime was that all the panto characters had started industrial action and gone on strike. At this point, if someone had shouted, 'Where's your career?', the answer would have been, 'It's behind me.' I was Jack from *Jack and the Beanstalk* and Ant was Captain Hook from *Peter Pan*.

*Oh no I wasn't.*

Oh yes you were. Sorry, force of habit. All the performances took place at a truly unique venue – the local mental health hospital, St Nicholas's. The play was put on to raise money for the hospital, but you won't be surprised to hear it didn't go well. The plot would have confused most audiences so, for the fragile patients there, it was a tough watch. Ant came out as Captain Hook, shouting, 'Aarrrggghh,' which completely freaked them out. Before we knew it, we were longing for a return to the Munchkin City.

*The most disconcerting thing, though, was that the audience also had a tendency to get up and wander around during the middle of the performance, which is really offputting when you're on stage. The whole experience was just bizarre – both for the cast and, no doubt, for the audience.*

All in all, we put their treatment back five years . . .

# Chapter 8

Throughout our disastrous dabblings with the world of theatre, there was one thing that kept us going: 18 November. That was when Ant would turn eighteen and, in the eyes of the law, civilized society and, most importantly, Telstar Records, would become a man, which meant we could finally sign the record contract and start our new life as pop stars.

I don't think I've ever been so excited about someone else's birthday.

*In the mean time, we kept going to college. It was important that we got an education and a commitment to college was a sign of that.*

*Oh, and we had nothing better to do.*

*Well, I had nothing better to do. The same couldn't be said for Dec.*

I'll admit that I always took a 'laid-back' approach to college, and by 'laid-back' I mean I laid back on the sofa, watched daytime TV and didn't bother going. Once we had the offer of the record deal, I wasn't really into college.

*He was never really IN college, never mind into it. He was supposed to give me a lift there and, most days, ten minutes after he was meant to be at mine, I'd get a phone call and hear the words I was dreading: 'I don't think I'm going to make it in today,' so I'd have to run for the bus.*

*It takes a special talent to keep someone waiting and make them late without even leaving your front room.*

What can I say? I have a gift.

During one of my rare appearances at college in the first term, the lecturer, Shirley, sat us and the rest of the class down and told us they were putting together an end-of-term show and that all the students had to take part. We *had* to do it, otherwise we risked failing the course. It was an old-time music-hall show, and it would go on tour around a collection of venues that are traditionally overlooked by plays, bands and comedians travelling the region – the old people's homes of the North-east.

Yes, after terrifying the patients of St Nicholas's mental health hospital, we were now moving on to the new task of scaring pensioners all over Tyneside.

*We had to come up with an act and, as usual, we had no idea what to do, so Shirley suggested we did a double act. We both reacted in exactly the same way:*

*'A proper double act? Us two? That's never going to work.'*

But, in the absence of any other credible ideas, we decided to give it a go. We put together a traditional old-time-variety double act. We may have wowed the BBC Club with the risqué love triangle that consisted of me, Ant and Mrs Jones, but this was a proper double act. Think Abbott and Costello, Dean Martin and Jerry Lewis, or Morecambe and Wise. Only nowhere near as funny.

The act itself was very simple: I'd stand on stage and try to read a poem and Ant would keep coming on and . . .

*. . . interrupting.*

I can still remember that poem now:

There's a one-eyed yellow idol to the north of Kathmandu,
There's a little marble cross below the town;
And a broken-hearted woman tends the grave of 'Mad' Carew,
While the yellow god forever gazes down.

*And then I would come on and deliver my hilarious catchphrase: 'What's going on here then?' Probably my finest moment in the act was when I walked on stage with a cabbage on the end of a dog lead. Dec would ask*

66

me what I was doing with a cabbage on the end of a lead, and I'd reply, 'Cabbage? They told me it was a collie!', and walk off.

Admit it, you're laughing, aren't you? No? Well, the residents of those old people's homes loved it, probably because the jokes were the only things older than they were.

We went all over the North-east with that show, and that was our first tour, long before we tasted life on the road as PJ and Duncan. I always thought we should have sold merchandise — a branded checked blanket perhaps, or slippers with our faces on but, strangely, no one else shared my vision.

They say, 'What goes on tour, stays on tour,' but on this occasion, I am prepared to do something those OAPs did every lunchtime: spill the beans.

One of the biggest problems was that, as with the mental hospital, the audience weren't always 100 per cent focused on the show. They'd either get up and walk around or start talking to each other and, in their case, it was never a whisper. We were starting to think it might have been the quality of our performance: we'd often come a poor second to a plate of Rich Tea or a packet of Werther's Originals.

There was one performance where we faced a particularly tough crowd. We were doing our act, and one of a gaggle of old ladies in the front row started making this mad sound at the most inappropriate moments. 'Eee, eeee, eeee,' she would cry, really loudly, again and again and again. We were in the middle of the cabbage-on-a-dog-lead gag and all we could hear was 'Eee, eeee, eeee.' It went on at intervals right until the end, and then we just couldn't help it, we cracked up laughing. And once we started, we couldn't help ourselves. The act stopped, the audience was silent, even the eee-ing had ceased. One of the other residents, who was sitting next to 'eee woman', seemed angry with us, and shouted at the top of her voice, 'Hey, man, yous cannot laugh at her, she hasn't got a tongue!'

Not our finest hour as a double act.

Finally, after a few more, less eventful, music-hall performances and even, in my case, a few days at college, the big day arrived – Ant's eighteenth.

*I had a party at a social club in Benwell, which is in the west end of Newcastle, on Joanne Street, as it happens, and quite a lot of the Byker Grove cast came, although if they were hoping for another singsong from the Munchkin City, they were going to be sorely disappointed. My family were there, too. Even more important than the party, though, was the fact that we could finally sign the record contract.*

*We'd got a lawyer to look at it, and he'd recommended that we didn't sign. He said it wasn't particularly lucrative or creatively liberating and, on the whole, it looked like a pretty bad contract. However, he also said that he'd completely understand if we did sign. That was the kind of sharp-minded legal genius we'd paid good money for. The thing was, it was the best offer on the table, because it was the only offer on the table. Plus, we'd waited months for this moment, so we decided to sign. A milestone like that deserves plenty of fanfare, and an extravagant location where you can put pen to paper. Unfortunately, we didn't get either of those things. We signed it in Dave Holly's office.*

*By this time, Dave had moved premises to a new office opposite the central station and above the Baker's Oven, a baker's in Newcastle – he was obviously splashing out with the money we were earning for him – so we signed our lives away and celebrated with a cheese pasty and an iced finger. We were now officially recording 'artistes', and 'Tonight I'm Free' was scheduled for a Christmas 1993 release. We'd been given permission to miss college when we had music work to do, so we immediately organized performances and promotion to try and get people to buy the single. It was time to hit the road – again.*

*Our first ever gig as PJ and Duncan was at the Birmingham Dome on the TV Hits Roadshow.*

We've all seen pop stars travelling in limos and being flown around in helicopters, so as we sat in a packed train carriage on the 2.38 from Newcastle to Birmingham, we couldn't help wondering if there'd been some sort of mistake. It was just the two of us – no burly bodyguard, no record-company assistant, no tour manager, no nothing. Just us with our leather Head bag and a change of clothes. Still, we might not have had an entourage, but we definitely felt we were going places.

And the first of those places was Birmingham New Street station.

We arrived there, jumped in a taxi and turned up at the stage door with our CD in our bag and said, 'Hello, er, we're here to sing?'

We were only doing one song that particular evening because, well, we only had one song. We were sharing the bill with a couple of solo acts and a group called Menergy.

*They were a bunch of ex-male strippers.*
*They were men with energy.*
*They were Menergy.*

Backstage beforehand, we got chatting to all the other bands, bombarding them with questions about how they were feeling, and if they were nervous too. The thing that struck us was how calm they all seemed and, in Menergy's case, how much baby oil they were getting through.

I suppose they'd done it so many times before. We, on the other hand, were completely new to all this.

*Eventually, our big moment arrived and, in the last few seconds before we went on, I remember thinking, 'Well, this is it, we've got to just do it now.'*

*We gave the CD to the sound engineer and told him it was 'track one, full mime', words we would come to use many, many times over the next few years. The nerves had really taken hold by now. We hadn't done any rehearsing, because we were just going to do the routine we'd done on Byker Grove, which hadn't been that long ago, but now we were beginning to wish we had. It sounded like there were thousands of people in the venue. We were young, we had no experience and we had absolutely no idea what to expect. In spite of all of that, right there and then we set sail on a voyage of pop discovery that would last far too long.*

*As we stepped on to the stage, the whole place went bananas. It was incredible! Before we'd even opened our mouths to start miming, the crowd was screaming and, for once, it seemed to be the good kind of screaming. Because* Byker Grove *had been so popular and our parts had become so big, there was clearly this recognition between the audience and the two of us. We couldn't believe it.*

*We did the song, but the whole thing was just a blur, it was over in a matter of minutes — two minutes and forty-three seconds, to be precise. As an added bonus, we didn't hear 'Eee, eee, eee' once.*

We came off stage on a complete high, unable to fully comprehend what had just happened to us and how well it had gone. We spent most of the train journey back talking it all over. The venue, the crowds, Menergy's outfits . . .

We treated ourselves to a burger each and just buzzed all the way home.

*From the gig, not the burger.*

We got back to Newcastle, and it felt like our lives had changed overnight. We were eighteen, and we were pop stars. But we didn't celebrate, we didn't get drunk, we just went home and had an early night. Not necessarily because we wanted to . . .

*. . . but because we had to do our double act at another old people's home the next day.*

*The music-hall tour hadn't finished, and we'd made a commitment, so we got out the dog lead and the cabbage, and off we went.*

*We were leading a bizarre double life of musical-hall double act by day and fledgling teen idols by night, although the audiences for both gigs had a lot in common: they both liked screaming, eating sweets and, occasionally, someone would wet themselves.*

*Our second gig was in Stockton-on-Tees, near Darlington, and we knew this one was a big deal, because East 17 were headlining. When we were on stage, there were girls fainting and crying. This was pop hysteria at its finest.*

*Slowly but surely, we were growing into the roles of pop stars. At first, I wasn't sure how to act before and after the songs, or even during the song. But before you knew it, you'd be striking those boy-band poses you'd picked up from somewhere.*

Probably from East 17 . . .

Next was the Hammersmith Palais in London, and the hysteria seemed to really go up a notch. There were security guards pulling girls out of the crowd, and at first I thought, 'They seem very keen to leave,' but then I realized they were fainting with excitement at seeing PJ and Duncan. It was a strange feeling but, if I'm honest, it was also a real thrill.

And after the gig, we just couldn't get out of the venue.

*The doors were locked.*

*I'm joking. We couldn't get out because there were so many girls at the stage door. They had to use extra security to get us into the car. If there's one thing you need when you're faced with a small group of pop-crazed fourteen-year-olds, it's half a dozen security guards, preferably with extensive military experience. Trust me, those girls could get very, very vicious. And they seemed like proper fans – they knew our real names, they'd read interviews with us in magazines. It felt, for the first time, that the attention was focused on us two. We weren't holding on to the coat tails of a bunch of male strippers like Menergy. Besides, holding on to Menergy's coat tails was usually a mistake – they were attached with Velcro and came off at the drop of a hat.*

*Don't get us wrong: we knew our fans were just girls of a certain age who get obsessed with pop stars, and we knew they were seeing other boy bands behind our back, but it still felt good.*

Finally, after more roadshows and more old people's homes, 'Tonight I'm Free' was released. We couldn't have been more excited. We'd had such an amazing reaction at all the roadshows that we just knew the single would do well; it was simply a question of *how* well. That Sunday, we both sat down in our front rooms to listen to Mark Goodier doing the Top 40 on Radio 1. He counted down the first ten places from 40 to 30: no sign of it, which meant our debut single had made the Top 30 – brilliant.

Then they ran down the next ten, and we still weren't mentioned, which meant it would be in the Top 20 – even better.

Then another ten went by, and still no PJ and Duncan, which meant our first ever release had made the Top 10. We were stunned: this couldn't be happening.

*It turned out we were right:*

*It wasn't happening.*

*We hadn't even made the Top 40 – 'Tonight I'm Free' went straight in at number sixty-two.*

*We were devastated.*

I sat at home that Christmas and watched the *Smash Hits* Poll Winners Party on TV. I think our invite had got lost in the post. Take That won everything that year, and you certainly couldn't imagine them going to college, running for the bus or touring old people's homes.

After just one single, it seemed like our career could be over – and the reality of becoming successful pop stars seemed further away than ever.

# Chapter 9

With our careers in the music industry hanging in the balance, this was a time for calm reflection and a chance to consider the future. Whatever happened, we were still on the B-Tech in Performing Arts. If the music didn't work out, that could provide us with a route back into acting, so getting that qualification was still absolutely vital. Bearing that in mind, I made a decision.

I left college immediately.

The tour of the old people's homes had pushed me over the edge, and I decided college just wasn't for me. Fortunately, at the same time, something else came along. Telstar, who clearly weren't taking any notice of our record sales, decided they wanted us to record a second single.

They'd seen the reaction we'd been getting at the roadshows, and they thought that, with the right track and enough promotion, we still had a chance of having a hit. With any luck, we might even crack the Top 60.

So, we recorded our second single. The deal was exactly the same as the first one: one single, without a commitment from them to release any more of our material. The song was called 'Why Me? (Is it justified?)' and, as you can see, like Bryan Adams' 'Everything I Do (I do it for you)' and a lot of *good* pop songs, part of the title was in brackets. Although 'Is it justified?' may just have been what Telstar's accountants said after seeing the sales of our first single.

After we finished recording it, we set off on another whirlwind promotional tour. When you're a pop star, that's the only kind of promotional tour you do: it's quick, and it destroys everything in its path.

*I was still going to college. I didn't have the same carefree attitude as Dec. He's always been a bit more impulsive than me, and I suppose I was conscious of still needing something to fall back on, especially after my career as a paperboy hadn't worked. And a part of me enjoyed student life, it was different from school. Everyone was there because they wanted to be – well, everyone apart from Dec, who wasn't there because he didn't want to be – and there was no teasing because I'd been on the telly.*

*After shining as the man with a cabbage on a dog lead, it was soon time for my next big role, the lawyer in Bertolt Brecht's* The Caucasian Chalk Circle. *In case you're not familiar with that play, it's an example of Brecht's epic theatre and is a parable about a girl who steals a baby but becomes a better mother than its natural parents.*

*At least, that's what it says on Wikipedia. I can't remember a thing about it.*

*At the same time as rehearsing for the play, I'd be off doing promotion for 'Why Me?' in the evenings. I must be the only performer in history to combine a Bertolt Brecht play with the Just 17 roadshow.*

*When it came to opening night, I was ready for my debut as a serious stage actor, and Dec even came to see me in it.*

**It was awful, absolutely bloody awful.**

*He's right, it was.*

**I was joined in the audience by Matthew Robinson, the producer from** Byker Grove, **a man who knew all about drama, stage acting and great playwrights.**

*I never did find out – what did he make of it?*

**He left at the interval.**

*I can't blame him, I didn't enjoy it much either. I almost felt nostalgic for the heady days of being the coroner of the Munchkin City. I caught Dec's eye during the performance, and I could see he was thinking, 'You poor sod.'*

Actually, I was thinking, 'Where's Matthew gone?', and 'How long does this drivel last?', but I did feel sorry for Ant.

*Anyway, not long after that I decided to leave the course as well – The* Caucasian Chalk Circle *convinced me that college wasn't my cup of tea. Looking back, I probably should've gone when Dec did.*

Too right you should have, then I never would have had to sit through that bloody play. I'll never get those two hours back . . .

*As soon as we really started on the music, we realized life was about to go one of two ways: we'd either end up on* Top of the Pops, *or the dole. So we started working. Hard. As well as the roadshows, we started performing at under-18s discos. Back then, they were a popular way to promote a new band, and they'd always be held at a local nightclub with sticky floors and the smell of stale smoke. I think it was actually a part of the contract. When it came to getting changed and preparing for the gig, we'd always enjoy the same lavish backstage facilities: the manager's office or the staff toilet.*

*These discos provided our first taste of the kind of extreme reactions we provoked from any lads who'd happen to be in the audience. And by 'extreme', I mean extremely hostile and aggressive. We'd take to the dance- floor – there wasn't even a stage – and perform our extensive back catalogue of two songs, then the teenage girls there would start screaming and shout- ing our names. With the lads, though, it was very different. They tended to show their appreciation by throwing ice cubes or ashtrays at us, and if they couldn't find anything to throw, they'd just spit at us. It happened every night without fail and there was nothing you could do about it – if someone spat at you, you'd just have to swallow it.*

Not literally, that would be disgusting.

We did have to put up with it, though, and in a way, we could see where they were coming from. They were teenage boys who'd been dragged along to this disco to watch their girlfriends scream at these two jokers from *Byker Grove*. It wouldn't have put me in a good mood either.

*Undeterred, we threw ourselves into life on the road, something we'd become very familiar with over the next few years. We had a driver who would ferry us from place to place and, for a while, we seemed to live in a non-stop cycle of motorway service stations, Travelodges and Ginsters pasties. We were living the life of an HGV driver, but stopping to get spat on once or twice a day.*

*After each gig, we'd go back into the manager's office, wipe the saliva off our clothes, check for ice cube- and ashtray-based bruises and get changed. Then our driver would head off towards the following night's venue. We'd drive halfway there that night and then stop at a Travelodge.*

*Naturally, there would always be two rooms booked — one for the driver and one for us two to share. Yes, we had to share — every night we'd toss a coin to see who got the bed and who got the fold-out sofa — the standard of our accommodation gave us another indication of how much faith the record company had in us. I sometimes thought we would have been better off getting a job as drivers for a boy band ourselves: at least that way we'd have got our own rooms.*

All the time we were doing the discos, we were chasing the Holy Grail for all pop stars, something so special, so powerful, so amazing that we were desperate to do it – an appearance at the Radio 1 Roadshow. Never mind *TV Hits* or *Fast Forward* magazine, Radio 1 was the big one. We knew if we could get on the bill, our record would be played on national radio to millions of listeners, which would result in our record sales going up, which would hopefully persuade Telstar to let us record a third single.

*As is normal practice in the music industry, the record company employed a plugging company. Where Telstar's job would be to choose tracks for us, organize contracts and decide on releases, the plugger's job was simple – get people to hear our records. Sounds simple but, depending on the record, it can be very difficult. Within the plugging company, you'd have different people for what, back then, were the three main ways to get your music heard – TV, radio and magazines.*

*Matt Connolly, our radio plugger, did some serious persuasion and managed to pull off an almighty coup, a spot at the Radio 1 Roadshow in*

*Glasgow. I don't know how he did it – maybe he had some compromising pictures of the head of Radio 1 – but he did it, and that was all that mattered. This was a big moment. It really felt like the start of something. Things were about to change and, if we played our cards right, we could even end up with the one thing we'd always dreamed of: our own rooms at the Travelodge.*

The plugging company told us we'd also been offered the chance to perform the song live on *Blue Peter* – yes, you read that right, *Blue Peter*. At the time, they didn't really have many bands on the show, and for us to be invited on was a bit special – either that or the Royal Highland Bagpipers had dropped out at the last minute.

Then, inevitably, the bad news came. *Blue Peter* was the same day as the Radio 1 Roadshow. They were the two biggest opportunities of our career so far, and they clashed. Obviously, we wanted to do both, but that seemed impossible. *Blue Peter* had booked us for the day, it was live at around five o'clock and we would need to rehearse beforehand. There was no way they would ever let us go up to Glasgow in between, in case there was a traffic jam and we missed the show.

Then we had an idea: what if we did the Radio 1 Roadshow without telling *Blue Peter*?

We asked the record company if it could be done and they came up with a plan. We'd do a rehearsal at *Blue Peter* in the morning, then fly up to Glasgow on a private jet, sing our song on the Radio 1 stage and fly back in time for the show at 5.10.

*At least, I think that was how the plan worked – we both stopped listening after we heard the words 'private' and 'jet'.*

*This was one of the most exciting things that had ever happened to us. We were going to fly on a private jet and stitch up Blue Peter. It didn't get much more rock 'n' roll than this.*

When the day came, we did it all as planned. After we'd finished our rehearsal, the *Blue Peter* production team asked us if we needed anything. Did we want any lunch? We were suddenly very cagey, saying, 'No, no, we're . . . er . . . going out for lunch – in London, that's where we'll be – in London, and definitely nowhere else. Anyway, we've got to fly, I mean go, we've got to go – 'bye!'

And off we went. We caught the jet, which was just about the most decadent thing I had ever experienced in my whole life. It had plush leather everywhere, there were only eight seats, it was totally luxurious. We got to Glasgow, did the show, and it went like a dream. The Scottish crowd gave us the most amazing response, as they would continue to do every time we performed there. We left Glasgow on a high, over the moon that phase one of our evil masterplan had been completed.

We felt like a pair of Bond villains.

Well, if you can imagine Bond villains in baggy jeans and fluorescent shirts . . .

*We arrived back in West London and at* Blue Peter *in good time, feeling very pleased with ourselves – until word got back to us that the producers had found out exactly what we'd done. They were furious. They threatened to pull us off the show, which would have been a desperate blow to our promotion plans. We were embarrassed, but also angry. Who had snitched on us? Someone had gone behind our backs and told* Blue Peter *about the Radio 1 Roadshow. We had to find out who.*

*Then the penny dropped. They'd simply listened to Radio 1. They heard us on the radio, then immediately went to check our dressing rooms. It didn't take Hercule Poirot to work it out. So, despite their anger, and partly due to the fact it was too late for them to book anyone else, they graciously let us perform on the show. Afterwards, they told us we'd never perform on* Blue Peter *again but, frankly, we didn't care, we'd been in a private jet and, thanks to them and Radio 1, our new single had been heard by millions of kids.*

Mark Goodier had been the DJ at the Radio 1 Roadshow and, from that gig onwards, he and his producer, Fergus Dudley, championed us, playing our singles on Radio 1 whenever they could. After all the hard work and our shameless deception of *Blue Peter*, 'Why Me?' went into the UK singles chart with a bullet at number twenty-seven. Okay, it might not have been superstardom but, after number sixty-two for the first single, we felt like we'd just sold out Wembley Stadium. We were in the Top 30, and things were moving in the right direction.

Telstar immediately took up the option for a third single, which meant it was time to go back into the studio. Little did we know that we were about to record a track that would become our biggest hit, and would follow us around for the next fifteen years . . .

# Chapter 10

Watch us wreck the mic.
Watch us wreck the mic.
Watch us wreck the mic.
P–S–S–S–yche.

*It's up there with 'Bohemian Rhapsody', isn't it?*

*'Let's Get Ready to Rhumble' was our third single, and most probably our last chance of making it as pop stars (if you didn't count the last chance we'd had on the second single). It was certainly our catchiest track yet; once it got inside your head, it wouldn't go away, a bit like a nasty migraine. But it was a great pop song.*

*By this stage, we also had something else in our favour – a music manager. We hired Kim Glover to take care of some of the stuff we didn't know about, like the entire music industry. Kim had managed New Kids on the Block in Europe so, when it came to complicated stuff, like white boys in baggy jeans trying to rap, she knew what she was doing. She was a fiery little redhead who also managed Let Loose, whose lead singer had written 'Tonight I'm Free'. Kim had seen the reaction we'd got at some of the roadshows, she'd been around the industry for a while and the whole thing seemed like a good fit.*

*Kim always wore a bumbag and a black beret and carried a clipboard and a mobile phone that never had any battery left. She'd call everyone 'gang', so we always knew we were leaving somewhere when we heard a shrill, 'Come on, Kim's gang, we're going.' We'd all stop what we were doing and follow her to the next gig, or photo shoot, or signing, or possibly all three in one. With Kim's arrival came more gigs, more interviews and more hard work at the sweaty coalface of pop semi-stardom.*

**It wasn't long before that hard work started to pay off, and we were now getting screamed and spat at in some of the UK's very**

finest dodgy nightclubs. After weeks of non-stop promotion, it was time to release 'Rhumble' – that's what I'm going to call it from now on, I can't be bothered to say 'Let's Get Ready to Rhumble' every time we mention it, okay? Good. For the week of release, we'd been booked to appear on *Live & Kicking*, the BBC1 Saturday-morning show with Andi Peters. The Saturday-morning shows were a big battleground for pop stars at that time because, naturally, kids would go out and buy records on Saturday afternoons, so the hope was that our performance would convince them to buy 'Rhumble'. When it came to that week's Top 40, it rocketed straight into the charts at number eighteen. We weren't exactly setting the world on fire, but we were making progress. Slowly.

*We had listened to the chart on Sunday night, and on Monday lunchtime Kim rang us with some news. We had been booked to appear on that Thursday's* Top of the Pops. *Top of the Pops! We couldn't believe it. It was news we had always hoped for but never really expected. We'd grown up watching this show and it was amazing to be invited on it. In the week leading up to it, we promoted like we'd never promoted before. Trust me, if you were aged between about five and fifteen in July of 1994, me and Dec were unavoidable.*

*Top of the Pops* was, of course, a dream come true. There was just one teensy, weensy problem: we would be required, as everyone was, to do live vocals. Yes, rapping on the telly live, rather than miming. This was something we weren't used to, so we started rehearsing straight away. We got a tape of the instrumental version of the track, and we went to work.

The only trouble was we were out on the road doing gigs and sleeping in Travelodges, and we didn't have a tape machine, so we had to practise in the only place that did have a tape machine – our van. The hired burgundy Toyota Previa, a kind of people carrier – well, I suppose all cars carry people, but you know what I mean – we went everywhere in doubled up as our rehearsal studio. I was in the driver's seat, with Ant in the passenger seat, and we sat in a hotel car park practising our live rapping. We must have looked like a right couple of halfwits.

*When it came to the day of the show, we spent a long afternoon rehearsing in the studio in front of the cameras. We weren't used to rapping and dancing at the same time, so we had to make sure we could pull off all the moves and the vocals without getting too out of breath, which is harder than it sounds. That was actually the most embarrassing part of the day. The* Top of the Pops *crew had seen everyone in that studio down the years, like Madonna, U2, David Bowie, so watching a couple of former child actors cough and splutter their way through five renditions of 'Rhumble' was hardly likely to impress them.*

*The show was filmed at Elstree Studios, which was also home to the* EastEnders *set. It was a bit of a thrill in the canteen at lunchtime spotting people like Dot Cotton (salad) and Ian Beale (chicken Kiev).*

*The number-one record that week was Wet Wet Wet's 'Love Is All Around' and, appearing on* Top of the Pops *with us were Clubhouse, Bad Boys Inc., The Grid, CJ Lewis and Skin. Bizarrely, the show was hosted by Julian Clary. I just remember feeling incredibly nervous before we did it, mainly because everyone around us seemed incredibly nervous too. Kim, Les Molloy our TV plugger, Adam Hollywood our A&R man and everyone connected to PJ and Duncan seemed to be on edge. At the time, I just thought it was because the show was such a big deal but, looking back, I imagine they were worried about the live rapping and us being a bit crap – with good reason.*

*Finally, after what seemed like an eternity of hanging around, it came to our performance. The butterflies in our stomachs were going mental as we stepped on to the stage and got into position. The opening bars boomed through the speakers, and immediately my mouth went desert-dry and my top lip stuck like glue to my front teeth. We took deep breaths and launched into the first line. And we rhumbled like we'd never rhumbled before. Nobody could accuse us of being half-hearted – we flung ourselves around the stage like a couple of rapping rag dolls. The audience was full of PJ and Duncan fans, who played their part brilliantly, screaming and cheering in all the right places. We grew in confidence throughout the song and finished* with our tightly choreographed dance break and a few 'rhumbles' to fade. The camera moved off, and Julian Clary linked to a VT.

We'd done it. We were breathless and sweaty but ecstatic. We'd made our Top of the Pops *debut*, we'd given it everything we had and we had absolutely smashed it. We were exhausted, but we were buzzing. Until the floor manager made an announcement to the packed studio: 'Thanks, everybody, we'll just do that one more time.' Bollocks! Thankfully, the second time went even better than the first, and we went off home with our Top of the Pops *cherries well and truly popped.*

But had it been enough to propel 'Rhumble' up the charts? We sat down on Sunday night to listen to the Top 40 in that most exotic of locations – the forecourt of South Mimms service station, just off the M1.

I can still hear Bruno Brookes' crazy DJ voice now: 'The highest climber of the week, up nine places to number nine, it's PJ and Duncan with 'Let's Get Ready to Rhumble'. I never did find out what Bruno Brookes was doing in the back of our car, but that's another story.

*Number NINE! That was a top-ten hit! This was big time, we'd officially made it as pop stars. This called for a major celebration, so, right there in the middle of the forecourt, we cracked open a bottle of something fizzy. I think it was Irn-Bru. And that was it. Now we had a top-ten hit, Telstar said six words that struck fear and excitement into our hearts: 'We need an album, by Christmas.'*

*It was already June, and we were worried. Recording an album meant a lot of hard work. There were lyrics to write and melodies to compose. How would the people who did all that stuff for us get it done in time?*

*Telstar told us that wasn't our problem, they'd get us into the studio when the songs were written and ready to go. In the meantime, we should stick to doing what we did best: more interviews, more photo shoots and, wherever possible, more TV appearances.*

During the summer of 1994, ITV had a Saturday-morning kids' show called *Gimme 5*. It was made at the old Tyne Tees studios on City Road in Newcastle, and we became regular guests. The producers always joked that we were only booked because we stayed with our mams and they didn't have to pay for hotels, but we knew they didn't mean it. We'd get involved in games and sketches and generally fool around with the main presenters, Jenny Powell, Paul Leyshon, Matthew Davies and Nobby the Sheep.

One Saturday we were on the show, there were a couple of executives there from the TV production company, Zenith North. Zenith North made *Byker Grove* and, after they saw us in the sketches, they invited us for a meeting. They said they thought we worked really well together and asked if we had considered doing anything as a double act that wasn't centred on music. We resisted the urge to start reciting: 'The one-eyed yellow idol . . .', as Ant stupidly didn't have his cabbage on a dog lead with him at the meeting. We told them it wasn't something we'd really thought too much about; we were just messing about. They thought there could be more mileage in it, though, and kept talking about the 'special chemistry' between us.

*I didn't even pass GCSE science, so all this talk of chemistry was baffling, but they wanted to pitch a TV show with us two in it. They thought we had something and, frankly, who were we to stop them?*

The idea appealed to us for a lot of reasons. TV was where we'd started out, it was something we had developed a passion for and, most importantly, there was no singing involved. Everything takes *ages* in TV, so nothing much happened there and then, but we told our management about it and hoped that, one day, something fun would come out of it.

*Meanwhile, we kept promoting. And promoting. And promoting. And then, just for good measure, we did a bit of promotion. We were travelling all over the country, and by now we had a permanent driver, a French bloke called Dominique, who'd got the job thanks to his extensive qualifications*

*– he was Kim Glover's boyfriend. Over the next few years, we spent more time in that Toyota Previa than anywhere else. Think of 'The Prev', as we imaginatively nicknamed it, as a character in our story. Just as Pete Best is often referred to as the 'fifth Beatle', so The Prev was the third member of PJ and Duncan.*

*After just a few days on the road, The Prev was completely covered in make-up from fans who'd found out it was our car and written messages and phone numbers all over it. At first we used to clean them off. By 'we', I mean our driver. But after a while it became pointless, because it would just get covered in lipstick again. That car wore more make-up than Lily Savage.*

**The Prev always represented sanctuary for us. When you were inside it, you were away from everything and you could relax, but the hard part was getting in there. When we left a TV studio, we had to make our way past screaming girls, who were still, without doubt, the most vicious creatures on the face of the earth. I've often thought this country could do away with its entire army and replace it with a crack team of teenage girls who've been told the enemy has kidnapped their favourite boy band.**

*Bear in mind, this hysteria was just for us two. If they'd seen the biggest boy bands of the time, Take That or East 17, I think their heads would have exploded with pure, unadulterated boy-band adrenalin. They would do anything to get a piece of you. At the time, I was wearing a lot of caps, which, as you can imagine, came with the territory if you were a streetwise rapper.*

**Or if you wanted to cover up a massive forehead . . .**

*They were helpful for that too. The fans would grab them. For them, it meant instant memorabilia and, for me, another trip to the cap shop.*

*There was no less hysteria when you were on stage either. We'd be up there mid-song, and we'd be looking out over a sea of banners that said things like, 'Point your erection in my direction.' Considering the age of most of our fans, you wouldn't point your finger in their direction, never mind anything else.*

*There was also a lot of fainting going on, and we saw a pattern emerge: girl faints during show, girl gets carried backstage by sweaty security guard, girl gets polo mint from St John ambulanceman and misses show. It became as much a part of our performance as the dance break in 'Rhumble'.*

One night we did a gig in a weird little venue somewhere, and the fainting girls were getting dragged out of the crowd by the security guards and taken backstage as per usual. However, the only access doors to the backstage area were at the back right-hand corner of the stage, so the guards were pulling these limp teenagers out of the melee, slinging them over their shoulders then running across the stage between us and off for a refreshing mint. We'd be in the middle of our finest dance move, and a sweaty bouncer would huff and puff his way across the stage. I don't mind telling you, it could be very offputting.

*I was miming to the ninth hottest pop tune in the charts and thinking, 'The health and safety facilities in this venue leave a lot to be desired.' I often got distracted during shows, especially in the early days, when we did the same three songs every night for weeks on end. You could slip into autopilot and let your mind wander. I'd be halfway through a rap, and I'd be thinking,*

*'I'm getting the double bed tonight in the Travelodge — he's had it the last two nights. I know what I'll do: as soon as we get in there, I'll put my bag on the bed, then what can he do?'*

*I suppose I've always been one of life's deep thinkers.*

Our fans may have been prone to bouts of nausea, but they were very generous. In one magazine interview, we'd been asked about our favourite sweets.

*Those interviews were pretty highbrow — I think the favourite-sweets question came right after our answer to the problems in the Middle East.*

I'd said my favourite sweets were chocolate buttons, and Ant had gone for Smarties, and for a while after that interview, at every gig we'd get our favourite sweets thrown at us by the fans. It was a step on from eggs and potatoes, but we still seemed to spend a disproportionate amount of our early career having food thrown at us.

*On the up side, we were never short of sweets, but on the downside, a flying tube of Smarties can be quite painful, especially if it hits you in the face. It's no fun trying to get through some pretty intricate dance moves when you're having the entire confectionery section of Woolworths hurled at you. Don't get me wrong, I was grateful they'd gone to the trouble of buying the sweets; I just wish I'd said I liked marshmallows or flumps or something else less likely to cause bruising. They never went to waste, though, we'd come off stage filled with the euphoria of another successful gig and say to the security guards, 'Quick, go back and get the sweets, we'll eat them in the car.' After all, driving around in The Prev all week, we had to make sure we had a balanced diet. Back then, Ginsters pasties and a tube of Smarties counted as two of our five a day.*

Along with our favourite sweets, our fans would also buy us teddies and red roses and as a result, The Prev looked like it had ramraided Clinton Cards on Valentine's Day. The boot was full of flowers and teddies, which we would eventually get round to dropping off at the local hospitals.

*When we arrived at the hospitals, we always had two questions: 'Do you want this lot?', and 'What's the best thing for excessive Smarties bruising?'*

We'd also get underwear thrown at us on stage, and Ant regularly had bra-related accidents – but part of the reason is because he is particularly clumsy. He once slipped on a banana skin. Really. I thought that only ever happened in cartoons, but he genuinely did it.

87

*I think my favourite fan ever was the girl who changed her name, by deed poll, to Declan Donnelly.*

You've just brought that up because I mentioned the banana skin, haven't you?

*It was absolutely hilarious: you've got to admit, that's dedication. He used to get Valentine's cards: 'To Declan Donnelly from Declan Donnelly'. I'd wind him up and ask him why he was sending valentines to himself, and he'd snap at me.*

*Getting cards from obsessive fans was all part of being in a boy band – or boy duo, as we were – and, around this time, we also learnt one of the first laws of the boy-band jungle: Thou shalt not have a girlfriend.*

That particular boy-band commandment was going to be a bit of a problem for me. I'd been with Clare for a couple of years, and the record company and Kim said, 'You mustn't talk about her. Whenever you're asked, say you haven't got a girlfriend.' I was used to being told what to do, so I accepted it. I thought, 'Okay, that seems straightforward enough. I'll just run that past Clare. I'm sure it'll be fine.'

Not as easy as I thought. She wasn't happy and, looking back, I can understand why. Ant and me were now bona fide pop stars, but it began to cause a bit of friction between me and Clare. She did reluctantly agree to go along with the 'no girlfriend' story, but it was probably pretty selfish of me to ask her.

Once we'd had our first top-ten hit with 'Rhumble', went on *Top of the Pops* and were on the front of magazines, it all went mad. The fans that knew about Clare could be really vicious. She'd come to our gigs when she could, and she'd usually sneak in through the stage door, although fans would still catch sight of her and shout horrible names. Most of the time she'd try and shrug it off but, inevitably, it got to her now and again. There'd be times we'd be leaving gigs in The Prev and Clare would be lying on the floor, hiding under a pile of coats, so as not to be seen. Quite why she didn't tell me to sling my hook there and then I'll never know. I think it helped that she was a performer herself – she'd left *Grange Hill* and was now in the sitcom *2.4 Children* – so she knew all about the strange world of fame and understood we were just doing a job.

Magazine interviews could be a struggle. Young pop bands can be very naïve. We were no exception, and journalists exploited that. After you'd denied having a girlfriend, they'd leave a pause, and you'd hear yourself saying, 'Well, I've kissed a few girls recently,' even though it wasn't true, just because you wanted to give them an answer. Before you knew it, they'd have enough information for a page in *Smash Hits* about 'My girlfriend hell' by chocolate button-loving pop sensation Duncan.

With all the interviews, photo shoots and teddies, a lot of the time the music itself could feel like a very small part of what we were doing. I sometimes thought we could have put out any old rubbish and people would still have bought it.

*What do you mean 'could have' . . . ?*

After months of promotion, we couldn't wait to get into the studio and actually record the album. We knew it would be weird being in one place and not spending days on end in The Prev so, before we went to the studio, we insisted the staff wrote, '*PJ and Duncan 4 Eva*' in lipstick all over the outside of the building.

*Now we felt at home, and ready to record our debut album.*

# Chapter 11

In the late summer of 1994, with the music industry holding its breath, we went into a studio in London to record PJ and Duncan's debut album. For the duration of the sessions, the record company moved us into a hotel in Chelsea called La Reserve. After 'The Travelodge '94 Tour', life actually settled into a bit of a routine there, plus we had our own rooms, so there was no more fighting over who got the double bed. This was big time.

We didn't know London at all, so we'd just get dropped at the studio in the morning, and then back at the hotel at night. Once we were there, we'd be really careful to rest our vocal chords and drink plenty of warm honey and lemon. Sorry, did I say 'honey and lemon'? I meant Stella Artois.

*The album had twelve tracks, including our first three singles, and was called* Psyche. *It was pure pop, with a smile on its face. There were no moody black-and-white shots of us with our tops off, it was more baseball caps and wacky poses, and that was just the way we liked it. If you'd seen us with our tops off, then that would have been just the way you liked it too.*

*A lot of the album was written by Nicky Graham, who had produced the top-65 smash, 'Tonight I'm Free', and his songwriting team of Deni Lew and Mike Olton. We were never really what you'd call singer-songwriters.*

To be fair, it was a push to call us singers.

*We did have a go at writing though and, one night, back at the hotel, I was convinced I'd written a hit. I was in the toilet, where I get most of my good ideas, and suddenly a melody popped into my head. It was a really catchy tune, and I began to hum it out loud. I got louder and louder as the melody seemed to take on a life of its own and progressed from a little ditty to a full verse, bridge and chorus. 'This is it,' I thought to myself, 'this is a hit.' I washed my hands and began to write some lyrics down. Legend has is that when Paul McCartney wrote 'Yester-day', he just sang 'scrambled eggs' over and over to the tune until he thought of the words. Well, I had gone one better: the lyrics were flowing like a cheap wine and pouring themselves all over the page. I'd heard people say that when the genius takes over, a great song can come together in three minutes, and this is exactly what was happening. I felt a rush of adrenalin as I harnessed the genius and let it flow. This was my Lennon and McCartney moment! I rang Dec, and said, 'Come to my room, I've just written us a number-one single.'*

After I'd finished laughing, I put down the phone and went to his room.

*I was so excited, I started singing my song to Dec, and all I could think was 'Hit, hit, hit.'*

I was thinking of a word that sounded very similar, but had an extra letter at the beginning. Ant was convinced the song was going to be a massive hit, and he was right, it *was* a hit, a huge hit – for Boyz II Men, the American R&B group, whose 'I'll Make Love to You' was in the charts that week. Their lyrics went like this: 'I'll make love to you/Like you want me to/ And I'll hold you tight/Baby, all through the night', and Ant was standing there in his hotel room singing 'We will go right through/That's what I will do/You are such a sight/Girl, I'll see you right' to the exact same tune.

*I couldn't believe it, I'd nicked their melody – without realizing it, obviously. I just wanted to say that in case any of the Boyz or the Men's lawyers are reading this. I 'borrowed' their melody, and I'd written completely new lyrics to it. I was gutted; I thought I'd had my first moment of genuine musical inspiration.*

Unfortunately, we're both still waiting for that one.

We weren't musicians by any stretch of the imagination, but we did enjoy being in the recording studio. Later on, we did get to do a lot more songwriting, and it had a huge impact on our career and would completely change everything: we would stop selling records.

*If we thought an album meant an end to dodgy gigs, we were wrong. It was around this time we played one of the worst gigs of our career – and, believe me, there's some very stiff competition for that title. It was a roadshow, as always, and it was promoting Ribena Spring, which is basically fizzy Ribena. The roadshow was being held in Peterborough, at an event called Truck Fest. I know, I know, Ribena Spring, Truck Fest, PJ and Duncan, none of it makes sense, but neither did most of our career up till then. At the time, if you had a roadshow to book, no matter where it was, however inappropriate the audience or whatever the quality of the venue, you could always rely on PJ and Duncan. We were like the A-Team of pop: 'If you've got a problem and no one else can help, maybe you can book PJ and Duncan.' Whenever we voiced even the slightest concern, we were always met with the same phrase: 'The record company thinks it's a good idea.' Whenever we heard that sentence, we knew one thing – it was a terrible idea.*

We arrived in Peterborough to discover a venue that was, and there's no other way of saying this, a field. And not a field in a Glastonbury way, more a field in a field way. Straight away, it seemed like we may not be the ideal performers for Truck Fest. It was full of truckers, looking at trucks, talking about trucks and touching each other's trucks; in fact, it was the most heavily truck-themed event I've ever seen. This motley crew were about to be exposed to PJ and Duncan – Live, and I was just praying they weren't going to throw Yorkie bars at us. That would make a tube of Smarties look like small potatoes, which, of course, we'd also had thrown at us when filming *Byker Grove*.

*When we got there, we both thought, 'This is going to be a disaster' and, judging by the looks on the truckers' faces, they were thinking the same.*

92

Dec: Me, aged three.

Ant: *He's cute, he's lovable, he's ...clan Donnelly.*

Ant: *That's a nice hat you're wearing.*

Dec: That's my hair.

Dec: Me, aged four, in a school music project. We were so poor we couldn't afford a classroom.

Dec: Christmas 1978 I was going ... the 'young Mark Knopfler meets ...oody from *Toy Story*' look.

Dec: My first Holy Communion and my first girlfriend.

Ant: *She looks like she's having the time of her life . . .*

*Ant: Me, aged nine months.*

Dec: You're not even strapped into that deckchair on wheels.

*Ant: Me, my sister Sarha and my Nanna Kitty at her caravan in Amble. As you can see, the entire 1970s was sponsored by the colour brown.*

*Ant: Me with my Granda Willy.*

Dec: Curtains *and* blinds? Very posh . . .

*Ant: Me and Sarha were taught from an early age to keep our elbows off the table . . . and on other people's plates.*

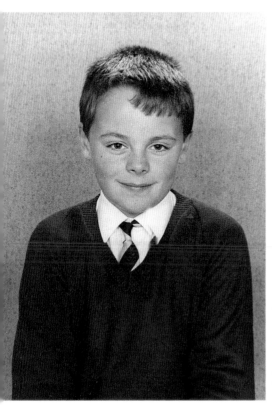

*Ant: Me, aged eleven, in my first Rutherford Comprehensive school uniform.*

Dec: The cow that had licked his fringe seconds before is just out of shot.

Ant: *Me, Sarha and Robbie on holiday.*
Dec: Are those free McDonald's sunglasses? I had a pair of those . . .

Ant: *Me and Sarha thinking exactly the same thing, 'I wish someone would tell Davey there's nothing on the end of that fishing line . . .'*

7 Hawthorn Place
~~Cradles Park~~
Newcastle upon Tyne
NE4 7HR
9/4/89.

Tel no. 091 272 4521

Dear Mr. Robinson,

I am writing with reference to the article in the Evening Chronicle on Thursday March 30th refering to the new B.B.C programme 'Byker Grove'

I am a 13yr old boy and attend St. Cuthberts Comprehensive School Benwell Hill.

In the past I auditioned with Sue weeks for a BBC Look and Read programme called 'Geordie Racer' as the part of Spuggy Hilton, unfortunately I did not get the part but was lucky enough to be one of three finalists chosen. I was encouraged by Sue weeks to keep trying for auditions as she said I was very talented.

I would be very grateful for any information of auditions being staged

Yours Faithfully
Declan Donnelly

Dec: The first draft of my letter to the BBC.

BRITISH BROADCASTING CORPORATION
BROADCASTING CENTRE
BARRACK ROAD
NEWCASTLE UPON TYNE NE99 2NE
TELEPHONE: 091-232 1313
TELEX: 537007
FAX: 091-232 5082

3rd May 1989

Dear Declan

I am pleased to confirm that you are on our short short-list for the cast
of "Byker Grove". In order to help us make our final selection, we are
holding a workshop-party at the BBC in Newcastle on Saturday, 6th May
from 2 p.m. till 6 p.m.

There is no script to learn as we will be spending the afternoon engaged
in drama exercises, improvisations, and playing extremely silly party
games! Tea will be provided.

I would be delighted if you could attend. If you can, please read the
following carefully:

1. Please do not talk about "Byker Grove" to anyone from the time you
   arrive at the BBC to the time you leave.

2. Please come prepared to be energetic and therefore in appropriate
   clothes.

3. Please be prepared to abandon your shoes on arrival and to the spend
   the afternoon either in socks or bare feet.

4. Please come knowing your height (in feet and inches) and your weight
   (in stones and pounds).

5. Please do not panic when, on arrival at the BBC, you are given an
   identity badge bearing a name which is not your own.

6. Please come prepared to entertain us all for one minute with a solo
   act (for example, a joke, a song, a poem, a bit of magic).

7. Please bring one wrapped silly present (maximum value £1) with a blank
   gift tag attached.

I look forward to seeing you at 2 p.m. sharp on Saturday.

Yours sincerely,

Matthew

Matthew Robinson,
Director,
"BYKER GROVE"

Dec: The BBC's reply. Scarier than anything Stephen King's ever written.

Dec: Matthew Robinson directs the epic 'Duncan and Spuggie waterfight' in Byker Grove.

Dec: The aforementioned Spuggie and Duncan (I'm the one on the right).

Dec: A cast trip to the log cabins in Clennell Hall with Craig Reilly, who played Winston. And yes, that is a bandana. A red bandana.

*Ant: Debbie and PJ – the Posh and Becks of Byker Grove.*

Dec: Me, Craig Reilly, David Oliver (Marcus) and Rory Gibson (Lee). Ant got knocked out of that year's 'Silly Smile Competition' in the early stages.

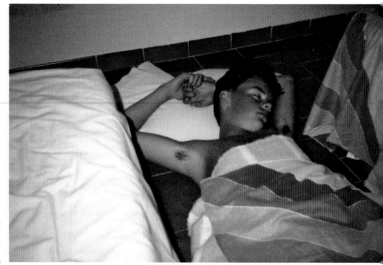

Dec: Ant lying on his back. On the floor.

Ant: Dec lying on his belly. In a bed.

Dec: At my brother Dermott's ordination to the priesthood in 1992.
Ant: Where's your tie, you tramp?

Dec: Gran Canaria 1992. I quickly became accustomed to the taste of tequila.

*Ant: No, you're not.*

*Ant: More drinking in Gran Canaria.*

Dec: Hold on, who took that photo? Only two of us went on that holiday . . .

Dec: My legendary MG Metro Turbo. See how it has Turbo written down the side.

*Ant: Funny, it's not quite as cool as I remember . . .*

*Ant: Boppa, me and Goody in my bedroom.*

Dec: Did you sleep in a giant cot?

*Ant: Let's move on, shall we?*

Dec: Bacon sandwiches and beer for breakfast.

*Ant: You can take the boys out of Newcastle . . .*

Dec: Me and Sarha a wicked night out.

*Ant: What?!*

c: In a club in Tokyo with the head of Telstar Records, Graham Williams,
ebrating another top-fifteen smash.

c: Backstage at Newcastle City Hall.
o you like my funky shirt?
t: No.

Dec: Our last tour in 1997.
Imagine our embarrassment
when we turned up to the
gig wearing the same outfit.

*Ant: 'Now everybody scream!' Rhumbling on
the Just Seventeen Roadshow 1994.*

*Ant: A Japanese photo shoot.*

Dec: Why did we ev
agree to that?

*Ant: Big in Japan.*
Dec: And loving it!

*Ant: Interviews with Japanese magazi*
*could sometimes get embarrassing.*

Dec: Tell me about it . . .

Dec: A Japanese photo shoo
The record company 'thoug
it was a good idea . . .'

*nt: Ribena Spring Roadshow with Let Loose, 1994.*

*ec:* Down the pub with Si Hargreaves. Ant was
tting a round in, so we took a picture to mark
e occasion.

*Ant: Me and that long
fringe parted shortly
afterwards, due to
'creative differences'.*

Dec: Majorca, 1998, our post-pop star holiday with the girls. Ant celebrated in the only way he knew how – by riding an inflatable Dalmatian.

*Ant: I loved that dog. But I let her down.*

Dec: Ginger hair and a shaved head – our radical image transformation was complete.

*Ant: Me living out my dreams in a photo shoot.*

*Ant: On the set of* The Ant and Dec Show *series one.*

*nt: The cast and crew of* sm:tv.

Dec: The stars of the show.

*nt: The real star of the ow, Wonkey Donkey.*

Dec: With John Knight in the green room at *sm:tv.*

*nt: Celebrating the 100th show. Cat early celebrated with a spray tan.*

Dec: A catch-up with Cat at the Sky Bar, the Mondrian Hotel, L.A.

*Ant:* On TFI Friday *with Chris Evans.*

Dec: 'In a little over twenty-four hours, I'm going to be sick in your toilet.'

Dec: In Japan with Simon Jones on a Pokémon trip.

*Ant: Do Pokémon backstage passes always make you go that camp?*

Dec: On the streets of Tokyo, 'will Poké-rap for beer'.

*Well, that, and, 'Look at that other trucker's truck. I love trucks and trucking.'*

*As always, we were professional and, as always, we were stupid, so we did the gig. Or we tried to. It was meant to be the classic PJ and Duncan set: three songs, full mime, and back in The Prev before you could say, 'It's my turn in the front seat,' but it didn't work out like that. We were coming towards the end of our second track when we noticed the stage manager waving manically and mouthing to us. He was saying we had to come off at the end of the song. We weren't quite sure what the problem was but, as usual, we did what we were told. What was it that had interrupted our set? A health and safety issue? Had one of the truckers fainted? He took us to the side and told us he was terribly sorry, but the PA system was being turned off. This was clearly something serious. He looked at Dec and me and explained the shocking and tragic reason for the interruption.*

'I've got to turn the PA system off, because I promised the farmer there wouldn't be any noise when he brings his cows past.'

*It's hard to describe just how belittling it feels to find out you're second on the bill to a herd of cows. And the truckers weren't happy either. All we could hear was them booing.*

It was either that, or the cows mooing. Eventually, we were introduced back on, and the boos got louder. I think I heard one of the truckers trying to persuade the cows to come back. Plus, by a cruel twist of fate, our third and final track was the premiere of our forthcoming single, 'Eternal Love', a heartfelt ballad. Picture the scene: a band of furious truckers staring at us, booing, while I belted out lyrics like these:

> *Suntan lotion that familiar smell,*
> *I made you a necklace from a chain of shells . . .*
> *I'll give you my love, an Eternal Love,*
> *From me to you, if you return*
> *A token of love, an Eternal Love.*

You get the drift. One trucker, who was sat on the grass near the front, physically turned his back on us. He couldn't even bring himself to look in our direction. Silly trucker. To say it was a low point would be an understatement.

*At least there were two of us – we only had half the humiliation, half the embarrassment and half of Truck Fest growling at us – and we were best mates so, whatever happened, we would eventually try and have a laugh about it. The fact that we've both been through all this bizarre stuff together still makes everything easier today.*

Whether it was to do with music or TV shows, we've never had to make decisions on our own, because we've always been each other's second opinion. When it came to music, we never took the whole thing, or ourselves, too seriously. We never actually believed we were pop stars, and we always did everything with a wink. Well, not everything – you couldn't spend your life winking all the time, people would think you were a right winker. There was just such a big gap between PJ and Duncan, the clean-cut, lovable boys next door, and Ant and Dec, who went back to the hotel every night and drank pints. Ant even smoked tabs. We were leading a double life: squeaky-clean pop stars by day and normal nineteen-year-old lads by night. It wasn't exactly Clark Kent and Superman, but it did feel like we were still playing characters, rather than truly being ourselves.

*Throughout our time as PJ and Duncan, we always had an eye on the door. To survive in pop, you need a great songwriter in the band – and if there was one thing we didn't have, it was a great songwriter in the band. And there were always elements we didn't enjoy – the music itself wasn't exactly to our taste and it could be a strain constantly pretending to be something you weren't.*

Still, we were determined to have as much fun as we could while it lasted, and on 7 November we released *Psyche*. At least, that's when I'm told we released it, we were so busy there was no time for a big showbiz launch party, or even a small showbiz launch party, we just kept promoting and performing. We also released two more singles, 'If I Give You My Number' and 'Eternal Love', and announced our first headline tour of theatre venues around Britain. The press releases were despatched, the TV and radio shows were informed and the teddy-bear and rose suppliers were put on red alert.

Going on tour, our own tour, was a real thrill. We had a support band, which for them must have ranked as one of the lowest gigs on the musical ladder. I bet they'd rather have been headlining Truck Fest. They were an American boy band, and they'd go on half an hour before us to warm up the crowd, which wasn't an easy job – most of the audience had come straight out without any tea and had to be up for school in the morning. On the first night, our new tour manager John McMahon came to find us so they could show us what these crazy American kids were doing on stage.

There were five of them, and they employed a trick used by a lot of boy bands at the time: they'd pull a girl out of the crowd, bring her up on the stage and then sing to her. It was corny, it was slushy and it took cheesy to a whole new level. These jokers made us two look like Oasis.

*They had a table on stage with a checked tablecloth and a red rose in a vase on it, and the lucky girl would sit down while one of the band sat opposite her and the other four posed as waiters. The whole thing was very unrealistic. For a start, most restaurants only give you one waiter at a time, and there wasn't even any food on the table. The service was terrible. They were all singing a cappella to her, and we were watching from the side of the stage, laughing our heads off. This was the most clichéd, hammy rubbish we'd ever seen. Someone needed to tell these flash Yanks that this stuff was too cheesy for a UK audience. It was embarrassing and, if their little boy band didn't buck its ideas up, it'd be going nowhere fast.*

That 'little boy band' was called The Backstreet Boys.
They've sold over 100 million records.
They are the biggest-selling boy band of all time.

*And you wonder why we ended up on telly?*

# Chapter 12

*It was towards the end of 1994 that I met the love of my life, Lisa Arm-*
*strong. Meeting Lisa changed everything, and was the most amazing*
*thing that's ever happened to me (I hope you're reading this, pet). We met*
*in the most romantic of circumstances – the* Smash Hits Poll Winners
Party Tour. *Lisa was in a two boys, two girls band called Deuce, who were*
*on the tour with me and Dec. We got talking, and I was attracted to her*
*immediately. She was beautiful, she had a great sense of fun, and she was*
*different from any girl I'd ever met (I hope you're still reading, pet). I*
*remember one late-night game of pool on the Isle of Wight being the*
*moment I knew she was the girl for me. It was nothing to do with pool,*
*that was just the moment I remember falling for her. Although, in case*
*you're wondering, yes, I did let her win (I hope you're not still reading*
*this, pet). We swapped numbers and, after the tour was finished, we'd*
*spend hours on the phone talking about love, life and the best way to pot*
*the black if you were snookered.*

*After a while Lisa would come to our PJ and Duncan gigs – that's how*
*nice she was – and she'd get the kind of abuse any boy-band member's*
*girlfriend faced from teenage fans. She handled it brilliantly and, being in*
*a band herself, she knew that kind of thing came with the territory. Deuce*
*released one album before going their separate ways. Lisa always says Steps*
*came along and stole their thunder, but thank god Deuce did that album*
*– I never would have met Lisa without them, and she's been by my side*
*for the last fifteen years.*

And they make a beautiful couple. Not as beautiful a couple
as *me* and Ant, mind, but beautiful nonetheless.

By December 1994, after a year of working non-stop and
trying to get our music careers off the ground, we only had
one thing on our minds, and that was Christmas at home.
We'd spent the last few months of the year looking forward to

it, like a couple of kids looking forward to Christmas. Apart from the occasional weekend or a night here and there, we hadn't been back to Newcastle all year. We'd been far too busy seeing the world – the world of under-18s discos and single rooms at the Travelodge. We couldn't wait to enjoy the peace and tranquillity of home, a place where we wouldn't be bothered and where we were safe from the outside world. Basically, we saw Newcastle as a giant version of The Prev.

What we didn't know was that everything had changed for us at home. Don't get me wrong, our bedrooms hadn't been rented out or anything, but things were definitely different. Local fans had found out where our houses were, and they decided to celebrate that fact by standing outside them morning, noon and night. And these girls were tough. They stood there for weeks on end, despite the fact that December in Newcastle is what a weatherman would call 'absolutely bloody freezing'. They didn't care about that, though; nothing could cure their adolescent obsession with staring at the front door of PJ or Duncan's house. You were always caught in two minds about fans like that. On the one hand, they were the whole reason you sold records and had a career; on the other, when they were in your garden or sticking their noses to the kitchen window, it felt like a bit of an invasion. The best approach was to go out, sign some autographs, pose for a few pictures and hope that a trade-off like that would be enough for them to – how can I put it? – Go Away.

*It wasn't always that simple, though. There was one day during that Christmas holiday when my mam took pity on a couple of the fans. I came home one afternoon, walked into the kitchen and found two girls, who both let out huge screams when they saw me. I thought I'd walked into the wrong house at first, then my mam explained. She'd seen the girls freezing outside and invited them in for a cup of tea and some quality time in the McPartlin kitchen. It was an act of great compassion and generosity, which was to be applauded. Although obviously not by me – she'd left me alone with two of Newcastle's biggest PJ fans. I stood in the kitchen with them for the longest twenty minutes of my life. They spent the whole time in complete silence, which seemed strange, considering the talent they'd previously displayed for making noise. I stood there trying to make small talk about digestives, and they just carried on staring at me. The whole thing was very awkward, I couldn't stand the heat but, unfortunately, I couldn't get out of the kitchen.*

That Christmas was hard work. Everyone would be asking me about where I'd been and what I'd been doing and, to be honest, it was the last thing on earth I wanted to talk about. I was wanting a nice, relaxing Christmas. Frankly, I was sick to the back teeth of PJ and bloody Duncan.

*Going back to see my old mates felt different too. The first time I met up with Ginger, Boppa, Athey and Goody that Christmas, it took most of the night to get up to speed about what they were doing. They'd ask about Top of the Pops and, to their credit, they managed to keep a straight face but, generally, I tried not to go on about life in the Top-65 fast lane too much. I was especially keen not to tell them about being second on the bill to a herd of cows and getting spat at by the teenage boys of Great Britain. Partly because I didn't want to sound like I was bragging, and partly 'cos there was nothing to brag about. After all, I wasn't head over heels in love with every single part of pop-star life.*

And, in the pub, you just couldn't win. Either you got a round in and everyone accused you of being a Flash Harry, or you tried to just pay your fair share and they'd think you were being tight. When you're in your late teens, everyone's life changes pretty drastically – people get jobs, go to university or appear on *Top of the Pops* in large orange shirts. In Newcastle, I'd always just been 'Fonsey and Anne's youngest', just another one of the Donnellys, but now it seemed like people were looking at me differently, which is quite a disconcerting thing to happen. Suddenly nothing seems to be how it was, and when everything changes it can leave you a little disorientated and unsure of where to turn.

*One day of that Christmas holiday really stands out, because I was the victim of a heinous crime. I was at home, and my mam had just finished what is technically known as 'a big wash'. I came downstairs and, as I walked past the windows, I heard the by now familiar sound of the fans outside screaming – it always sounded like someone was showing horror films in our front garden. Walking into the kitchen, where most of the washing was drying, I suddenly saw this hand shoot in through the open window and grab a pair of my boxer shorts. My immediate reaction was 'That's burglary, I should call 999,' then I began to imagine the scene if the police were called out to investigate The Great Boxer-short Mystery of '94 and decided there was probably no point calling them. I always assumed it was one of the female fans whodunnit. She might even have been one of the girls who'd thrown bras and knickers at us on stage, but if she was trying to start some sort of underwear-exchange system, this wasn't the way to go about it.*

I managed to keep all my underwear, but I did have my own problems at home. Problems with, of all things, the telephone. My mam and dad were still in the phone book, so anyone could get our number – it was 0191 272 4321, in case you're interested. Fans would find the number, then ring the house and ask to speak to me. You'd think that sort of thing could be slightly irritating, but you'd be wrong. It was infuriating. I'm not exaggerating when I tell you that, on Christmas Day 1994, the phone rang solidly for fourteen hours. We got through the presents, breakfast, Christmas dinner and the Queen's Speech, all to the sound of the phone ringing. We had relatives trying to phone and wish us Happy Christmas, and they couldn't get through. The fans would just ring and say 'Is Declan there?', and I'd hang up, but before I could sit down, it would ring again. And again. And again. It never stopped, but my parents wanted to keep their number, because it ended in 4321, and they liked that set of numbers (at the time they were also huge fans of the chocolate bar 5-4-3-2-1 – they love a set of descending digits, my mam and dad). Only a month earlier, PJ and Duncan had released 'If I Give You

My Number', and people were taking it a bit too literally for my liking. I was keen to record a Christmas single called 'Please Stop Ringing My House, The Turkey's Getting Cold', but no one at the record company seemed very interested.

*1994 became 1995, as you might expect, in early January, and that was when we got a call from Dave Holly. He had some amazing news.* Psyche *had gone platinum. It had peaked at number five in the album charts and had now sold 500,000 copies. We were stunned, it felt like a real achievement. I think the Christmas-present market probably accounted for a lot of that – at the time, we were told that an estimated 300,000 people had been given* Psyche *as a gift.*

I think most of them rang my house on Christmas Day to tell me about it.

*To celebrate this, we'd been booked to go on* Top of the Pops' *special show on 5 January. We were due to perform heart-rending ballad and Truck Fest favourite 'Eternal Love', but it meant our Christmas was cut short. We had to leave for London immediately. In the space of a few days, I'd lost the rest of my precious holiday and a pair of boxer shorts. 1995 had not started well.*

By February, we'd released our sixth – yes, *sixth* – and final single from *Psyche*, 'Our Radio Rocks', and, if you thought a platinum album and a second appearance on *Top of the Pops* was exciting, what happened next was probably the single biggest achievement of our music career. The record company tipped us off about what was one of the freakiest occurrences in the history of British pop music – PJ and Duncan had been nominated for a BRIT Award. I couldn't have been more surprised if we'd made the shortlist for Rear of the Year. We were nominated in the category of Best Newcomer, and we just couldn't believe it. Clearly the record industry was starting to take notice of *Psyche*'s success, and the fact that we were shortlisted for a BRIT award was a fantastic accolade.

*The awards were held on 20 February and were hosted by TV's golden – or ginger – boy of the time, Chris Evans. Having been in the music biz for almost sixteen whole months by this point, we were pretty sure of one thing: when it came to winning a BRIT Award, we were a long shot but, you never know: we might just surprise everyone and take the title. Our management told us that, 'The record company thought it would be a good idea' if we did something that would get us some attention on the night, something that made a bit of a statement about PJ and Duncan – a statement that, for once, wouldn't include the words 'Geordies', 'pint-sized' and 'cheeky'. Telstar came up with a plan for us to make a splash – we were going to make a grand entrance by arriving in a mode of transport no one else would be using and that would guarantee press attention. We would turn up to the BRITS in an ice-cream van.*

It's hard to think of a worse idea than turning up to the BRIT Awards in an ice-cream van, but Telstar talked us into it, and the ice-cream van was booked. I doubt that was a difficult job; I don't suppose there's much call for ice-cream vans in the middle of February. The plan was we'd turn up in the ice-cream van, jump out of the serving hatch and have our photos taken, which would be hilarious and 'crazy'. I still have no idea why it had to be an ice-cream van; none of our songs had anything to do with frozen desserts.

*The night of the ceremony came around. It was being held in Alexandra Palace in North London. We were coming from a hotel in another part of London, and we told the record company there was no way we'd travel all the way there in the ice-cream van. After all, we had our dignity. Well, okay, we didn't have any dignity, we just didn't want to get cold. They arranged for a car to take us there – it wasn't The Prev, it was probably in the car wash having the lipstick removed – and the plan was to wait until we got round the corner from the venue and then get out of the car and into the ice-cream van.*

*To make sure it arrived on time, the van set off early from the depot – sometime in mid-January I think and, as planned, we met it round the corner from Alexandra Palace. That's when we faced our first problem.*

*What with the BRITs being a huge international music event and every-
thing, the traffic was horrendous. We were in that van for ages, inching
our way there. We'd had a few drinks back in our hotel before we left,
and a few more in the car, all of which meant that we were both desperate
for the toilet. It made a very slow journey very painful. I remember eyeing a few empty ice-cream tubs but resisted the temptation and, besides,
it would all be worth it because, when we arrived, we were going to get
so much press attention.*

So although we were stuck in an ice-cream van, perched on a
couple of boxes of cones, sweating our crushed velvet suits off
and dying for the toilet, we were dead excited. It took what
seemed like an eternity but, finally, we arrived at Ally Pally,
ready to make our big entrance. The van pulled up, we clambered out of the hatch and jumped down, striking our best
'wacky' poses, only to find there was absolutely no one there.
Not a soul. The journey had taken so long that all the celebrities had already gone in, the pit of paparazzi had emptied
and the red carpet was actually being rolled up. The only
people who saw our dramatic entrance were a few door stew-
ards and the driver of the ice-cream van, and I think *he* was
reading the paper.

We put it behind us, made our way inside, had a massive
pee and took our seats. The ceremony itself was brilliant. Blur
were the big winners that year. They won best album, video,
British group and single, for 'Parklife'. Finally, our moment
arrived, the Best Newcomer category. They showed a bit of
each nominee's video, and a nice little cheer went up in the
room for ours. Then it was time. The envelope was opened, I
remember my heart beating in my chest harder and louder
than it ever had done before and, although the sensible,
rational part of me was saying, 'We're not going to win, we're
not going to win,' there was still a mischievous voice saying,
'Maybe. Maybe you've won it. It could happen.' That's how
drunk we were.

Along with the three other bands in our category, the night

ended in disappointment. Us, Echobelly, Eternal and Portishead all left the BRITs empty-handed. As for the winners of the 1995 Best Newcomer Award, well, apparently they're still together and they're doing okay. They were a little band called Oasis.

Shortly after the BRITs, the PJ and Duncan adventure took a whole new twist, with a strange and unpredictable experience the record company called overseas promotion. Over the next few years, we were to get very used to punting our own unique brand of 'pop with a smile on its face' round the far-flung corners of the globe. We went round Europe, Australia and the Far East, and it was, at times, bizarre, surreal and insane – and that was just our choice of outfits. It was a great way to see the world. We saw TV studios in Germany, TV studios in France and even a radio station in Stockholm. It's true what they say: travel really does broaden the mind.

*We also learnt something about French pop-music policy. If you're not, and I sincerely hope you're not, a nineties-French-pop aficionado, you might not be aware of this, but 40 per cent of the songs played on French radio must, by law, be by French artists. It really is the law, and you go to pop-music prison if you break that law. After hearing that, our management had wisely decided that the chances of PJ and Duncan getting a look-in were about the same as me getting my stolen boxer shorts back. Then the record company got a call with news that surprised us all: 'Our Radio Rocks' was rocketing up the French charts. They told us to take our spectacular and visually stunning live show out there immediately, so Dec grabbed the CD, I dug out my favourite baseball cap, and we headed for the airport.*

I've never understood why you have to promote something that's already doing well, but 'the record company thought it was a good idea.' You can guess what's coming next, can't you?

*We arrived in Paris, where we'd been booked to appear on the French equivalent of the* Smash Hits *Poll Winners Party. I can't remember the name of the event itself, it may have been Le Poll Winners Partie de Smash Hits — my French is a bit rusty. It was in a massive arena that had been filled with ten thousand French teenagers, and it was being broadcast live on French TV. It was the same mime and the same dance moves we'd done a hundred times to 'Our Radio Rocks', so we didn't need any rehearsal, we were perfectly happy to just turn up and do it. We didn't speak a word of the language, but these French pop fans knew how much our radio rocked, so what could possibly go wrong?*

In a word: everything. We went on stage to the opening bars and struck our usual poses, ready to go into our normal radio-rocking routine. The song carried on playing and – there's no other way to say this – it was a track we'd never heard in our lives. I felt sick. Our dance moves didn't fit the music, the vocals had changed – the whole thing was our worst nightmare. The French TV producers had forgotten to tell us that the track that was doing so well in the French charts was the 12-inch dance remix. We were live in front of ten thousand screaming French teenagers and in millions of people's homes, performing to a track we were hearing for the very first time. And, because it was the twelve-inch *extended* mix, it seemed to last about three and a half hours.

On the off chance that any of you lovely readers aren't familiar with 'Our Radio Rocks (The Loony Toons House Mix)', then let me explain. As with most dance remixes, they'd stripped out almost all of the vocals, and when those vocals did come in, they were sampled and r-r-r-r-repeated, so they bore no resemblance to the original track. We quickly worked out that the best strategy was to keep the micro-phones clamped to our lips at all times, because we had no idea when the vocals would start or stop.

*It was a disaster. Deprived of our usual routine, we ended up inventing dance moves on the spot, and we were both completely out of time with the music and each other. There were cameras pointed in our faces and we had no idea what to do, so we kept criss-crossing the stage to try and stop the cameras following us. Vocals were coming in left, right and centre, and I was just thinking, 'Is that me, or is that Dec?' In a pop career full of unmitigated disasters, this was one of the largest-scale cock-ups of the lot. The whole thing made Truck Fest seem like a walk in the park. Or a walk in the field, which is actually what it was.*

Usually, after a gig, you'd come off stage and the other bands would congratulate you on your performance. That night, no one even looked us in the eye and, if they had, they would have burst out laughing. Our French pop career began and ended that day.

*Foreign promotion wasn't all disastrous live performances though. Just like in the UK, we used to do days on end of interviews. They'd start at nine in the morning and finish at six at night, and you'd spend the whole time being interviewed, previewed and reviewed. Believe me, there's only so long you can talk about what you do for a living. So, to keep ourselves amused, we started to make stuff up. For some reason, this tended to happen a lot in Germany. One interviewer asked about the most embarrassing thing that had ever happened to me. I said to Dec, 'Remember that time my trousers fell down on stage, and then I fell off the stage and then I landed on a fan without my trousers and ended up doing the rest of the gig in a pink tutu?' After a while, delirium would set in and we'd say anything to try and make each other laugh. I'm not sure we made a very good impression.*

*After a few more weeks of European promotion, we went back home to start a new chapter in our careers. And if there's one thing a new chapter in our career deserves, it's a new chapter in this book. So what are you waiting for? Go to the next page and get started.*

# Chapter 13

*1995 was shaping up to be our busiest year so far. So busy it felt like the expression 'kick-bollock scramble' had been invented just for us. With such a heavy schedule and hardly a day to ourselves, it became increasingly clear what we had to do – star in our own eight-part TV series for Children's BBC while simultaneously trying to keep our pop career afloat.*

*Those guys at Zenith Productions had finally made some progress with the TV-show idea. They said they were ready to pitch – telly speak for 'desperately try and flog' – The Ant and Dec Show to the BBC. This was incredibly exciting; we'd always felt more at home on the small screen. Plus, making a TV show might mean slowing down our musical output, which would be good news for people with ears everywhere. It turned out we were wrong: it just meant doing a TV show and our second album at exactly the same time.*

As you'd imagine, it was important to get the TV show right. It was the BBC, and our big chance to add another string to our bow, so we spoke to the record company, cancelled our press commitments, cleared our diaries and managed to free up a whole afternoon. We spent that afternoon in the Drill Hall, an old theatrical venue in North London, where we filmed a few sketches that had been written for us, using only an old video camera and, of course, our sparkling wit and repartee. The idea was to produce a short tape of the funny bits from this session and send it to Children's BBC. I imagine that tape lasted around thirty seconds.

Ant doesn't remember that day at all, but I suppose that's understandable: people often blank out traumatic or embarrassing moments in their life. I don't remember much either, but I do recall telling a joke to camera at the end of the day, and the BBC decided they wanted to make the show partly because they loved it. It was completely unsuitable for kids' TV, but it had made them laugh. This was the joke that sealed the deal:

I stayed in a hotel last night, and in the next room was James Bond. My friend asked me how I knew it was James Bond, and I said, 'Because all I heard all night was a woman shouting "Oh, Roger, more! Roger, more! Roger, more!"'

*And they say TV is full of stupid people. Next thing we knew, it was March, and we were off to the BBC to make our own show.*

We turned up at that famous old building in White City and were made to feel at home immediately. Little did we realize that this was the start of what became our full-time career. We discovered we had a natural talent for hanging round TV studios trying to make people laugh and eating free sandwiches. It was the first step on the road to becoming TV presenters and playing heightened versions of ourselves. We were still Ant and Dec, but everything was a bit 'bigger' and more exaggerated, because we were on the telly. It's a strange way to earn a living when you think about it. It wouldn't work with other jobs. You can't imagine a traffic warden jumping around saying, 'Welcome to the double-yellow line. Tonight, *you* could win a parking ticket,' but that's what you do on telly. Most people you see present an extreme version of their personality, although there are exceptions. There are people who are just as unpleasant on screen as they are off it. Not that we're naming any names, Mr Cowell.

*There was some debate about what we were going to call this show. It isn't an issue for most people on telly. Once they had Jeremy Kyle on board, I can't imagine it took too long to decide on* The Jeremy Kyle Show, *but for us it was never that easy. In* Byker Grove *and as pop stars, we were PJ and Duncan, but our real names, as our more observant readers will have noticed, are Ant and Dec. We were never keen to be* called PJ and Duncan as pop stars, but Telstar had insisted on it, and being in the middle of a performing arts B-Tech at Newcastle College at the time of that conversation, we weren't exactly in the strongest bargaining position. The names caused us problems for years, especially when we did foreign promotion and the audiences had never even heard of Byker Grove. You won't be surprised to hear that the everyday story of a youth club in the North-east of England wasn't a big hit on German TV. Now, all we wanted was to be known by our real names. After all, we'd had nearly twenty years' experience using them, and it seemed a shame to waste it.

It marked our first exposure as Ant and Dec. We went for Ant and Dec in that order, because it was PJ and Duncan – PJ was Ant and, well, you get the rest. I've been asked about this, but I never argued for it to be Dec and Ant, I've never even really thought about it. It's really not a big deal. Honestly. I'm fine with it, I really am. It's not like I still lie awake at night thinking about it, or it's secretly bothered me for years or anything like that.

The programme itself was a traditional sketch show, although it was different to the other children's programmes – it wasn't that funny. We pretty much just performed the scripts we were given. We didn't get properly involved with it the way we do with our TV shows now. We'd turn up to rehearsals, put in our own little bits – a cabbage on a dog lead, that kind of thing – and the next thing we knew, it was on the telly.

The thing was, we didn't really have that much confidence or faith in ourselves, we weren't a 'real' double act and we weren't comedians and, just like our TV show, this was no laughing matter. At the time, Vic Reeves and Bob Mortimer were huge. Hugely popular that is, not fat. People would ask us if we saw ourselves as the new Vic and Bob, but we were nothing like them. Yes, they were from the North-east and they both had three letters in their name, but there was one big difference: they were brilliant. They were, and still are, legends, and big heroes to us, and we were embarrassed to even be asked if we thought we were in the same league.

We were just a couple of young lads, and we certainly didn't have an 'act', not unless you counted miming to a backing track and doing the running-man dance moves as an 'act'. Yes, we had the required number of performers for a traditional double act, but we didn't see ourselves that way. We just didn't think we were good enough, and we thought if we said we were just two mates having a laugh then maybe, just maybe, no one would notice that we didn't have a clue what we were doing.

One of the most influential people on *The Ant and Dec Show* was the director, Anne Gilchrist. Anne saw us for exactly what we were – a couple of frightened young actors pretending to be pop stars who had a TV show to host. It's no wonder we had a bit of an identity crisis. Anne was incredibly supportive and a constant source of encouragement, always saying stuff like, 'You can do this', 'You can make it work' and 'Why are you crying?' She was absolutely vital to the success of the show and, when it came to TV, she gave us two things we'd never had before – a bit of self-confidence and our own dressing room.

*Being on the BBC, and especially Children's BBC, also brought its own issues for us. We'd never really enjoyed sending mums and aunties out of the room, saving old cereal boxes or using sticky-backed plastic. The BBC always seemed very traditional and educational to us, and we wanted to be a bit dafter than that. Plus, we couldn't make a cardboard rockery to save our lives.*

*At the time, we loved shows like* The Word, The Big Breakfast *and* Don't Forget Your Toothbrush. *These were programmes that seemed to break all the rules of TV, showing viewers the cameras, the backstage areas and the crew. They deliberately avoided being slick and, when things went wrong, they'd revel in it. They represented a new kind of telly, and we wanted to put some of that into our show. Of course, it was still 4.35 on Tuesday afternoon, we weren't exactly the Sex Pistols, but we tried to push things as far as we could. We also had guests in the studio with us – including Rolf Harris, Sean Maguire, Bernie Clifton, Su Pollard, Dani Behr and Bill Oddie.*

One routine I do remember from that series was when Bill Oddie came on. We asked Bill how Madonna was, then he gave us a confused look and said he'd never met her. 'But she sang a song about you,' we told him. Then, to the tune of Madonna's single 'Erotic', we sang, 'Bill Oddie, Bill Oddie, put your hands all over my body . . .'. I remember being very pleased with that gag.

But, despite our Oddie-baiting and our intentions to rip up the rulebook, the series still ended up being a bit too BBC and too young for our liking. Whenever we did something funny, which was about once a fortnight, the kids in the audience would react with a staged 'ha-ha' because the floor manager had told them to laugh at everything. I can only assume he bribed them. It was a difficult environment to work in – we could never tell what our audience was and wasn't finding genuinely funny. I don't think Chris Evans was losing any sleep.

At the same time as rehearsing and recording the TV show, we were making our second album, Top Katz. As you can tell from the title, we were becoming serious recording artists by now. I'm pretty sure Radiohead were quaking in their Doc Martens. Doing two things at once meant we spent all day in script meetings, rehearsals or recording the show, and then, at nights, we'd go off to the studio and work on the album. As a result of this, a lot of the mid-nineties is a bit of blur. It's been said that Keith Richards 'doesn't remember the seventies', and 1995 is a bit like that for us, but slightly less rock 'n' roll. We spent the whole time living in hotels in London and developed a varied and extensive knowledge of salty bar snacks.

We recorded the album in bits. The first single was 'Stuck On U' and was produced by Ray 'Mad Man' Hedges, who'd written for Boyzone. Don't worry, Ray wasn't actually insane, it was just a crazy music-biz nickname he'd given himself. Ray was very happy to let us get involved in writing, so we'd contribute lyrics and come up with the odd melody. Some of them were very odd. Maybe it was because we were going a bit mad ourselves, spending our days desperately trying to put together our own TV show and our nights recording our album. Oh yes, we were multimedia long before our time.

*In a lot of ways, the TV show and the pop career never really sat comfortably with each other. We'd do sketches about boy bands on the TV show and then, the next day, we'd be back on the boy-band treadmill ourselves. During* The Ant and Dec Show, *we did a sketch called 'How to Make Your Own Take That Video'. Take That's 'Back For Good' was the classic boy-band video of the time. It was all black and white, slow motion and pouring rain. Our sketch had me on a stepladder pouring water over Dec while he danced in a 'strange way' wearing a 'really big coat', all shot in black and white. It worked quite well, but the problem was that, as pop stars, that was exactly the kind of video we would have made – if only we'd had the budget, fan base, good looks and songwriting skills of Take That. Looking back at the video for our ballad 'Eternal Love' it showed that we were living those boy-band clichés too. Everyone else could ridicule our music career – and lots of people did – but to be doing it ourselves was dangerous territory.*

Pop stars should be unattainable and glamorous, whereas TV presenters should be approachable and down to earth. With a TV show, you're inviting the hosts into your home – not literally, although if anyone reading this does want to invite us round, mine's a black tea and Ant prefers coffee with one sugar. In 1995, though, on one hand, we were saying, 'We're glamorous pop stars – put our posters on your wall and throw different types of confectionery at us,' and on the other hand we were saying, 'Hey, we're just like you, we're a couple of normal blokes who happen to be on telly.'

*While we were filming* The Ant and Dec Show, *we lived at the Olympia Hilton, and our time at that hotel taught us one thing: the BBC had more money than Telstar.*

*I remember one time, Rory Gibson, who you may remember as our co-star in* Byker Grove *and the third member of our* The Doors-meets-The-Chippendales *log-cabin triumph, came down from Newcastle with a mate of his.*

This mate of Rory's thought he might get hungry on the train, so he took precautions. He brought a plastic bag full of meat with him. I can still see him now, walking towards me carrying a sweaty white plastic bag full of sliced turkey, sausages and boiled ham. Judging by the amount of meat that was still in that bag, neither Rory nor his mate *had* got hungry on the train. Either that, or they'd both become vegetarians somewhere around Darlington.

*But the meat was just the start of it. Once they'd seen the kind of diverse food and beverages on offer in the capital, they went mad – and invested in a loaf of bread and a block of cheese. I'm not sure how Dec pulled this one off, but Rory and his mate both ended up staying in my room on that trip. With three pairs of teenage socks in one place, it would have smelt of cheese either way, but a large block of Cheddar certainly didn't help keep the McPartlin residence fragrant that day.*

*Me and Dec went off to the TV studio one morning and, against my better judgement, I left Rory and his mate in my room. Understandably, they weren't keen on paying for a room-service breakfast at the Olympia Hilton – I think a bowl of cornflakes costs around £92 in most of those hotels – so they decided to improvise. Armed with the bread and cheese, they searched the room and discovered an iron and an ironing board in the cupboard. The next thing they did was insane and ingenious at the same time. They used the iron and its board to make cheese toasties. If only Dragon's Den had been around then, I'm sure those two entrepreneurs would be millionaires by now. It was just a good job I didn't have to do any ironing when I got back, although I did pity the businessman who next stayed in my room: I could just picture him trying to press his shirt with a souped-up Breville sandwich-maker.*

*The Ant and Dec Show* went on air in April 1995 and went out every Tuesday on BBC1 for eight weeks. It did well in the ratings and even went on to win a Children's BAFTA award, but most of that passed us by – we never saw the show go out, and we missed the BAFTAs. As soon as we'd finished the series, we had to get out there and convince people to buy our new single, 'Stuck On U', which, like convincing anyone to buy any of our singles, took absolutely ages.

*It was while we were doing that promotion that we faced one of the biggest challenges of our entire career, something neither of us has ever forgotten. We had our first fight.*

# Chapter 14

*Whenever we're interviewed, or whenever we meet new people, they always ask us the same question: 'Have you two ever had a fight?' Don't get me wrong, they usually say hello and stuff first, it's not like, 'Nice to meet you, have you two ever had a fight?', but it always comes up sooner or later, and it's only right we tell you the full story. So strap yourself in, here goes.*

We were in the middle of this whirlwind promotional tour (as we've established, there is no other kind) for 'Stuck On U', and we'd been booked to appear on one of the biggest music events of the year, if not the decade – *GMTV's Fun in the Sun*, live from Torremolinos, with Anthea Turner. We arrived in the middle of a baking Spanish summer, expecting to do the usual full day of promotion, crossing our fingers there were no dance-music remixes involved. Then we were given a rare treat: Kim, our tour manager, told us we had the whole day to take in the local surroundings and do some sightseeing. 'This is a great chance to immerse ourselves in the local culture and discover the real Spain,' I thought, as I ordered two pints of Heineken in Terry's Bar and Grill.

*One drink led to six and suddenly it was ten o'clock at night and we were tucking into a plateful of the local delicacies– a full English breakfast, with chips. Once we'd finished our fry-ups, we went back to the hotel bar, where Kim joined us, to 'keep an eye on things', which, roughly translated, meant 'make sure we didn't get too drunk'. The night wasn't getting any younger and, after a whole day of drinking in the sun, with a live performance on GMTV early the next morning, we did the sensible thing, and ordered some shots with our next round of beers.*

It was practically dawn when I finally stood up and announced I was going to bed.

*I slurred, 'Where are you going?' back at Dec, ignoring the fact he'd just told me and Kim exactly where he was going.*

I told Ant I was going to bed, although I'd had so much to drink that it might have come out as 'Boing to ged', and started to head towards the lift.

*I asked him why he was boing to ged. He told me we had to be up at 5 a.m., which, by this point, was probably about an hour and a half away, and then he walked off, turning his back on me. Something in me snapped. I followed him, with Kim right behind me.*

*'Don't you dare walk away from me when I'm talking to you,' I shouted after him, and I got my wish – he turned round and started ranting at me by the lifts.*

I've got no idea what it was about, but I do like a good rant when I'm drunk. I eventually finished, and then, right on time, the lift came, and us two and Kim got in it.

*I turned to Dec and said, 'If you've quite finished, I'd like to have my say.' I started slurring something, and I think Dec's response tells you a lot about him as a person.*

I put my hands in my ears and started going, 'La, la, la, la, la, can't hear you.'

*I was furious. I quickly decided that actions spoke louder than words, and punched Dec in the chest.*

I was stunned, but I pulled myself together and came back with a move that Muhammad Ali would have been proud of, as I tried to knock Ant's cap off. The problem was, I was so drunk that I only managed to catch the peak of it, which meant the only injury Ant sustained was a slightly wonky cap. Suddenly, an act of incandescent drunken rage had turned into a Chuckle Brothers sketch. Kim started shouting, 'Break it up, break it up,' and, of course, like all young lads, once we knew there was no chance of an actual fight, we started mouthing off to each other, doing what's known as 'giving it the big 'un'. Poor Kim was completely freaked out – she'd never been exposed to raw, graphic violence like this. Once the lift arrived at our floor, we all went to our respective rooms. I spent the next hour in mine trying to work out what the hell had just happened.

*The next morning – actually, later the same morning – I woke up after about an hour's sleep, feeling remarkably good. Of course, that was because I was still drunk, but I was too drunk to know that at the time. I put on my Day-glo shirt and headed for make-up at the GMTV studio. When I arrived, Dec was already there, and the two of us sat side by side, not speaking to each other. Believe me when I say that a make-up room is one of the campest environments to try and maintain a moody, testosterone-charged silence in.*

*By the time we had made our way to the set, both our hangovers were starting to kick in, and we were feeling truly awful. Over the years, a lot of people have speculated on the best cures for a hangover – a Bloody Mary, a fry-up, a strong black coffee – but I'm pretty sure no one's ever suggested performing PJ and Duncan's 'Stuck On U' live on GMTV in Torremolinos. It was the last thing in the world either of us wanted to do, and over that shared feeling of dread and embarrassment, we put our friendship back together. I turned to Dec just as the track was starting up and said, 'Thank god we're still pissed.' We both started to laugh, did the song and, after that, we were mates again.*

And there you have it, that's our only big fight. We did have an argument over a *Who Wants to be a Millionaire?* board game in the late nineties, but let's not give you all the gossip at once.

'Stuck On U' was released in July 1995. We'd been away from the charts for almost six months and were genuinely worried people might not remember who we were. 'Pop years' are pretty much the same as dog years – six months in human time actually equals five 'pop years'. We needn't have worried though, the single got to number twelve, further proof that we still weren't number-one material, but we were managing to stay out of the bargain bins – and that was good enough for us.

*In October, we released another single, 'U Krazy Katz'. Despite our disastrous summer trip to Spain, Telstar's promotional plans included another stab at world domination, and this time we were starting in Germany. At the time, it was considered the second biggest market in Europe for pop music, and Telstar seemed certain we'd do well there, sell millions of records and become superstars of German pop.*

A big German teen magazine had decided they wanted to do a feature on us and our home town of Newcastle. At the time, Newcastle United were doing well in Europe – which gives you some idea of how long ago this was – and there was a buzz about the city. They wanted to come over and do an article where we visited our old schools and the football stadium, and it sounded great. It meant invaluable exposure, some great PR and, most importantly, the chance to see our mams. Then, as always, came the twist: Telstar told us the magazine also wanted to do an 'At home with PJ and Duncan' photo shoot in the flat we shared in Newcastle. We calmly pointed out that we didn't share a flat in Newcastle, but the record company didn't seem too bothered – the whole thing was about the city, so we'd have to find a flat there and pretend we lived in it. When I look back now, I find it amazing we agreed to this, *and* that it was left to us to find a flat we could pretend we lived in. It was like they were trying to turn us into Britain's first estate-agent pop stars.

*Finding a flat in Newcastle was going to be a very tall order and, eventually, we went to the only people we could rely on – our families. At the time, my mam's boyfriend, Davey, who's now my stepdad, had a flat he lived in with his son. Robbie and I talked Davey into letting us use it and I made him promise that he and Robbie would make themselves scarce*

*when we went to do the shoot. The plan was to get there before the pho-*
*tographer and the journalist, give the place the onceover, litter it with a few*
*personal possessions and make it look like we lived there. Of course, we*
*never had time, and we all ended up arriving at once.*

*It was a two-bedroom place, and we started by giving them the guided*
*tour. I walked into Davey's bedroom and said, 'This is my room.' It was*
*quite obvious that was a lie. There was a wardrobe with suede jackets and*
*Kicker boots in it, and the decor, from the bedspread to the wallpaper, said*
*one thing: 'I'm a middle-aged man and I last decorated this room in the*
*1970s.' I could see they were already starting to smell a rat. Before they*
*could ask me any questions, I said, 'Come on, let's get you a drink. Dec,*
*put the kettle on.'*

*I should add that the kitchen is not Dec's natural habitat. As I've men-*
*tioned already, even beans on toast pose an insurmountable challenge to him.*
*And don't worry readers, that epic tale is now just a matter of pages away.*

I really think you're overselling that beans-on-toast story . . .
Before I could even make the tea, they said, 'Where is your
room, Dec?' That was a question that spelt trouble, because I'd
never been to the place in my life. Behind their backs, Ant was
pointing to the left in an attempt to let me know which room
was 'mine'. It was like a French farce, with a couple of German pop journalists in the middle of it. I tried to act confident
and said, 'My room? It's just down here. Follow me.' I opened
the door to 'my' room, and there it was. A He-Man bedspread,
Airfix planes hanging from the ceiling and a toy castle on top
of the chest of drawers. The journalist took one look at the
room, one look at me, and said, 'This is not your flat, is it?'

*We'd messed up France with the dance remix, and now we were never going*
*to make it in Germany. After this fiasco, there'd be no more interviews, no*
*more photo shoots and no more TV in the land of sausages and sauerkraut.*
*It was another country off the list when it came to foreign promotion.*

We were over the moon.

# Chapter 15

After October had seen 'U Krazy Katz' storm to number fifteen, November marked the release of *Top Katz*, the album, which was a whole different kettle of fish. That went to number eleven. Never worried about overexposure, we also released a third single, 'Perfect', and no, before you ask, it wasn't a cover of the Fairground Attraction classic, it was another ballad. This one reached number sixteen, which showed we were nothing if not consistent.

*But releasing an album paled into insignificance next to our other big project. After living in each other's pockets for five years, we decided to take the plunge and move in together. Telstar agreed to rent a flat for us, because apparently that's what happens when you're a pop star, and it seemed like a great idea to me and Dec — we were best mates and we were inseparable. Besides, Telstar told us they couldn't afford two flats.*

*One of the great things when we first moved down to London full time was the anonymity. It was almost as if people didn't have a clue who we were. Our flat was in Fulham, and it's not uncommon for there to be pop stars, actors or celebrities knocking about in West London, so we got a lot less hassle than we ever did anywhere else. Having said that, people were a lot less friendly. You couldn't just walk into any pub and have a chat with the landlord (obviously we tested that theory with dozens of boozers, just to be on the safe side). The other problem was our accents, which were stronger back then. If you ordered a drink with a Geordie accent in West London, you'd often get situations like this:*

*'Can I have a Coke please?'*
*'A cork?'*
*'A Coke.'*
*'A cork?'*

*'A Coke.'*

*'A cork?'*

*'Forget it, I'll have an orange juice.'*

I'm sorry; I can't have that, that's simply not true. You would never order soft drinks in a pub. The stuff about accents is right though.

*We were delighted to leave the hotel and get our own place. This was perhaps the one and only instance where on hearing the sentence 'The record company thinks it's a good idea' we wholeheartedly agreed.*

The flat was great, but we didn't have a lot of room. You could definitely have swung a cat in there, but I wouldn't have tried to swing any bigger animals. One bedroom was much smaller than the other, so we tossed a coin to see who got the bigger room, which I still say was a very unfair way of deciding.

*Dec lost the toss . . .*

I was devastated. I still say it should've been best of three.

*The main thing is you've put it behind you.*

*As soon as we moved into the flat, we decided to decorate it. To most people, that would have meant a trip to B&Q or Homebase, but not us. We went to the local newsagents, bought a copy of that week's NME, which had three free posters in it, of Supergrass, Oasis and Black Grape, put one in the hall, one in the kitchen and one in the front room, then sat back, had a can of lager and admired our handiwork.*

I could've done with a fourth poster, because my room was a right state. It had pink curtains and two single beds pushed together. And people think pop stars live in luxury. These days, my life is very different and my bedroom is a million miles from that one – I've got three beds pushed together now and blinds – pink, obviously.

That flat very quickly became an absolute tip and, before long, it was filthy. I don't think we bought a single cleaning product in the entire year we were there. At one point, we started to wonder if *Men Behaving Badly* was a documentary based on our lives.

*Lisa would tidy up when she came round, but we didn't even have a Hoover, so she would go round picking stuff up off the carpet – bits of food, fluff – I'm ashamed to say she was the human Hoover back then.*

*We spent most of our time doing what any sane twenty-year-olds with their own flat in London would do – drinking cans of lager and watching our favourite TV shows. Tuesday night was always the high point, because that was* The X-Files *and* The Fast Show, *although we also watched the consumer-affairs programme,* Watchdog. *Give us a break; there was no such thing as satellite TV in those days, okay? One week,* Watchdog *did an item about sofas that broke fire regulations. Lynne Faulds Wood, the presenter, explained that if a sofa didn't have a particular tag, then it wasn't flame retardant and that made it a fire hazard. We both got up off the sofa – it took something special to make that happen – and immediately checked the sofa. There was no tag: we were living with a fire hazard. This was a serious issue, so serious, in fact, that it took almost thirty seconds for us to order another takeaway and forget all about it.*

We survived almost exclusively on takeaways in that flat, although we weren't complete idiots when it came to food. We still managed to maintain a strict and balanced diet. It went like this: curry, Chinese, pizza, fish and chips, then curry, Chinese – you get the picture. I once ate so much I was physically sick. That's how good life was back then. Our new-found independence did have one other profound effect on our lives. We put on two stone each.

*Eating so much junk food was the closest we got to an Elvis phase and, if you look at photos of us from around that time, well, let's just say we were both carrying a bit of extra timber, which wasn't good news, because* chubby pop stars sell even fewer records than skinny ones. Having said that, we didn't spend all our time in the flat. Hey, we were two young lads living in swinging nineties Britpop London, one of the most cosmopolitan cities in the world, so we decided to go out into the big bad world and get stuck in. 'Getting stuck in' mainly involved going to an old mans' pub at the end of our road. It was called the Prince of Wales, was run by Irish Vince, and had regulars like Chinese Pete. Not everyone who drank there had their nationality at the front of their names – we weren't English Ant and English Dec – but for some people it just seemed fitting.

We loved the Prince of Wales. It was full of men in their forties and fifties. They had no idea who we were, and it was a beer-serving, salty snack-selling slice of heaven. Chinese Pete ran the chicken and rib takeaway next door, which meant our balanced diet now included a fifth dish to fall back on. It wasn't long before we were invited to lock-ins, where Chinese Pete would pop next door and bring loads of chicken back to the pub. So we'd sit in the pub with a load of middle-aged men, eating free chicken and ribs. To borrow a catchphrase from our favourite TV show of the time, 'We were very, very drunk.'

**It might sound like fun, but life in the new flat wasn't always a bed of roses. Let's just say there was an inevitable period of adjustment.**

Too right there was – Dec was impossible to live with at first, mainly because he's the least domesticated man in the history of western civilization. There are tribes living in mud huts on the Amazon who know more about housework than Declan Donnelly. For a start, he would pee all over the toilet seat, and he'd leave the lid off the margarine.

**Not the lid off the margarine? I'm no better than an animal.**

His clothes would pile up in the corner of his room, and I had to show him how to do everything, from how to work the washing machine, to – and this is no lie – how to wash up. I mean, how do you get through the first twenty years of your life without being able to wash up?

Well, I think I can be excused for the first five years – you don't let toddlers wash up – and then, well, I quickly worked out that I had six brothers and sisters and a mum who would get there before me.

*Even the washing-up pales into insignificance compared to the first time Dec tried to 'cook' beans on toast. I think most people reading this book will agree it's not a complicated recipe. In fact, it's not even a recipe but, to the galloping gourmet here, it was a major project. I walked into the kitchen one night and, straight away, I was met with a sight that shocked me – Dec had managed to open a tin of beans and get them into a pan without losing any of his limbs which, by his standards, was like cooking a six-course meal on top of Mount Everest. But then he looked at me, then looked at the beans and uttered the immortal words, 'What do I do with these?' A few suggestions sprang to mind, but I won't repeat them in print, so I told him to just heat them up and put them on the toast. He looked at me as if I'd just suggested rubbing them into his hair, and then he said, 'Don't be stupid, you've got to cook them properly – how will I know when they're cooked through? I don't want to catch salmonella . . .' I tried to stay calm and told him the clue was in the title – they were BAKED Beans, they'd already been cooked and he was just warming them up, but he wasn't having any of it. He took one more look at the pan and made a big decision.*

I rang my sister and asked her how to cook beans on toast. She told me exactly the same thing Ant had. Much to Ant's annoyance, I decided to believe her, and it's been my signature dish ever since. I know what you're thinking, lady readers: I'm a real catch, aren't I?

Of course, while we were living in the flat, one constant remained – we were out and about promoting our records, and the record company had a whole new way to push our music on to an unsuspecting public: competitions. There'd be 'Win a signed CD', 'Win a telephone call' or, by far the worst, 'Win lunch with PJ and Duncan'. They would be run by magazines like *Just 17* or *Smash Hits*, and would always strike fear and dread into our hearts. It's true what they say:

there really is no such thing as a free lunch. They were some of the most painful meals of my life, and I've had breakfast with Terry from East 17.

*The lunches were always in London, at Planet Hollywood or the Hard Rock Café, basically anywhere that served burgers, chips and fizzy drinks – me and Dec insisted on it. The winning fan would turn up, usually very nervous, with a friend there for moral support, and it would be up to us to make conversation. It was like a two-course version of the girls in my mam's kitchen. We'd have to make all the running, so we'd open with the very original question, 'How are you?', followed by the classic 'Which school do you go to?' The waiter would come over to take our order and we'd always say, 'No starters, let's skip straight to the mains, shall we?' We were determined to get in and out as quickly as possible.*

There was one exception though, a lunch we had with two fans who weren't nervous at all, mainly because they didn't give a toss about PJ and Duncan. This girl had been bought lunch with us by her dad at a charity auction. She turned up at Planet Hollywood with her friend and, pretty much immediately, we could tell she really wasn't bothered. They looked even more bored than we did. I was tempted to say, 'Look, you're both clearly not arsed and we'd rather be somewhere else, shall we just call it a day?', but we stuck it out to the bitter end, all the way through the ice-cream sundaes.

Away from the embarrassment of lunch with fans, we found sanctuary in our flat in Fulham. We kept ourselves to ourselves and didn't really know any of our neighbours, apart from an Australian bloke who lived upstairs. His name? Peter Andre. These days he may be better known as Jordan's one-time other half but, back then, he was a fellow pop star and, apart from the deafeningly loud R'n'B he used to play, Peter was the perfect neighbour. We'd often bump into him in the foyer of an evening – he'd be off to the gym for a swim and a workout and we'd be on our way to the Prince of Wales for eight pints and a bucketload of free meat. Looking back, that was another warning sign we weren't cut out for pop stardom. Peter was working out to keep his six-pack stomach in shape, while all we could think about was Chinese Pete's six-pack of chicken wings. The fact that the record company put us in a flat with a gym was a hint that we never really took.

While we were in Fulham, I bought my second car. You won't be surprised to hear that the MG Metro Turbo never made it down to the big smoke. My second car was a Suzuki Vitara jeep. It had the flared arches, wide wheels, lowered suspension and beefy twin exhaust – but there was just one problem: I was too scared to drive it in London, which meant I hardly ever took it out.

*It was the most useless purchase Dec has ever made. One evening, I'd planned a romantic evening with Lisa. She had just got back from touring with Deuce and we hadn't seen each other in ages. I'd booked dinner at one of our regular haunts, Mr Wings Chinese restaurant. It was going to be a special night for the two of us. She came round to the flat, we had a nice glass of champagne and, when we were both ready, I rang a taxi. Dec overheard me and insisted I cancel it; he'd take us in the jeep.*

It was less than a mile away – I might have been scared of driving in London, but I was sure that even I could manage such a short trip.

*So I phoned the taxi firm to cancel. The controller said the car was just round the corner. I told him I didn't need it because I was getting a lift from a friend instead, and the bloke at the taxi firm flipped. 'You can't do that,' he shouted. 'You can't just order a taxi and then cancel it 'cos you've sorted out a lift. It's already on the way.' I didn't much like his tone, and I didn't appreciate him telling me what I could and couldn't do. I said I could cancel it and I was cancelling it, and we parted on bad terms.*

*Dec had already gone downstairs to pull the jeep round to the front door. Lisa and I got our things together and headed down for our lift. We got to the ground floor, and there was Dec, keys in his hand and no sign of the jeep. 'Bad news,' he muttered. The battery was flat. The car hadn't been used or even started for so long the battery had drained and it was useless. There was no other option: I had to ring a taxi. I called the taxi firm back and tried to order another one, but the bloke on the phone was still so furious that he refused. Me and Lisa had to walk a mile to our special dinner.*

**It was probably for the best. I was secretly still really scared of driving in London.**

*I did however manage to get my own back. A few weeks later, me and Dec went out for a curry on the King's Road after a night down the pub, and the food was amazing. As usual, by the end of the night we were a little bit the worse for wear. We paid the bill and, before we left, Dec nipped to the toilet, and while he was away, I filled his coat pockets with cutlery – just enough so that it would fall out when he put his jacket on as we left the restaurant. I then sat back, feeling that kind of smugness you only get when you play a trick on one of your mates and you can barely stop yourself from sniggering*

**I came back from the toilet, and we were just about to leave when the owner came over. We thanked him for a lovely meal, and he brought us over another drink. The three of us chatted for a while and then eventually we got up and left.**

*The cutlery didn't fall out of his jacket. I was gutted.*

**I didn't even notice the extra weight in my coat. We were in a taxi on the way back and, as I searched my pocket for my wallet, I found the cutlery. It took me a couple of seconds to click what he had done, and we burst out laughing. I turned to Ant and said, 'Very funny.'**

*It was very funny – very, very funny – and I didn't know it then, but this was a gag that was going to keep on giving.*

**We got home, and I unloaded the cutlery out of my coat pockets. We were actually both quite chuffed that we had**

clean knives and forks in the flat for the first time since we'd moved in.

The following weekend, Clare came round to stay and said she fancied a curry. I remembered the amazing food and hospitality we'd been shown on our night at the Indian restaurant and said to her, 'I've got the perfect place, me and Ant went last week, you'll love it.' We headed down to the King's Road in Chelsea. When we arrived at the restaurant, it was crammed full of people but, immediately, the owner recognized me.

'It's you!'

'Yes, it's me,' I replied. 'I'm back!'

'Get out or I'm calling the police.'

He glared at me angrily. He was dead serious.

'Get out or I am calling the police.'

He reached for the phone next to the till. The whole restaurant went silent and turned to look at us. Clare looked at me, as the excited smile I was wearing on the way in slowly disappeared from my now puzzled, not to mention embarrassed, face. Then the penny dropped . . .

'Oh! The cutlery! Don't worry, I'll bring it back.'

'Get out! Get out! Or I'm calling the police.'

We turned and left sharpish as he started to dial 999. Naturally, Clare asked what the hell all that was about. I tried to explain what had happened, but Ant's mock cutlery-theft didn't sound so funny after the shame of being chucked out, not to mention nearly arrested, in front of the whole restaurant. We cancelled our curry plan and headed back to the flat. Ant and Lisa were in front of the telly watching *Stars in Their Eyes*.

*'That was quick – nice curry?' I said to Clare. She gave me the dirtiest of dirty looks and said 'Don't you dare talk to me about curry.'*

*We might not have had much of a fan base at the Indian restaurant but, as pop stars, we were capable of attracting the occasional – how shall I put it? – obsessive stalker. I was once sent a notebook by a female fan who, I hasten to add, was older than most of the people who normally bought our records and, let me tell you, this was no ordinary book. The outside was covered in pictures from the Kama Sutra and, inside, was a story she'd written. The plot seemed to involve kidnapping me and using me as her sex slave. At least I think that's what was going on – I certainly wasn't going to read the whole thing.*

I read most of that book, and it was hilarious. When it came to sex slavery, this girl had a very vivid imagination.

*From what I could gather, her plan was to feed me just enough food so that I'd be capable of performing sexually but not so much that I'd have enough energy to escape.*

I'm no dietician, but getting that nutritional balance right would be a very fine line – surely escaping requires fewer calories than being a sex slave?

*I suppose that depends what your sex-slave duties involved. You're right, though, wouldn't it be much easier to jump out of a window than have a bit of how's your father? We should have finished the book; I'm sure she had it all worked out.*

*The second half of 1995 saw our new album perform less well than* Psyche, *even though it still shifted over 100,000 copies and reached number eleven. We started 1996 by turning our attention back to what we did best, or what we did least badly anyway: television. We had our BAFTA from the first series of* The Ant and Dec Show, *which had secured good ratings, so, displaying the same showbiz nous we always did, we decided not to do a second series because of our reservations about the quality of the first one. Then someone pointed out that if we didn't do another one, the show would look like a failure, so we agreed to do a follow-up series.*

This time, though, like the mini multimedia moguls we were, we also made a few demands. We wanted a new time slot – 5.10 instead of 4.35, because we thought the extra thirty-five minutes would make us more grown-up. We wanted a new producer, and new writers. Remarkably, the BBC agreed, and without even once suggesting we find new presenters. Once they'd given the go-ahead for that lot, we demanded a jacuzzi full of champagne and a Rolls-Royce to the studio every day, but they told us to quit while we were ahead.

Finding a new producer was tough. We needed someone experienced and funny. Eventually, the job went to a man called Conor McAnally, a tall, well-built Irishman who always wore a cap and had made a lot of kids' shows in Ireland. Conor was a bit of a maverick and, once we got to know him, we realized he liked to take risks, although we should have known that from the start: wearing a cap in my company was always a big risk after what I'd done to Ant in Torremolinos. Working with him was a breath of fresh air. In our first meeting, he told us he thought the first series had been a bit of a mess and suggested that, for series two, we pretend that Ant and I share a flat – although he stopped short of letting us bring *The X-Files* box set and a crate of Stella Artois to the studio, which was disappointing.

*Anne Gilchrist, the director we'd enjoyed working with so much on the first series, also brought two new writers on board. The first one was a fellow North-easterner called Dean Wilkinson. Dean was from Stockton-on-Tees, and he was very different to the writers we'd had on the first series: he was funny, for a start, and his style was a little more surreal, which we loved. This was the start of a working relationship with Dean that would last for the next seven years. I don't know if he smashed a mirror sometime in 1995 to get that kind of bad luck, but he was stuck with us for a long time.*

*Dean was the first person who wrote what could be called proper double-act material for us. We'd had reservations about it in the first series, but there was no point in denying it any longer: we were performing on TV, and there were two of us so, whichever way you sliced it, we were a double act. Writing for kids, it's important to get inside their heads, and that means laughing at the same things they do, which, in short, consist of farts, burps and hitting people over the head with frying pans. Dean found all that stuff funny because he had the mind of a big kid, and that was really important for the material. The other great thing about Dean was that we could have a laugh and a drink or ten with him, which always formed a vital part of any professional relationship we created.*

The other writer was, to be blunt, downright odd. He was a cross-dressing frustrated performer who would always be very disruptive in meetings. He'd spend most of his time drawing 'suggestive' pictures of Conor and showing off to whoever was in the room. As I've already told you, performers are all neurotic, insecure and self-obsessed, and he was no different. The important thing was we found him hilarious. His name was David Walliams. You might have heard of him; he's done a few little bits and pieces on telly since *The Ant and Dec Show* in 1995.

David was, and if he's reading, still is, a great writer, but there was one drawback – he always tried to write himself into the sketches. There was a sketch we started doing in the second series called Retro Cops, which was basically a *Starsky and Hutch* spoof, with us two dressed up in afro wigs, flares and platform shoes. Despite a reluctance when it came to dressing up in the first series, we'd jumped at doing this particular sketch simply because we found it funny.

In one edition of Retro Cops, David had written in the part of a vicar, and we agreed to let him do it. In the sketch, we had to stop the vicar, who was driving down the street, and take his car. It was like *Heartbeat* meets *Life On Mars*. A bit. On the day, David turned up with his own glasses and comedy teeth. We had to steal his car, while he was trying to do the same with the limelight.

*We went to our starting positions, and the director called out 'Action!' David, dressed as the vicar, drove the car into shot as planned. We stopped him, and pulled him out of the car. What we didn't know was that while we'd been getting ready to film, David had got into the car and taken his trousers off. So when we pulled him out of the car, the top half of him was a vicar, and the bottom half was just pants and socks. We started laughing our heads off, and the poor director was shouting*

*'Cut! David, put your trousers back on'* – not the last time someone in the TV industry would say that to Mr Walliams. When he said he wanted to impress everyone with his part, we hadn't realized that was what he had in mind. But there's a time and a place for vicars in their underpants, and it's not on Children's BBC at 5.10 on a Thursday afternoon. Just like Dean, David had to constantly be reined in, and that was exactly what we wanted. We were finally getting the kind of risqué show we'd hoped to make first time around and, if the price we paid for that was seeing David Walliams in false teeth and underpants, well, we were prepared to pay it.

If I remember rightly, David came to the wrap party of that series and sprung two surprises on us. Number one, he was wearing a pink tutu, which gave us an early glimpse of what a convincing laydee he made; and number two, he brought his girlfriend, which was a shock, because we'd always assumed he was gay. He was great fun to have around and, whenever we see him today, we have a laugh reminiscing about the old times, as we remind him how he owes his whole career to us, while he maintains he was the only decent thing on *The Ant and Dec Show*.

*We started having guests on the second series too. When it came to booking them, the only real criterion was that we wanted them to be people we were keen to meet. Unfortunately, Bill Clinton, the Sultan of Brunei and Peter Beardsley were busy – so we went with the kind of old-school showbiz legends we'd always enjoyed watching as kids. That meant we were lucky enough to perform with the likes of Frank Carson and Lionel Blair. Guests like that were always professional, dedicated and, above all, available. In the case of Lionel Blair, we finished the show with a song called 'Get inside a Bin', which we performed, as you might have guessed, from inside bins. Even Lionel got inside one, from which he delivered the line, 'Hi, I'm Lionel Blair, and I hope you are too.'*

That's still one of my favourite lines of that series. We'd done some research, and by 'we', I mean some people from the

BBC we'd never met, and discovered that the audience for the first series was made up predominantly of girls, so we were told to try and make the new series a bit more male-friendly. That was music to our ears.

*When it came to pushing things, our first target was our old nemesis,* Blue Peter. *Yes, this was some of the sharpest satire on TV. Katy Hill was one of the presenters and, at the time, was considered the pin-up of Children's TV. We did a song on the show one week called 'I Love Katy Hill, she's a* Blue Peter *presenter', and in the song, I had a line that said she was 'gagging for it'.*

We knew it was completely inappropriate for Children's TV, and that was exactly why we did it. 'Gagging for it' wasn't even a double entendre – it was a very single entendre, and we got into proper trouble for saying it pre-watershed.

*I think the Tom Jones-esque pelvic thrust you delivered with the line might have made things worse.*

Hmmm, do you think so? Let's be honest, it was about 95 per cent of the reason we got into trouble. But this paled into insignificance after we introduced a feature called Beat the Barber. Before we'd started making the new series, we knew we had to do something to get it talked about, and this was it. It's been said that there's no such thing as bad publicity and, with this item, we tested that theory to the limit. The premise was very simple: we asked kids from the audience hair-related questions, while the 'barber', who, miraculously wasn't played by David Walliams, hovered over them. If they got the questions wrong, he shaved their heads. We'd had to fight hard to persuade the BBC to let us do it, but eventually they said yes. The kids and their parents all gave permission before they played the game, and the first three contestants were boys. Then, we had a girl who entered. That was when we knew things would really kick off.

*I don't know why the fact that the girl, whose name was Laurie Slater, had ginger hair made it better, it just did. On the day, she failed to Beat the Barber, which meant it was out with the clippers and off with her long, flowing red locks. When the show was transmitted, there was an uproar. We received a record number of complaints for a kids show, and Conor had to go on the Channel 4 TV show,* Right To Reply *and the BBC's own* Points Of View *to defend Beat the Barber, and the Katy Hill incident. For Conor, as the producer, it was tough to go on these shows and defend our ideas but, for us, sat at home with a beer watching them, it was strangely exciting.*

The thing was, the item could be justified: these kids and their parents knew what they were getting into when they played the game. To us, it was all part of not talking down to kids, which has always been really important to us. Laurie even went on *Right To Reply* with Conor, although I can't remember how much of her hair had grown back by then. It has to be said, when the BBC, the papers and the whole TV industry went mad about it, it probably wasn't our wisest move to issue a statement simply saying, 'Keep your hair on.'

*By the end of that series, we felt like we'd found our feet as TV presenters and knew it was something we really enjoyed doing. In fact, we enjoyed it so much, we seemed to be taking our work home with us, because we were always playing pranks in the flat, and the girls were often the victims.*

*Lisa was staying one night and needed to get to bed early so, like the considerate and respectful souls we are, Dec and me made ourselves scarce and went down the pub. Several hours later, we got back and decided that it would be the funniest thing in the world if Dec impersonated me and got into bed with Lisa. He asked me what I'd normally say when I got into bed. I told him that I would usually call out softly, 'Hello, babes,' and that I would then slide an arm around Lisa. I nipped to the toilet while Dec prepared for his role. I could hear him practising his 'Hello, babes,' in what he felt sounded like my voice.*

An actor of my calibre takes every role very seriously.

*When Dec was happy with his impression of me, he went into my room, got into bed, put his arm round Lisa and delivered his line.*

I was very good, if I do say so myself.

*Then I burst in, turned the light on and shouted, 'What the bloody hell's going on here?' Lisa jumped out of her skin, while us two laughed our heads off.*
  *I don't think she spoke to me for about three days.*

Once we'd finished our TV series, and scaring the life out of poor Lisa, it was time to get back on the pop-star treadmill, which meant yet again endless hours of interviews, photoshoots and personal appearances. It was a daunting thought but, on the bright side, we'd decided to indulge in a showbiz crime we'd been waiting three years to commit.

*We were about to kill off PJ and Duncan.*

# Chapter 16

*Killing off PJ and Duncan wasn't the only big move we made that summer. Together we took an important decision – we parted company with our music manager, Kim Glover. We'd felt for a while that things weren't really working out with Kim and we were keen to try and take our music in a new direction – preferably one that didn't involve miming, corny dance routines and roadshows. Our solicitor, Paul Russell, who still takes care of our legal business, handled the whole thing. Paul's got so many things going for him – a law degree, plenty of experience and two first names. He's also got our best interests at heart; at least that's what it says on the contract I'm currently reading aloud from.*

*We sat down with Paul for a few hours – standing up for that long seemed unnecessary – and said that we wanted to split with Kim. He then explained our position in clear legal terms that any simpleton could understand. Then, when he saw the baffled looks on our faces, he tried again. What we needed to do was sack Kim and Dave Holly, to make a clean break, and then re-employ Dave, who we wanted to keep. This was all for 'legal reasons'. The lawyers among our readers . . .*

**Who are you trying to kid?**

*. . . will know why we had to do it; the rest of you can just do what we did – and take Paul's word for it.*

On his advice, we rang Dave and said, 'No hard feelings, but we're sacking you – and then giving you your job back next week.' Dave understood, plus it gave him a week off from us two, which was probably why he was whooping and cheering down the phone. Then, Paul sent a legal letter to Kim confirming what we'd discussed. If you're wondering what the difference between a normal letter and a legal letter is, the answer's simple – about three hundred quid.

Like the mature adults we were, once we knew the letter had been sent, we did the decent and honourable thing – and ran off to Marbella for the weekend. It wasn't that we'd done anything to be ashamed of, but we were twenty-one, so rather than face the music, we decided to get out of the way and let the dust settle. Looking back, if we'd been older and wiser, we might have handled it differently. But at that age, we decided to jump on a plane and leave our problems behind.

*When we got back, we got down to the serious business of killing off our evil alter egos. Ever since the first single, we'd been desperate to use our real-life names, and now, with two hugely successful albums – okay, two albums – behind us, Telstar agreed. We were thrilled, although in hindsight, it seems odd that we were so excited about using our real names. No one in our real lives called us PJ and Duncan – well, not unless they were really trying to wind us up.*

It wasn't just our names we were being honest about either. We came out as full-blown heterosexuals who had girlfriends. We were really living on the edge now: using our own names, mentioning those of our girlfriends – talk about pushing the boundaries.

To help us do all this, we had a new press officer called Simon Hargreaves, and he encouraged us to be a bit more ourselves. The mid- to late nineties was an era characterized by what the press christened 'lad culture'. It was all about drinking, partying and reading *Loaded* magazine, and it suited us down to the ground. Simon got us featured in *The Face*, *Loaded* and, unbelievably, the *NME*. We were trying to rely less on *Smash Hits*, *Just Seventeen* and *Mizz*, and Si pulled off the miraculous trick of making music journalists take us seriously. In his spare time, he also turns water into wine and walks on water. After years of giving sugar-coated interviews to girls' magazines, we could finally let people see us for what we were – two young lads who liked drinking lager, partying hard and playing cutlery-based pranks on each other.

*Telstar also took some big decisions – and they decided that our third album would have something neither of the first two had.*

More than one top-ten hit?

*Don't be ridiculous. They decided to spend some serious money on a big marketing campaign with one central message: 'Two men in their early twenties are going to use their real names.' We also persuaded them to let us change our music and aim for a more mature sound.*

We decided it was probably a good time to change our image. We went for dinner with Si and the then editor of *Smash Hits*, Kate Thornton, who went on to host ITV2's coverage of *Pop Idol* and, later, *The X-Factor*. As editor of the most powerful pop magazine in the country, Kate gave us her thoughts on what sort of image her readers would respond to. It was a long and complex discussion that took in many schools of thought and stylistic influences and, in the end, we reached a major decision.

*It was all about the hair.*

A few days later we were going to shoot the video for our first single as Ant and Dec, 'Better Watch Out', and we were also scheduled to do a photo shoot with Rankin, a genuinely cool and respected photographer, so there was no time to spare.

*I'd wanted to shave my head for a while, so this was the perfect excuse. There were only two problems: with a forehead like mine, a shaved head isn't a good look, and Lisa hated it. She told me I looked like a Romanian orphan, and refused to kiss me until it grew back, although she did express an interest in adopting me. We'd known the Rankin shoot was coming for a while, though, and we really liked his work, so we both stayed off the beer and lost some weight. We were determined to look good in the shots.*

Ant had it easy with his shaved head. I didn't have it so good. The plan was to dye my hair a lighter shade of blond but, when it was finished, I looked in the mirror and just had one question for Ant:

'Is this ginger?'

*To which I replied, 'Yeah, it is.' And then left the room, so I could laugh loudly and properly.*

I got it lightened slightly on the day of the shoot, but there wasn't much you could do. I was gutted. The image change we'd been so excited about ended up with me looking like a young Mick Hucknall.

Even though our third album, *The Cult of Ant and Dec*, wasn't released until May 1997, 'Better Watch Out' came out in August of 1996, and it made the top ten. Okay, it was number ten – but that's still technically the top ten, and no one can take that away from us. I've got such happy memories of that summer – our music was changing and we had our sights set on the big time.

*When it came to the rest of the album, we worked with a couple of writers called Biff and Matt. Music-industry professionals called them Stannard and Rowe, so they insisted we stuck with Biff and Matt. They helped us try and develop the more mature sound we were after. I know what you're thinking, 'What, more mature than "Our Radio Rocks"? You'd have to write an opera.' Biff and Matt even encouraged us to write a few tracks ourselves – and some of them weren't even Boyz II Men covers. In the past, we'd written a B-side here or a lyric there, but this time we were much more involved, and it was great fun.*

*We wanted to make music that was more like the stuff we were listening to, which was bands like Oasis and Blur. That's just how ambitious, deter-mined and downright stupid we were.*

Towards the end of the year, I got the chance to make some other big changes, to correct some of the mistakes I'd made in Ant's and my first few years as pop stars. For a start, I got the big bedroom when we moved out of our flat in Fulham and into a new one in Chelsea. Finally, I could put the coin-toss catastrophe behind me. But before we'd fully moved out of the Fulham flat, or 'vacated the property', the lady from the estate agents came round to check that everything was spick and span. It was neither, but there wasn't any lasting damage and we always had the fire-hazard sofa up our sleeves if things got, well, heated.

She was going round the kitchen, checking everything still worked when she did something that shocked Ant and me to the core. There was one small door that we'd tried and failed to open when we first moved in, and she did it straight away, and said, 'Yep, the dishwasher's fine.'

*We couldn't believe it. We'd been there twelve months and we hadn't known we had a dishwasher. I was devastated. Just think of the time I could've saved teaching Dec how to wash up.*

*When we moved into our new flat in Chelsea, we were still leading the* Men Behaving Badly *lifestyle. We spent a lot of time in various pubs, but one of our most popular haunts was Sainsbury's. It was at the end of the road, so we used to go down there and stock up on essentials like bread, milk and, of course, beer. We'd fill up a trolley and wheel it back to the flat – it was quicker than driving there. Although, if Sainsbury's lawyers are reading this, I'd like to point out that we did always return the trolleys.*

*After a few months, though, disaster struck: Sainsbury's introduced a system that meant that, when you took the trolley out of the car park, the wheels locked. Presumably it was designed to stop people stealing the trolleys, although as I say, we always returned them – I don't think we were the cause of the new system being introduced. Anyway, as you'd expect, the new trolleys deterred most people from taking them off the premises. Most people. But not us. It just meant we would half push, half lift our trolley down the road, the wheels scraping the pavement. Those trolleys could have had elephants attached to them for all we cared – nothing would have stopped us getting our beer home.*

In between trips to the supermarket, we were also busy trying to keep our TV career afloat. After all the furore – or the mild bit of attention – we'd got from Beat the Barber, we'd had a meeting with the BBC, and their policy was very clear: 'We want to keep you, but you've got to tone it down.' Our policy was equally clear: 'We're not going to tone it down, so we're leaving you.' We'd often thought about flirting with other channels behind their backs, but this time we went the whole hog and committed to a full-blown relationship with another broadcaster.

At the time, Channel 4 was the home of the edgiest, riskiest shows on TV – *The Word*, *TFI Friday* and *Countdown*, to name but three. In our first meeting with them, we asked Lucinda Whiteley, who was the Head of Children's, if they'd let us shave people's hair off. Her response? 'You can shave their pubes for all we care!' That was good enough for us, and we signed a deal with Channel 4. We also started our own production company, the cunningly titled Ant and Dec Productions. We were twenty-one, we had a new TV deal and we were the managing directors of our own TV company.

*I hate us, don't you?*

*November of that year marked my twenty-first birthday, and I had a surprise party, which was organized by my mam and Davey and held at FM's bar in the centre of Newcastle. I was really pleased that my dad was invited, as it was the first time I'd seen him for a few years – it was a big surprise, even at a surprise party. It was a bit awkward at first, but it worked out fine. He told me that he'd sit away from everyone and keep himself to himself. He said he wasn't there to cause a scene, just to say happy birthday and tell me he was very proud of me, which I appreciated.*

*In a way, that night sums up my relationship with my dad. We still talk from time to time, but he doesn't try and force his way into my life. I know that, down the years, he's been offered money by newspapers to talk about me, and he could have made a tidy penny, but he's always turned them down. He's a plumber, and there've been times when he's been out of work and the money would have come in handy, but he's never done it — and I respect him for that. I know that, one day, we'll probably see each other more regularly. My sister Sarha's started seeing him since she had her son, Ethan, and I completely understand why, because whatever's happened, Ethan is my dad's grandson.*

*The highlight of the evening came about an hour into the party. An enormous — and clearly cardboard — cake was wheeled towards me, and everyone started singing. I remember thinking, 'What is this? Am I the only one who's spotted that this cake is made of cardboard?' The singing ended, and I was getting ready to thank everyone when I noticed that something inside the cake was moving. For my twenty-first, I'd asked for a boxer, and I thought, 'Great, they've got me the dog.' The top of the cake flew off and I couldn't believe it when Lisa, who I'd been told had had to stay back home in Oxford, jumped out. Wearing a Newcastle United shirt. It was a fantastic surprise. I was over the moon, while at the same time thinking, 'I really wanted that dog.'*

In the same month as Ant's birthday, we released another single, 'When I Fall in Love', which hit number twelve. It seemed as though our new projects were working out very nicely, thank you. Despite our new image and our honesty in interviews, it hadn't affected our record sales too much. We had a new series on Channel 4 about to launch, and things were looking better than they had for a long time.

*We didn't know it yet but, within twelve months, the whole thing would collapse around our ears.*

# Chapter 17

*Tuesday 18 February 1997.*

*It's a date that's etched on quite literally no one's brain, but that was when our new show with Channel 4, Ant and Dec Unzipped, first hit the front rooms of Great Britain. The show went out every Tuesday at six, but because we were so busy completely reinventing British pop music, I can hardly remember a thing about it. Still, at least that's something we've got in common, eh, readers? Here's what I can recall: Conor McAnally was back on producing duties and Dean Wilkinson was writing for us, but there was one big problem with the show: rebellion. Or a complete lack of it, to be precise.*

*Ripping up the rulebook was a lot easier on BBC1 at 5 p.m. than it was on Channel 4 at 6 p.m. Channel 4 probably didn't even have a rulebook and, if they did, it would have been torn to pieces long before we arrived. Channel 4 was so edgy that nothing we did seemed particularly risqué. The idea for the show was that me and Dec lived together in a flat, although at least we knew where the dishwasher was in this one. We were joined by celebrity guests and, each week, we put on a different show — one week might be a costume drama, the next a whodunnit, and so on — and by 'and so on', I mean that's all I can remember. In many ways, the guests we had reflected our tastes at the time — there was Neil Hannon, the lead singer from the Divine Comedy, a great songwriter and someone whose work we really admired. And then there was Jo Guest. She was a topless model — and we admired her work too.*

Although we didn't feel it was our finest hour or, to be more precise, ten half-hours, the show still won a Children's BAFTA. Then something happened that's very common in telly — everyone changed jobs. It's just the way the industry works — I mean, it's not as if people would change their whole job just to avoid working with us . . . is it? After ten shows of *Unzipped*, we went for a meeting at Channel 4, and it was less 'Hi, guys, what do you want to do next?' and more 'Hi, guys, here's your leaving present.' After one series, our time at Channel 4 looked like it was coming to an end.

*We decided to take solace in song, and we went back to our music career. Fortunately, Telstar were about to put out* The Cult of Ant and Dec, *from which we'd already released two singles. There was a general election called for 1 May 1997, and we held a big launch party for the album at Chelsea Town Hall on the same night. Anyone who's anyone was there, or at least anyone who didn't give a toss about politics – I know Sophie Dahl and a policeman definitely turned up, because I had my picture taken with them. I still can't believe Tony Blair didn't make it, mind, apparently he had 'better things to do'.*

All night at the party, you'd hear the same sentence: 'Who's going to get to Number Ten?' I remember thinking, 'I'm hoping for top five, to be honest.'

The album came out, and we released our third single, 'Falling'. A tour followed, with a live band, which was a different experience for us. We could interact with them on stage; we could drink with them after the show; and the whole thing made us feel like proper musicians. Despite the fact we toured and did monstrous amounts of promotion, though, *The Cult of Ant and Dec* didn't do well.

In hindsight, we probably confused the audience a bit. We were trying to go a bit more *Cigarettes and Alcohol* and a bit less *Teddy Bears and Chocolates,* and it just wasn't working out. We sold around 60,000 albums, which, considering the first album had shifted over half a million, wasn't what you'd call progress. We ended up a bit like the England football team at the previous summer's European Championships – we came up short in the quest for success. That's where the similarity ends, by the way: we weren't managed by Terry Venables – he's a great football coach, but try asking him to get you a spot on *Top of the Pops* – it's a complete waste of time.

We decided to drown our sorrows. Our regular watering holes in Chelsea included pubs like the Man on the Moon and the Magpie and Stump, plus a sports bar called Shoeless Joe's. I don't know who Joe was or how he'd lost his shoes, but they had a huge screen, so we watched a lot of football there. Unfortunately, we had to stop going to Shoeless Joe's. We watched a Newcastle game there one Sunday afternoon and, at the end of it, the owner started slagging off Newcastle United and, most heinously of all, Kevin Keegan. I took offence and started a bit of an argument with him. It ended up with me and the owner standing face to face, screaming at each other. At one point, I thought we were going to have an actual fight.

*For once, this wasn't little-man syndrome, this was protecting Kevin Keegan syndrome – something all Newcastle United fans will be very familiar with.*

Ant and me did leave without any blows being traded and, in my mind, with Kevin Keegan's honour restored. But a few days later we were in the Man in the Moon when the landlord said to us, 'I see you've been barred from Shoeless Joe's then.' We didn't have a clue what he was talking about. He produced that night's *Evening Standard*, and showed us an article about celebrities who'd been banned from various pubs and clubs. On that list was 'Ant and Dec – barred from Shoeless Joe's in Chelsea.' We must be the only people who've ever been barred from a pub via a newspaper. I wouldn't want to drink anywhere that slagged off Kevin Keegan anyway. I did miss the big screen, though.

*After three albums, our three-album deal with Telstar was understandably at an end. We were starting to think it might be time to reconsider our career choices but, at the time, we had no other offers, so Dave Holly started trying to negotiate a new contract for us while we went back on the road. We had a long-standing commitment to do a tour of the Far East, a*

*part of the world we'd never been to before, and a place where, for some*
*reason, we'd been selling a lot of records. It seemed like it might be the last*
*corner of the globe where people would actually be pleased to see us, so we*
*packed our bags and headed for Japan, aware that this might well be our*
*last throw of the pop-music dice. We were accompanied by John Knight,*
*who worked for Dave Holly and was in charge of our schedule – he should*
*have been knighted for dealing with that alone – and Mike Faux, who was*
*our tour manager, which involved doing security and keeping hold of the*
*DATs we mimed to.*

*If you've never been, Japan is fascinating and, to us, as a couple of*
*twenty-two-year-olds from Newcastle, it was like a different planet. It's*
*fast-paced, crowded, there are neon signs everywhere and, if you don't*
*speak Japanese, you haven't got a clue what's going on, or where you are.*
*We got off the plane and were met by an interpreter and an MTV Japan*
*crew, who had apparently been given permission to film a documentary*
*about our time there. I'm not sure who'd given them permission, but I*
*know one thing: it certainly wasn't us. After twelve hours in the air, we*
*got straight to work. We didn't even know what jet lag was back then. I*
*remember waking up for the first few mornings at 4.30, wide awake, and*
*I'd ring Dec's room, and he'd be up too. We'd go to the spa at the hotel,*
*use the gym, jump in the hot tub and be sat there thinking, 'This is*
*great, you can get so much done getting up this early.' Then, by 8.30,*
*when all the interviews with magazines and radio stations started, we'd*
*be falling asleep.*

While we were over there, we'd been booked to appear on
what we were told was the biggest TV show in Japan. We
soon discovered on this promotional trip that every TV show
was 'the country's biggest TV show'. We went to meet the
producers of this particular one, and they told us that they had
a rule; any Western artist they had on the show had to perform a cover version of a Japanese pop track – in Japanese.
Live. They suggested we did a track by a pop duo called the
Kinki Kids. From what we could gather, they weren't kids, and
I don't even know if they were particularly kinky, but then
we'd spent years not being PJ and Duncan, so we already had

something in common. Still, we told them we couldn't possibly do it – mainly because neither of us spoke Japanese. Strangely, it hadn't featured much on the Newcastle school curriculums of the eighties. Plus, we didn't know the song.

They told us that didn't matter, they could write out the lyrics phonetically and put them on big boards next to the camera. Those boards are called 'idiot boards', which, looking back, should have started alarm bells ringing.

*We still said no, but then the record company came up with a compromise. We were scheduled to have the following day off, but they suggested we went into a studio, recorded a version of this Kinki Kids track, and then mimed to it on the show. That way we could be sure we'd get the words right, and avoid offending anyone by mispronouncing the lyrics. Plus, when it came to recording a track, getting an engineer to make it sound like actual music and then miming to it on TV, we were the best in the business. We agreed and spent our only day off in the studio painstakingly recording this track. There was us two, an engineer, a producer and an interpreter, so every time someone wanted to make a point, it had to go through three people. It was one of the longest days we'd ever spent in a recording studio.*

*It came to the night of the show, and we arrived in the TV studio feeling confident – the hard work was done and now all we had to do was mime to the track and enjoy our Japanese TV debut. As usual, we did a soundcheck before it started. The backing track started playing, and it soon became very clear that this was just the instrumental version, not the one we'd recorded with our lyrics on. Our translator came over and said, 'The TV producers want to know why you aren't singing.' We politely told her that it was because we were supposed to be miming. Suddenly everyone from the TV show looked very ashen-faced. They spoke to the translator, and she came over and said, 'No one mimes on this show.' It turned out that the record company had never cleared the mimed-track plan with the producers.*

We said again we couldn't sing it live – we didn't know the song and, strangely, in the forty-eight hours since our first meeting, we still hadn't become fluent Japanese speakers.

They told us there was no choice: if we wanted to appear on Japan's biggest prime-time entertainment show, we were going to have to sing live. In Japanese. The words were written out on the appropriately named idiot boards, and the next thing we knew, we were on live TV, stumbling through a version of 'Garasu No Shounen', which included such lyrical gems as:

> Ame ga odoru bus stop,
> Kimiwa dare kani dakare
> Tachi sukumu boku no koto
> Minai furi shita.

Good luck singing along at home.

*People tend to overuse the term 'toe-curling', but during that performance I honestly could feel my toes physically curling up inside my trainers. I remember there were only two English words in the whole song – 'bus' and 'stop'. I don't know if the Kinki Kids were ex-bus drivers, but it seemed like a strange choice. Either way, I just hope the Kinki Kids never saw it, I'm sure we must have ruined their song – well, apart from the bus-stop bit, which I'm proud to say we pronounced perfectly.*

Despite our Kinki Kids catastrophe, our Japanese fans were amazing. They'd buy us the most elaborate presents, and the best thing about that was that it's offensive in Japanese culture to refuse gifts. We'd get designer clothes, games consoles, sunglasses, CD Walkmans and, best of all, there wasn't a teddy bear in sight.

With the exception of getting very, very good at receiving expensive gifts, it's fair to say we didn't exactly immerse ourselves in the local culture. We'd never eaten sushi before, and we weren't too keen on the idea of raw fish for dinner, so we tried our best to stick to our usual strict dietary regime – wall-to-wall junk food. We found out one of the receptionists at the hotel spoke English, so we got her to write the Japanese for 'Take me to McDonald's please' on the back of a business card for the hotel. We'd leave our rooms, go down to reception, get a taxi, show them the card and then, when we'd bought our food, flip the card round to show the address of the hotel. It made getting a Big Mac feel like being in a James Bond film.

*But we couldn't eat McDonald's for ever, and one night we were taken to a dinner by the chairmen of Avex Trax, our record company, and some of his fellow executives. I think it's fair to say that, when it came to observing Japanese customs, we weren't the most sensitive of foreign visitors. We arrived at the restaurant and, as is the custom, everyone took off their shoes. One of the female executives who worked for the record company had a hole in her sock, which I immediately pointed out with a gleefully loud, 'Look, you've got a hole in your sock!' Our translator then took me to one side and said, 'Please. You should not point that out. She will feel so full of shame now.' We hadn't exactly got off on the right foot, if you'll pardon the pun.*

*We sat down, and they all started handing their business cards over to us, which we later discovered you have to take with two hands, because taking them with one hand is disrespectful. Apparently, using them to pick bits of food out of your teeth is disrespectful too, but we weren't to know that at the time, were we?*

*The restaurant didn't have menus, and the waiters suddenly appeared with tanks of live seafood. Me and Dec just looked at each other, thinking, 'Why have they brought their pets to work? Where's the food?' The penny dropped when we were asked to pick which one we wanted to eat. It looked like we weren't going to be the only fish out of water at this meal. The idea was that you'd put the food you chose into this huge bubbling vat of boiling water and cook it yourself. We couldn't have looked more worried if they'd asked us to perform the entire Kinki Kids back catalogue live.*

They also brought out some strips of raw beef, or Beef Shabu Shabu, as it's known in Japanese cuisine.

*'Japanese cuisine'? Someone's been on Google. The beef was good, and eventually we were persuaded to try some of the seafood, which, despite our reservations, was delicious. Throughout the meal, we'd keep getting little*

*bits of important cultural advice from the translator: 'Don't play drums with your chopsticks' — that kind of thing. Japan is such an amazing place, and such an exciting culture, and I'd love to go back now but, in 1997, I'm sorry to say, it was wasted on us.*

Our tour of the Far East also took in Taiwan and one of the most luxurious hotels I've ever stayed in. When we arrived, the manager and the whole staff were lined up in the foyer waiting to shake our hands — I felt like the Queen at the Royal Variety Performance.

*Then there was Singapore, where we had a whole floor of the Raffles Hotel to ourselves. We had an enormous suite each, and our own twenty-four-hour female butlers outside. We'd keep ringing each other's rooms and saying, 'Have you used your butler yet?' 'Nah — have you?' 'Nah — I can't think of anything.' I think, in the end, we sent them out to get some chocolate, just to give them something to do. And yes, before you ask, it was a tube of Smarties and a bag of chocolate buttons.*

The next stop was Indonesia, where we'd been booked to do a gig at the Hard Rock Café in Jakarta. We might not have been hard, and we certainly didn't rock, but we *were* partial to a cup of tea and a bacon roll, so at least we had the café bit sorted. On the day of the gig, we were scheduled to do a press conference.

*Throughout the tour, we'd had a different artist-liaison representative from each record company in each country. Their job involved organizing our schedule as well as being the main point of contact for the duration of our visit. The guy who was in charge of us in Indonesia was, to put it bluntly, an obsessive fan, so you don't need me to tell you he was a couple of sandwiches short of a picnic. It's highly unlikely he'll be reading this book, so I'll tell you exactly what he was like — he was short, chubby and had a smarmy little grin that would test the patience of a saint. You'd look round in the car on the way to a gig, and he'd just be staring at you, smiling, with a slightly maniacal look in his eyes.*

*On our way to one press conference, he snapped out of his silent trance and remembered he was at work and started to brief us. Then he said: 'AntandDec, you sing a cappella for them.'*

*What?*

*'What?'*

*'AntandDec, you sing a cappella for the press.'*

*'We don't sing a cappella.'*

*'But the press will love it, AntandDec. The Backstreet Boys did it here last week, AntandDec, please sing a cappella.'*

We told him again and again, getting more exasperated every time. We were professional singers and we had principles – the main one being 'Don't let anyone find out we're terrible singers.'

*Eventually, he gave up, we presumed he'd got the message and we went to the press conference. The journey had rattled us a bit and, when we arrived in a hot room with broken air conditioning and dozens of stern-looking journalists and TV crews, things weren't looking good. The first few questions didn't go too well, but then I made a crack about Dec looking like Michael J. Fox, and it brought the house down – people always found that funny in the Far East. Before long, they were all laughing along with us and, at one point, we even got a couple of rounds of applause. Suddenly the room didn't seem so hot and the journalists didn't seem so unfriendly.*

Despite the presence of this annoying little superfan, we'd given the press exactly what they wanted and we'd won them over with our dazzling charms. We stood up, triumphant and ready to leave. We must have been about halfway to the door, with the applause of the journalists still ringing in our ears, when we heard a familiar voice echo across the room.

'AntandDec, before you go, maybe you could sing a cappella for the press?'

We turned round, and there he was – his fat face full of girly glee. We couldn't believe it. The whole thing had gone perfectly, we were a couple of paces away from safety and now this little nutter had ruined it. The room started to feel hot again. Maybe no one else had heard him and we could pretend we hadn't either?

We took a quick glance over our shoulders and the entire room was on its feet, clapping and chanting, 'A cappella! A cappella! A cappella!', while our man grinned like some evil pop-music genius. I eventually managed to bring a halt to the chanting and said they should all come and see our show that night – I thought that would calm them down. Miraculously, it seemed to work. We had almost made it to the door when that sound echoed across the room again.

'AntandDec, please sing a cappella for the press!'

*The press started chanting and clapping again and staring at us expectantly. It was excruciating. Things were now getting really tense, and I could feel sweat running down my back. There was only one thing for it: me and Dec turned our backs on them and walked out of the room – fast. By the time we reached the door, the whole room was a cacophony of booing – and it was all the fault of Indonesia's biggest PJ and Duncan fan.*

We stormed down the corridor and went back to our dressing room. We were livid. How could this smug little stalker stitch us up like that? We were still sitting there, fuming, when there was a knock at the door and we heard that voice: 'AntandDec, can I come in? AntandDec, pleeease let me come in.' His whining got progressively more desperate. Despite still being furious, we decided to give him the benefit of the doubt – he obviously had seen the error of his ways and wanted to come in and apologize. I took a deep breath and opened the door.

'AntandDec, AntandDec, please let me come in . . . I've left my coat and my bag in here.'

Something in me just snapped. Ant had to physically hold me back from hitting him in the face. I threw the coat and the bag into the corridor and told him that there was no way we'd be doing the gig that night. If it hadn't been for him, the press conference would have gone off without a hitch, and we'd ended up being booed out of the room – it was degrading and humiliating.

*Still furious, we went back to the hotel and did something we'd never done before, something that was very out of character for us two and something we're not proud of. We had a game of tennis. There was a court on the roof of the hotel, and smacking a few tennis balls around was a great way to get rid of our frustration. We were in the middle of the first game when we heard a voice.*

*'AntandDec, I'm sorry, AntandDec, please come to the Hard Rock Café, AntandDec.'*

*At first I thought I was hearing things, but it was him all right – he had his mouth poking through the wire fence at the side of the court. Dec and me just started laughing our heads off at the ridiculousness of the situation. The more he pleaded, the more we laughed. As we walked off the tennis court, the last thing we felt like doing was a gig at the Hard Rock Café in Jakarta, so we did what anyone else wouldn't have done in that situation.*

## A gig at the Hard Rock Café in Jakarta.

*The whole Far East tour lasted about six weeks – it was one of the most surreal experiences of my life. When we got back, everything was still up in the air with music. Dave was still negotiating with Telstar and various other record companies who were interested in signing us. We were in a taxi when we got a phone call from Dave telling us Telstar had offered us another deal. He said, 'It's not a great deal, but it's a deal.' By this point, we weren't exactly seen as the next big thing. I listened to what Dave had to say, told him we'd think about it and put the phone down. Then we had a conversation that changed the rest of our career.*

It was quick, simple and to the point. I can still remember exactly what we said, which was this:

'I'm not enjoying this any more.'

*'Neither am I.'*

'Shall we knock it on the head?'
'*Aye.*'

And that was it. With those seventeen words – don't bother going back to count them, I've done it for you – we decided to stop being pop stars. It was time to bring the curtain down on the greatest Newcastle-based, ex-children's drama actors turned pop-star double act this damn country's ever seen.

The taxi stopped at the flat. We climbed out, paid the driver and gave him a tip: 'If your third album doesn't sell, it's time to retire from pop,' I said. I think he would have preferred money but, you never know, one day that advice may prove to be priceless.

*When we got back to the flat, we got a KFC and a couple of beers, and it felt like the biggest weight in the world had been lifted off our shoulders. Believe me when I tell you those beers were the coolest, sweetest-tasting lager I've ever drunk – and, trust me, I've done years of research. And the KFC? Well, it couldn't have tasted better if it'd been cooked by Gordon Ramsay and served on plates made of gold.*

The next day we rang Dave, told him we were giving up music and that we wanted to concentrate on TV, which, considering we had no TV show, no TV deal and no TV prospects, was a bit of a risk. In fact, the only connection we had to TV at that point was that we had one in the front room of the flat. The main thing was, though, that we were out of music and, to celebrate, we went on holiday to Majorca with Clare and Lisa.

That holiday was the very definition of blow-out: we drank gallons of San Miguel, ate what we liked and generally let our hair down, free from the shackles of boy-band life. Ant, in particular, celebrated by eating. And eating. And eating. He'd polish off everyone else's food, always to cries of 'Calm down, Guzzle Guts' from the girls – and, to his credit, he never once complained. Mainly because his mouth was full of food.

*I put on about two stone. It was brilliant. Clare and Lisa had known for a while that we weren't happy with our music careers so, when we finally quit, they could see how liberated, relieved and in my case, fat, we'd become. It was the first time the four of us had been away together, the girls got on like a house on fire and Dec and I relaxed. It was the perfect holiday.*

We came back totally refreshed: we weren't pop stars any more and we were free to try and create the career we'd always wanted – there were no commitments, no record company and no one to tell us what to do next.

*We were absolutely terrified.*

# Chapter 18

*We may have been, in the immortal words of Chaper 17, 'absolutely terri-*
*fied', but 1997 did end with a tiny glimmer of hope – a one-off show for*
*Channel 4 called* Ant and Dec's Geordie Christmas. *All I can really tell*
*you about that show is that it was definitely on around Christmas time, and*
*that Ant and Dec were in it. Other than that, as with* Ant and Dec
Unzipped, *my memory is hazy – I was probably too busy concentrating on*
*my newfound hobby of eating.*

After our *Geordie Christmas,* the next decent bit of work came
at Easter. While the rest of the country was busy opening
Easter eggs and watching old films, we stood in as guest hosts
of Channel 4's *The Bigger Breakfast,* which was a longer, and
frankly bigger, version of *The Big Breakfast* that went out during the school holidays. Normally, *The Big Breakfast* would be
broadcast between seven and nine in the morning but, in the
holidays, *The Bigger Breakfast* would normally be from seven to
twelve thirty – five and a half hours of live TV. That's enough
to exhaust even the most professional TV presenters around
– so, as you can imagine, it left us two completely knackered.

The show was always live from a house in East London and
it gave us first-hand experience of the kind of raucous, fly-by-
the-seat-of-your-pants telly that we came to know and love
over the next few years. Because the whole thing was on so
early – it's called breakfast TV for a reason – everyone who
worked there was always in a kind of heightened state. The
whole place was loud, enthusiastic and chaotic, thanks to a
combination of sleep deprivation and sheer excitement.

Our co-host was Melanie Sykes, and she wasn't interested
in appearing in any of the sketches or games in the show, so
we did them all. *The Ant and Dec Show* and *Unzipped* had both

featured sketches and games, but *The Bigger Breakfast* had one key difference from those shows – it was live, so whatever happened, no matter what went wrong, we would have to carry on regardless – and that's an incredible learning curve for a presenter. We started to try and surprise each other on air, or try and make each other laugh. I'm not sure we would have had the confidence to do that if Melanie had been involved, because we'd never worked with her before, so if you're reading, Melanie Sykes, thank you for not wanting to dress up and do sketches, it gave Ant and me the chance to start messing about on live telly together – something we're still getting away with ten years later.

*A while afterwards, we were invited to a meeting at Channel 4 to discuss that familiar topic known as 'our future'. On the way there, I remember both of us were really excited –* Unzipped *hadn't worked out, but Channel 4 was the coolest, edgiest TV channel around and where we wanted to be, so we couldn't wait to hear what they had to say. We didn't have a regular job, and this looked like it could be a golden opportunity. We got into the meeting, which was with Graham Smith and Stuart Cosgrove, and after a bit of chit chat, they started telling us how much they'd enjoyed what we'd done on* The Bigger Breakfast, *and that they wanted to talk to us about taking on the job full time, because they'd made a decision – there would be no more* Unzipped.

Hosting *The Big Breakfast* was an incredible opportunity – not only was it one of the most innovative shows on TV, this offer also provided us with everything that was currently missing from our careers – the chance to get extensive experience in presenting live TV and, even more importantly, a full-time job. It was perfect. With all these things going for it, we made our decision. We turned it down. We thought it was too early for us.

*Too right it was – it was on at seven o'clock in the morning.*

However good the offer seemed, our instincts were telling us it was the wrong move. After that, there was nothing on the horizon. Before long, the invitations to parties and premieres stopped coming – suddenly our names weren't down and we weren't coming in. If *I'm a Celebrity* . . . had been on the telly back then, I reckon we would've been asked to do it. As if that wasn't bad enough, at the time, the papers were running stories saying we had no record deal and no future – and printing that sort of stuff was scurrilous, damaging to our reputations and, worst of all, it was true.

Dave Holly showed us our financial statements, and they weren't exactly what you'd call a good read. We never really made a lot of money from our music career and, when we looked at the statements, there seemed to be a lot of activity in the column marked 'Out' and not too much going on in the column marked 'In'. At that point, there was a very real possibility that we'd have to move back to Newcastle and get, dare I say it, proper jobs. We needed to find a way to make a living – and fast. We knew we wanted to stay in TV, so we set about trying to do something we knew no one else in the TV industry would be doing – coming up with ideas for shows that could be hosted by Ant and Dec. We went into the offices of Ant and Dec Productions, just off Baker Street in Central London, and started brainstorming.

*One of the ideas we came up with was a music show for ITV, a kind of rival to* Top of the Pops, *live on Sunday night to coincide with the new Top 40 being announced. We thought there was a gap in the market at that time of the week – after all, the only other things on were* The Antiques Roadshow *and* Songs Of Praise *– and neither of them seemed too interested in the singles chart. We ended up pitching – (desperately trying to flog) – the show to Nigel Pickard, who was ITV's head of children's programmes. Nigel told us he was looking for a replacement for* The Chart Show *on Saturday mornings, and he thought our show could be it. The problem, as we saw it, was that he wanted us to host a two-hour, live, Saturday-morning kids' show before the music programme so, showing our* *as ever razor-sharp career instincts, we said no. We thought we were too old to be introducing cartoons on a Saturday morning, oblivious to the fact that, if the work situation didn't improve soon, we'd be stacking shelves on a Saturday morning before too long.*

Thankfully, Nigel gave us a second chance, and when we told him we'd changed our minds, he commissioned the show. It might seem strange that we went from the showbiz dole queue straight to having our own Saturday-morning show, but that's honestly how the fickle finger of television fate worked for us two. And you know what they say, never look the fickle finger of fate in the mouth – at least, I think that's right; I've never been great with proverbs.

Once we knew we were doing the show, we needed so many things: ideas, a title, people who had a clue how to make Saturday-morning telly . . . We called the show *sm:tv*, because it was Saturday-morning television – clever, eh? The music show afterwards was a 'CountDown' of the UK singles chart, so that became *cd:uk*. Don't be confused by the word 'count-down' in it, though, we weren't going after Carol Vorderman's audience.

Although we'd worked hard on *The Ant & Dec Show* and *Unzipped*, *sm:tv* and *cd:uk* were the beginnings of how we still work today – being closely involved in getting the show on air – from initial ideas right through to what you see on your telly. Part of making that happen meant putting together a production team, Conor McAnally became the executive producer for both shows, and we also needed another two producers. When we'd appeared on *Top of the Pops* as PJ and Duncan, we'd encountered a producer called Ric Blaxhill, who could be blunt and overbearing, and could make pop stars feel two feet tall. He was perfect, and we hired him to run *cd:uk*. Further down the line, we made two other key appointments: David Staite, who'd worked on *The Big Breakfast*, to run *sm:tv*; and Phil Mount, who'd been on *TFI Friday*, to work on music. David and Phil also went on to become great friends of ours, which is obviously why we've described them as 'key appointments' rather than 'a couple of blokes'.

*It's also a law of telly that, on Saturday mornings, you need a female co-host, so we set about meeting lots of glamorous young female TV presenters.*

Boy, that was a tough gig.

*One of the first stunners – I mean, candidates – we met was called Cat Deeley. Her initials were CD, so she already had her name in the title of the show, which was half the battle. We didn't know it at the time but, before her audition, Cat had done her homework on us. A few months earlier, me, Dec and Si Hargreaves had spent the day in the pub watching Newcastle play football. They weren't playing football in the pub – the match was on telly. As any Geordie will tell you, when you're watching Newcastle United, it's often helpful to drink heavily so, by the time we got to the end of the evening and arrived at Mr Wings, the Chinese restaurant, we were what's known in Newcastle as 'mortal drunk'.*

To give you a rough idea of just how inebriated we were, while we were in the restaurant, I fell off my chair – and, remember, Ant's supposed to be the clumsy one. At the next table, there was a nice young couple having a romantic dinner (the bloke was French) and they understandably asked to be moved away from us. I'm not proud of it, but I'm afraid I was very rude to them – I certainly didn't pardon my French. When the food came, I took one look at it, and my stomach churned. I stood up and said, 'I've got to go home,' which wasn't easy – I love a chicken with black bean sauce more than life itself.

*Me and Si finished our meal, then we went back to the flat to find Dec's keys still in the door and Dec poleaxed, fast asleep on the sofa. I think it would be fair to say that, other than these basic facts, neither of us have the most crystal-clear memory of what happened that evening.*

To be honest, I could have killed a man that night and I wouldn't have remembered it. Don't worry, I didn't, but I could have. I wasn't very proud of my actions though, and tried to put the whole incident behind me.

*In that interview with Cat, after a few pleasantries, she said, 'I think we've met before. I was in a Chinese restaurant a few months ago in Ful-ham with my boyfriend – he's French – and you two were sat next to us. You were quite rude actually.'*

I went bright red. I apologized at least *ten* times, and I was mortified – here was a girl we might be working with, and I'd been rude, offensive and obnoxious to her. I usually waited at least a month before I let work colleagues see my real person-ality. Cat finally put me out of my misery. It hadn't been her at all; when she knew she was coming to meet us, she'd found out that Si Hargreaves was our press officer and called him up to get some dirt on us.

*After being tricked, embarrassed and humiliated by this girl in the space of five minutes, there was only one option – we gave her the job. We had other girls to see, but we didn't bother. Cat was perfect, and we knew straight away we had a lot in common – a love of mischief, a good sense of humour and, of course, a first name with three letters in it.*

For us, one of the great things about working with Cat was that the three of us clicked really early on – and, by 'clicked', I mean, went out drinking a lot. She knew me and Ant had been together for years – not like that, you know what I mean – but that was never threatening to her. Even though she's very pretty – and, goodness knows, with us two on screen, we needed some glamour on the show – she was always prepared to muck in and make a fool of herself. She was never precious about how she looked, or how she behaved, she was up for a laugh right from the off, and that was vital when you were doing a Saturday-morning kids' show.

*At first, it was only me and Dec who did sketches, but after a while we started to involve Cat in them. So, for instance, she became Jam Woman, a superhero who provided jam at the drop of a hat. She'd never done 'comedy' before, but we told her to just really throw herself into everything, and she went for it. Soon, she was putting in goofy teeth, wearing a dodgy wig and calling herself Cat the Dog.*

*There's no one in the world I would rather have worked with week in, week out on sm:tv. Well, maybe Alan Shearer, but he would never have fitted into those little dresses. Since Byker Grove, Cat's still pretty much the only person we've ever worked with regularly and, once the show found its feet, every week felt like the three of us were having a laugh for a living.*

So, with a new team behind the camera, a fantastic co-host and a set designed by Jamie Hewlett of Gorillaz fame, we were ready to launch the show. We had a cast-iron commitment from ITV to run the show for a full year, and on 29 August 1998, *sm:tv* and *cd:uk* hit the airwaves. It was make-or-break time, and we knew it. With presenters who were new to the time slot, a brand-new show and a channel that hadn't traditionally done well on Saturday mornings, the whole thing could easily have been a complete disaster.

*And it was.*

In the run-up to the first show, Ant and me were feeling very apprehensive, and Cat also seemed quite overwhelmed by the whole thing. She came in to the studio for the first time the week before and couldn't believe how big it was – before that, she'd been working in a much smaller studio at MTV. She said, 'Will everyone in the country be able to see this show?' Of course they will, we told her – it's on ITV, it's going to be live to the whole of Great Britain. Cat nodded. 'So my nan'll be able to watch it in Birmingham, then?' she asked.

*None of us got much sleep the night before that first show, and our breakfast had gone untouched: there was no room in our stomachs for food, they were all too full of butterflies. We'd done a runthrough the week before, so we knew the script but, about halfway through it, I had a moment of clarity. I thought, 'There's nothing in this show.' It had no real content, and that's never a good sign with a telly programme. You don't often hear people saying, 'Did you see that new show last night? There was nothing in it – it was brilliant.'*

*In those early episodes, we'd present the show on top of a little platform called Mission Control. It had buttons and handles, and it was supposed to be the epicentre of that morning's entertainment – we'd play all the cartoons from there, cue the pop videos and fade in and out of breaks; it was kind of a mixture between a TV studio and a radio station. The idea was that we were fully in control. The reality was that we weren't. None of the buttons or handles were connected to anything and we just pretended.*

I actually think it was quite a good idea, Mission Control. It was SkyPlus ahead of its time, but it was just too complicated for 9.25 on a Saturday morning, when kids just want to watch cartoons and be left alone. If you see any of the early shows, you'll notice that even we didn't believe in it. Eventually, and it took us a while, we worked out that there's a reason Saturday-morning kids' shows have certain conventions – like a sofa. And no Mission Control. Those things work, but we just hadn't realized it yet.

*After the first show came off air, I just had this overwhelming feeling of, 'Well, we got through it,' but nothing more than that. There was no feeling of achievement or success, just relief and a slight whiff of 'Mission Control's a bit rubbish, isn't it?' I spoke to Sarha on the phone afterwards, and she's always been very honest with me about the stuff I do. She would have been about twenty then – a bit older than our target audience, but still young enough to appreciate what we were doing. I asked her what she thought of the show, and she said, 'I didn't really get it.' I reckon that's just about the worst thing you can say about a TV show, other than, 'And, later, PJ and Duncan are performing live.'*

*In the vicious, no-holds-barred battleground of Saturday-morning kids' TV, we were slayed – and the people doing the slaying were the hosts of*

*BBC1's* Live & Kicking, *Zoe Ball and Jamie Theakston. Back then, the BBC on Saturday mornings was like Godzilla – a ruthless beast that crushed anything that got in its way. Looking back at the early days of our show, we were trying to be too clever and too cool for our own good which, of course, in the eyes of the kids, made us not very cool and not very clever. We'd spend the whole two hours of* sm:tv *building up to* cd:uk *and showing 'exciting' things that were coming up later on in our super-cool music show. What that essentially involved was filming pop stars getting in and out of their cars when they arrived at the studio. We may as well have called the show 'Celebrity Taxi Rank'.*

*One of the many things we hadn't realized was how much the audience changes through the course of a morning. At 9.30, when your viewers are all young kids, you've got to show cartoons, do big, daft things and make a fool of yourself – but we were making fools of ourselves in completely the wrong way: by not understanding our audience.*

Throughout the autumn of 1998, the BBC trounced us in the ratings. It was really difficult coming to work and hearing, week after week, that we were coming second in a race with only two runners. I don't mind telling you, I started thinking shelf-stacking might be back on the agenda. The BBC had traditionally dominated Saturday morning television and, with us at the helm, it didn't look like that was going to change any time soon. There was a very real danger that, if the ratings and the show didn't get better, then ITV would cut its losses and cancel the series. It was also our company making the show, so we were failing in the boardroom as well as on the telly. If Alan Sugar had been in that boardroom, we would have been fired pretty sharpish. Thankfully for us, he was far too busy running a successful business empire to get involved with Saturday-morning telly.

*There was one thing and one thing only that saved us from getting cancelled in the first six months. That thing had a beard and a huge dollop of blind faith, and was called Nigel Pickard. Nigel was tremendously supportive of the show. He must have been under pressure from his bosses to cancel us, and it would have been very easy for him to buckle, but he stuck to his guns.*

Years later, Nigel became Director of Programmes at ITV, which meant he was in charge of *Saturday Night Takeaway* and *I'm a Celebrity . . . Get Me out of Here!*, and we had a great relationship with him then as well. To put all of that another way: thanks Nigel, we owe you big time.

*Christmas approached fast, and the show was still dying on its arse. Then something happened that changed everything. We didn't hire new people, we didn't change our style, we did something which, although we didn't know it at the time, would have an enormous impact on the show.*

We did pantomime.

*Earlier in the year, when we'd been in that showbiz wilderness, we'd signed up to appear in* Snow White and the Seven Dwarves *at the Sunderland Empire – I'll leave you to make your own jokes about which dwarves we were. Our co-star, playing the part of* Snow White, *was a beautiful, talented and charismatic actress who had a complete and utter loser of a boyfriend. Her name was Clare Buckfield.*

Very funny.

*Thanks, Grumpy – or were you Dopey? I can never remember . . .*

That's enough now.

*Oh no it isn't.*

Don't start all that again.

*When we'd agreed to do the panto, we didn't know that, by the time it came around, we'd be hosting our very own unsuccessful Saturday-morning show, but we were professionals, we'd made a commitment and we were* determined to honour it. Plus, we thought sm:tv *could get cancelled any day so, for all we knew, this could be our last paid work for a while.*

Doing Snow White *and* sm:tv *at the same time made for a hectic schedule. We'd do two pantos a day, Monday to Thursday, then after the Thursday evening, drive through the night from Sunderland to London and spend all day Friday rehearsing* sm:tv. *On a Saturday morning we'd do the live TV show and, the second it finished, at 12.30, we'd leave the studio on the back of a taxibike and race to Battersea heliport in South London. There, we'd get a helicopter to Gatwick, a flight from Gatwick to Newcastle, then a car from Newcastle to Sunderland. Once we were in the car, we'd get into our costumes, arrive at the theatre with seconds to spare and walk on stage three hours after we'd left London. I'm getting tired just thinking about it. Despite the chaos, we made every single one of those Saturday matinees – not that audiences ever knew we'd even been on telly that morning. Most of them were far too busy watching* Live & Kicking.

As well as us two and Clare, the panto also starred our old sparring partner from Byker Grove *Billy Fane. He had written and directed the panto, and he was always on standby in case we didn't make it in time – although I never quite worked out how he would have managed to portray both of Dame Dolly Doughnut's nephews. Yes, that's right, I said Dame Dolly Doughnut's nephews – these were parts so demanding, so intensely theatrical that I can only assume Daniel Day Lewis and Anthony Hopkins were busy.*

Like all pantos, this one ran through Christmas and into the New Year, which meant I spent Christmas with Clare. It was wonderful. She bought me a great present that year – a brand-new stereo, which came in various separate parts, or, as they were called back then, 'separates'. There was a radio, a tape player, a CD player, an amp and a set of speakers. (For younger readers, stereos were complicated affairs in the days before iPods.) Anyway, Clare had ordered the stereo from a shop in the centre of Newcastle but, when it came to collecting it, she realized she couldn't manage it on her own. She couldn't ask me for help – it would have spoiled the surprise

– and Ant was busy making sure he didn't get roped into carrying a stereo round Newcastle.

*That's right, I was.*

In the end, Clare did the sensible thing and enlisted the help of the only other people she knew were available – the dwarves from the panto. So Clare, or Snow White, as she was known to our audiences, turned up on the main shopping street in Newcastle with a band of dwarves in tow, to collect the stereo. I never did find out if they sang 'Hi-ho' all the way there and back, but I'd like to think they did.

*Saturday mornings may not have been going well, but the pantomime was breaking box-office records. The shows were packed out, and the audiences were loving it.*

*At the end of every performance, we'd do the song sheet, where we'd get kids from the audience up on stage to help with a song – a cover of the Fat Les classic, 'Vindaloo'. During the song, and for a few minutes afterwards, we'd have a chat, a laugh and a joke on stage with the kids. After a few shows of talking to different groups of kids, the penny suddenly dropped: they were our audience for Saturday mornings –and, on our TV show, we just weren't talking to them properly. We were talking to twenty-two-year-olds with hangovers, not these kids.*

*When you're face to face with kids, day after day, you realize exactly what makes them laugh – and what makes them laugh is fart noises, toilet humour and anything big, silly and visual. They didn't seem too interested in the latest Jamiroquai B-side. We'd always prided ourselves on knowing who our audience is and understanding what it wants but, this time, we'd got it completely wrong.*

When we went back to the TV show after Christmas, we talked to the producers and told them we needed to change everything. We introduced a game called Giant Grabbit, where we hoisted kids into a giant pit of balls to scramble for prizes. We also showed lots of episodes of *Sabrina the Teenage Witch* and, more importantly, engaged with it. We did sketches where I was obsessed with Sabrina and wrote her love poems. We did as much as we could around this crazy teenage witch, because we knew that was what the kids would change channels to see.

*Just as the seven dwarves had saved Snow White from the clutches of the evil queen, so the panto had saved Dame Dolly Doughnut's nephews from being killed off by the evil* Live & Kicking. *And, like all the best stories, this one would have a fairytale ending.*

The ratings started to pick up a bit, that's what Ant's trying to say – and more kids started watching. We were slowly but surely starting to get the hang of Saturday-morning telly.

# Chapter 19

*It was at the start of 1999 that we made another huge and very, very dif-
ficult decision — to part company with our manager Dave Holly. He'd
always said that, if ever we felt we'd outgrown him, to just tell him, and
we both felt the time had come.*

**It was a very tough decision, and not one we took lightly. We
were very fond of Dave, his assistant Margaret and his family,
and we'll never forget what he did for us. He had a huge
input into the first ten years of our careers, and we'll always
appreciate that.**

*After we'd made the break from Dave, we started looking for new man-
agement. The first meeting we had was at a company called James Grant
Management, which was run by Peter Powell, the former Radio 1 DJ,
and his business partner, Russ Lindsay. It was a good meeting, even if
Pete did keep giving us traffic news and the highest chart climbers of the
week, but I suppose old habits die hard. The company had clients like
Zoe 'the enemy' Ball and Philip 'not the enemy at all' Schofield, and
a track record for taking presenters from Saturday mornings to prime-time
TV. Even though sm:tv wasn't exactly setting the world alight, we
knew that was exactly the direction we wanted to go in. In that first
meeting, we also met Paul Worsley and Darren Worsley, who are both
from Bolton, about the same age but, despite their surname, strangely,
not related.*

   *Pete, Russ, Paul and Darren explained they were looking for new,
younger clients to represent, and they liked us as performers. Their company offered a full service to their clients and didn't just represent them but
took care of every aspect of their life. We nearly blew the whole thing when
Dec asked if that included washing dishes and cooking beans on toast, but
thankfully they didn't hold that against us. At the end of the meeting,*

*Pete said, 'Well, I'm sure you've got loads of people to see, but we'd love to sign you, so let us know when you've seen everyone.' We said, 'Oh yes, we've got lots of people to see,' and went on our merry way, but the truth was they were the only people we'd arranged to meet. Me and Dec were walking down the stairs of their office, when I whispered, 'Shall we go with them?'*

'One step at a time,' I said to him.

*I didn't know if he meant the agency or the staircase. After all, I am very clumsy.*

We pretty much decided there and then to go with James Grant, and we had a moment of déjà vu. Matthew Robinson had told us about the Telstar offer on the stairs at *Byker Grove*, and here we were, making another big decision on the stairs. Even now, when we have to make our mind up about something, we go straight to the nearest staircase.

We didn't actually tell James Grant for a few days – after all, we might have gone upstairs for a coffee, but we weren't going all the way on the first date. We led them on for another forty-eight hours or so and then signed – and we've been there ever since. Once we'd joined the agency, we were assigned an artist manager, Alison Astall, and, to this day, Ali is absolutely vital to everything we do. She knows the two of us better than anyone.

*Except my beautiful wife, of course.*

Of course. Ali is our Girl Friday. Although the truth is, she's more like a girl Monday, Tuesday, Wednesday, Thursday, Friday. And often Saturday and Sunday too. Ali takes care of everything – she's in charge of our schedule, she comes to Australia with us for *I'm a Celebrity . . .* she even sorts out when we get our hair cut. It's no exaggeration to say that, without Ali, our lives and our career would be total chaos.

*Things were beginning to fall into place. At the beginning of 1999, we also settled into our first ever houses. Thanks to the money from panto, and sm:tv being commissioned for fifty-two weeks, we knew that, even if the show was axed after a year, we'd be able to save up enough money to pay the mortgages for a while. We'd actually bought them in November, but because of the panto and Christmas at home, it didn't feel like we moved in properly until the New Year. They were in Chiswick, in West London, and for the record, they were not next door to each other – that would be absolutely ridiculous. They were two doors away from each other. People have always teased us about living so close, but we're best mates and there's no point in living on the other side of town to each other. Just like Dec with his big family and cousins round the corner, and me with my Nanna and Granda living across the road, we both grew up in houses next to the most important people in our lives, and I suppose this is an extension of that. We never sat down and decided to live next door to each other, it's just worked out that way, and that's how we like it.*

There was about twenty paces between the two houses, which was great – it was almost like sharing a flat, but with houses, and this time, there was no toss for who got the big bedroom. Living right next to my best mate, I always had someone to talk to but, more importantly, I had somewhere I could open my tins, because for the first year I lived in my house, I didn't have a tin opener. As you can tell, I wasn't exactly quick to adapt to the demands of living on my own. I didn't have any curtains for about six months, so I stuck together a load of flattened-out cardboard boxes with Sellotape and fashioned a makeshift blind. I was really proud of it.

*It would have taken less time to go and buy a blind than he spent making that one, but that didn't occur to him.*

I remember getting back from the pub one night and Ant and me went home. I fancied a sandwich, so I got some ham and a packet of cherry tomatoes out of the fridge and then a knife out of the cutlery drawer. Due to having had a couple and to not being a domestic goddess, I decided to use the biggest knife I could find to cut the tiny little cherry tomatoes. The end result was that I missed the cherry tomato and the only thing I ended up slicing was the top of my thumb. It started pouring with blood and it wouldn't stop. I'm not good with the sight of blood – it makes me feel very faint, almost as faint as the idea of cooking, in fact. I rang Ant, who came over with Lisa and bandaged me up.

*He was whiter than the slice of Mother's Pride on his chopping board when we got there.*

Before long, and partly for my own safety, Clare was staying a lot of time at the house, Lisa was at Ant's, and the four of us were spending loads of time together. Clare used to cook a Sunday dinner at mine, we'd watch videos at Ant's, or go out for dinners in Chiswick together.

Lisa and Clare always got on well, which made everything so easy – and they're still very close friends now. Back then, it also meant me and Ant could go to the pub, watch the football and leave them in one of the houses together. They were usually very happy to get shot of us two and tuck into a bottle of wine.

*Lisa and Clare would always tease us for spending so much time together, but what they never seemed to notice was that, nine times out of ten, when we were hanging out together, they were hanging out together too. If I spent the weekend in Oxford with Lisa, where she's from, and Dec went to Hertfordshire with Clare to see her family, when we got back, me and Dec would go for a pint on the Sunday night, and Clare and Lisa would say, 'Are you happy you're back with your little friend now?' but, at the same time, they would be together having a girlie gossip, back with their 'little friend' too. It still annoys me now to think about it.*

I can see that – my little friend.

*The four of us were great together, though, and having our own houses also meant we could have lots of people round. Almost as soon as we moved to Chiswick, everyone started coming back to my house after a night out and, specifically, coming back to my kitchen. Don't ask me why everyone liked to spend time in the kitchen, not the living room, but that kitchen had more drinking done in it than most pubs in London, so much so that we nicknamed it 'The Vortex', because once you got in there, time stood still. We'd get back from the pub after closing time, and the next thing you knew it was three o'clock in the morning.*

Years later, when Ant and Lisa moved out of that house, leaving that kitchen behind, it did wonders for my liver.

*Although there's one thing I miss about The Vortex, which is Dec and Lisa doing drunken Michael Jackson dancing. I never got involved personally — I'm not really one of life's dancers.*

Maybe we should enter *Britain's Got Talent* next year, Lisa and me. What do you think?

*No comment.*

With a new home, new management and, thanks to panto, a newfound love of childish humour (okay, we'd always had the last one), we set about trying to make the only Saturday-morning show that kids would actually want to watch. Along with Dec's love poems to Sabrina, we started to dress up as characters from *Pokémon*, the Japanese cartoon that kids everywhere loved in the late nineties. I still couldn't really tell you a single thing about *Pokémon*, but boy did the kids love those little, er, thingies. This meant that, like the consummate professionals we are, we got very good at pretending we loved those thingies too.

*One of the ways we did that was through the Pokéfight. David Staite, our producer, had come up with it, and it was written up by, appropriately*

173

*enough, our writer, Dean Wilkinson. It involved me and Dec dressing up as* Pokémon *characters and having a fight. Sounds funny already, doesn't it? What do you mean, 'No, not at all'?*

*Normally, with any sketch we do, we have a lot of input but, with this one, we had to take a leap of faith, because we had no idea what* Pokémon *was or how it worked. Taking a leap of faith on telly is hard enough, but when you're taking that leap dressed in a wig and talking in a cartoon character's voice, it's ten times harder.*

*That morning, we rehearsed it in front of the crew, who were always a good barometer of whether a sketch was funny or not. The Pokéfight went down like a lead balloon. Even worse, it was too late to change anything about it. I remember coming back after the ad break, getting ready to pokéfight live, fearing the worst, and Sticky, our floor manager, said, 'Right, everyone, here we go: 10–9–8–7 . . .' then he stopped mid-count, turned to me and Dec and said, 'You're going to die!', then carried on with "6–5–4–3–2–1.' Despite the crew's reaction, and Sticky's scaremongering, the Pokéfight went on to become a massively popular part of* sm:tv.

As well as *Pokémon*, we also had a cartoon called *Digimon*, which was a *Pokémon* spin-off. Really, don't ask. After the closing credits of one particular episode, it was my turn to back-reference it, which isn't easy if you've never watched a single episode. In the end, I went for the safe option: 'More *Digimon* next week. Ah, I love *Digimon.*' Quick as a flash, Cat turned to me with a glint in her eye and a cheeky smile and said, 'Do you? Which one's your favourite?' I obviously didn't have a clue – I couldn't even take a guess at a name – so I replied: 'What?' Cat calmly repeated, 'I said, who's your favourite *Digimon* character?' I just thought, 'You cheeky bitch,' while stuttering, 'Oh, I love them all.'

We all loved winding each other up and she'd got me a treat. Cheeky bitch.

*We did our fair share of stitching Cat up too. If there was ever a big competition that involved reading out lengthy questions, rules and regulations,*

174

*we'd always make Cat do it. I think the moment she rumbled us was after a particularly laborious read for a* Pocahontas On Ice *competition. She shouted, 'How come I always get this shit to do?'*

*Slowly, thanks to our clever plan of making a show that actually appealed to children, the ratings started to improve. In the spring, Zoe and Jamie announced they'd be quitting* Live & Kicking *at the end of the current series and, once that happened, we really started to believe we could win the battle against the Beeb. A few months later, Conor ran into the office shouting, 'We've done it, we've beaten them!'*

*After months of slogging our guts out, we were beating* Live & Kicking *in what TV bosses would call the 'key demographic' – kids aged between five and fifteen. This was huge – audience research told us that kids that age were in charge of the remote control on Saturday mornings, and the received wisdom was that if we got* them *watching, then the next age group – the sixteen to thirty-fours – would follow. I assume because they couldn't find the remote, but we didn't care why, we just wanted people to watch our show.*

By the time the summer came around, *Live & Kicking* had gone off air and been replaced by a show called *Fully Booked*. We were now winning every week, and we never looked back. All our hard work was starting to pay off – we'd work on the show from Tuesday to Saturday every single week and it was a great buzz when that commitment was rewarded with victory in the ratings battle.

*The sketches we did improved, our performances and our ideas for the show got better, and we still had Dean Wilkinson as our main writer. As Dean was such a big, naughty kid,* sm:tv *was the perfect show for him. He had a childish and mischievous sense of humour that made Saturday mornings the perfect showcase for his talents.*

Looking back now, there are so many parts of that show that we both genuinely *loved* doing – Splattoon, All Hands on Dec, Fart Attack with Neil Pumpcannon, Captain Justice, Dec Says, Eat My Goal, the Postbag dance. One of the best-loved was

Wonkey Donkey, an idea that came from Richard Preddy and Gary Howe, two of the other writers. Wonkey Donkey couldn't have been simpler – there was a different toy animal on a plinth every week, and we'd have made up a two-word rhyme, one word the animal and the other one that rhymed with it – for instance, slow crow, or sly fly – and the kids had to call in and guess which two words described the animal.

*What really made it work was Dec acting like a furious older brother when the kids got it wrong – teasing them and insulting them. That was some-thing we'd brought with us from* The Ant and Dec Show *on the BBC – not talking down to the kids. This time, though, we stopped short of shaving their heads – we'd learnt our lesson with that one.*

*The biggest and most fondly remembered part of* sm:tv *was surely our weekly sketch* Chums. *The American sitcom* Friends *was huge at the time and* Chums *started out as a rip-off or, as telly people say, a spoof. The idea was that the three of us lived in a flat together. Dec was always trying to get together with Cat, and the whole thing was played like a farce, so there'd constantly be people coming in and out of doors and getting caught doing things they shouldn't be. We also did the whole thing live, which was unusual for what was essentially a mini-sitcom. Of course, the whole show was live, but* Chums *was so much more complicated than anything else we did. It had pop stars, sportsmen and women and comedi-ans doing lots of acting and learning big chunks of script – all of which meant we'd often crack up laughing in the middle of scenes.*

*It quickly became the highlight of the week. In many ways, it summed up* sm:tv *at its best – it was big and daft and had plenty of punch-ups and pratfalls, but it was also full of double entendres, which had become a staple part of our act. That kind of thing appealed to our older viewers, and it was on around eleven o'clock in the morning, which meant they were actually awake, which is always a good quality in any audience. What really made it, apart from our incredibly realistic performances in the roles of 'Ant' and 'Dec', was the celebrity guests.*

As *Chums* went on, anyone who was anyone appeared on it, people like Mariah Carey, Kylie Minogue, Sting, Tom Jones, the Spice Girls, Jamiroquai and Jerry Springer (who of course got his own special *Jerry Springer Show*-style episode) and, after a while, people were approaching us and asking to be in it. We bumped into the cast of *Cold Feet* at an ITV summer party, and they all wanted to be part of it. It was incredible – some of the finest performers from one of ITV's best ever shows . . . were talking to the cast of *Cold Feet*. *Chums* became *the* place to be seen on telly. Well, on kids' telly . . . on Saturday morning . . . for ten minutes, but it was very popular.

*By the time we got to August 1999 and the end of our first year on the air, the ratings had gone up enough for us to turn down another panto, and ITV commissioned another twelve months of the show. All of this was down to lots of different factors: an incredible amount of hard work from a very dedicated production team (I hope you're all reading) and a huge amount of support from ITV; the lessons we'd learnt from panto; and the great relationship we had with Cat. Oh, and Zoe and Jamie's retirement. After each show, me, Dec and Cat would all go out together, and we were as good mates off screen as we were on it.*

All of this meant we were experiencing a strange sensation, something we'd never had throughout our time as pop stars.

*We were enjoying what we did for a living. We were almost – whisper it – proud of our career.*

I know, weird, isn't it?

# Chapter 20

*With* sm:tv *live and* cd:uk *finally working and people actually watching it, the producers made a move that, to be perfectly honest, was risky and brave. They started putting some more of* our *ideas on the show. One of the first examples of this was an item that involved me, Dec, eleven simple questions and an unsuspecting schoolkid. The two of us were in the middle of our regular ideas meeting – I think Dec was just coming back from the Gents and I was getting some pork scratchings and a couple of pints – when we came up with it. I said to Dec I'd like to take on kids in a proper general-knowledge, question-and-answer quiz. I was never going to make* University Challenge, *so I thought if I went up against kids, there was a chance I might actually win. I was also genuinely intrigued to see who knew more – the kids or me. Anyone who knew me at the time would have simply said, 'The kids – next question,' but I had faith in myself. In the pub that night, we devised a mini-gameshow that became a new feature on* sm:tv. *I'd put myself forward as the king of common knowledge, by which I mean kids' general knowledge – cartoons, pop music and computer games – not* What's the capital of Peru?*-type stuff. It's Lima, in case you're wondering.*

**Google?**

*Yep. The kids would ask me ten questions and, for every one I got wrong, they'd win a prize. At the end, they could gamble their prizes on asking me a killer question. If I got that wrong, they'd win the star prize, which was usually a games console. Like the men who came up with it, the format was very, very simple.*

The twist, if you like, was that if Ant got the killer question right, which he very occasionally did, the kids won absolutely nothing, and he would gloat over them, parading around in his crown and king's robes. Oh yeah, we didn't mention that, as the 'king' of general knowledge, Ant would wear a crown and a robe.

*I've still got that crown at home. Not that I ever parade around in it behind closed doors and pretend I'm a real king or anything.*

We called the game Challenge Ant and, when we first told Conor about the idea, he said, 'But if they lose, you give the kids something at the end, right? A consolation prize?' We told him they wouldn't get anything, and he said, 'People don't do that to kids.' Our reply was 'Exactly.' So, if the kids beat Ant, which of course they often did . . .

*What do you mean, 'of course'?*

If they beat Ant, they got to sing, 'You're thick, you're thick, you're thick, you're thick,' to him, and they loved that. In fact, the only person who loved it more than the kids was me.

*I, on the other hand, wasn't amused – I took the whole thing very seriously.*
*    My weak point was Harry Potter and, before long, the kids got wise, and questions on Harry Potter became the easy way to score points in Challenge Ant. Whenever they came up, I would choose one of a set of four words, even though I had no idea what they meant – they were 'Ron Weasley', 'Dumbledore' or 'Hagrid'.*

That was fine when the questions were about Harry Potter, but slightly embarrassing when he had to name a female member of Steps.

*The item was an immediate hit and, as sm:tv became more successful, we even had celebrities doing it. Alan Shearer, Victoria Beckham, Kevin Keegan and Michael Owen all had a go, and even Sarha, who must've been about twenty-three at the time, challenged me. Clare and Lisa had a pop too and, even worse, they won. In fact, I think I still owe them a skiing holiday, but let's not dwell on that. What was so great was that it was a daft idea we'd had in the pub and now it was on the telly and the audience loved it.*

As well as playing games with celebrities and our girlfriends, something else happened to us when *sm:tv* became the must-see Saturday-morning show, something we'd never encountered in the whole of our career. We started getting a little bit of respect from grown-ups – male grown-ups, what's more. As ex-pop stars and kids' TV presenters, our fan base had always been made up of girls and young children. As you'll remember from earlier on in the book, blokes had always thought of us as, well, a variety of things – just trust me when I tell you none of them are worth printing.

One incident around this time summed up the way men started to not completely hate us. We were in a pub in Chiswick one night when a bloke came up to us and asked us if we remembered a terrible moment we'd experienced as pop stars. We told him this could take hours, he'd have to be more specific. This bloke told us it involved two lads in Fulham who'd thrown a chair at our car and called us a pair of wankers.

*I actually remembered the incident. At the time, I thought, 'Why does this lad hate us so much?' Even though it came with the territory, and the chair-throwing was just a bigger, wooden version of the ashtrays, ice cubes and saliva that had been aimed at us in the past, it was still upsetting. One of the lads in particular just looked so angry. His face was contorted with rage, and we couldn't believe that, even taking our music into account, the sight of us just driving past had made someone so furious.*

This guy we were talking to in the pub had a confession to make – it was him who'd thrown the chair, and he wanted to apologize. As he confessed, we both reacted in exactly the same way – by immediately checking there weren't any empty chairs within grabbing distance. But he was completely genuine – he said he was really ashamed of what had happened when we were PJ and Duncan. 'Join the club' was our reply.

He was determined to set the record straight. He'd seen us on *sm:tv* and thought we were, in his words, 'all right blokes'.

Suddenly the world had become a nicer place for us. Sometimes, blokes would even offer to buy us a pint. At long last, we were showing people our real personalities rather than a sugar-coated pop version of who we were, and they liked us.

*As well as the man in the street, there was another section of the population who we suddenly seemed popular with – TV executives. Now that the show was doing well, ITV would invite us to corporate events, the first of which was the advertisers' autumn launch. This is where ITV announces its new programmes to the advertisers and agencies who spend serious money advertising their product on the channel. It's a major event for any commercial broadcaster. We were wheeled out, along with some of ITV's biggest names, to appear.*

*It was being held at a theatre in the west end of London and, when we arrived, we headed upstairs to a plush room where all the talent were being fed and watered. Before we even got in there, we heard the famous 'bongs' of* News At Ten, *which meant Sir Trevor McDonald was there. Des Lynam was also in attendance and, not long after us, Chris Tarrant arrived. Back then, Chris was hosting* Who Wants to be a Millionaire?, *which we loved – and liked to think of as similar to Challenge Ant, but with a bit more at stake. We'd met Chris before, and he always had a laugh with us, by which I mean a laugh at us. He'd gone from* Tiswas *on Saturday mornings to prime time and was a bit of a hero of ours. He'd come straight from his Capital Radio breakfast show, and he walked in, put down his tan leather briefcase and greeted us with a 'Hello, you talentless little tossers.'*

He didn't mean it, but you should've heard what he called Sir Trevor McDonald. One by one, these titans of telly went downstairs to the main stage to do their bit for the advertisers and, after Chris went down, we were left alone in the room. It seemed to take ages to get to our bit, and we began to get slightly bored. As part of hospitality, there was tea, coffee, fruit, pastries and an enormous plate of muffins in the room, which Ant started tucking into.

*I kicked off with a blueberry one but, after one bite, I wasn't impressed, so I picked up another. Banana. Still wasn't doing it for me, so I moved on to apple and cinnamon. I took one bite of that and realized that, by now, I was quite full and, even worse, I was stuck with three half-eaten muffins, so I decided to put them back on the plate.*

'You can't do that,' I told him. 'Des Lynam and David Jason'll be back any minute – they don't want to see your half-eaten-muffin mountain.'

*Suddenly, I had a brainwave, I put them into Chris Tarrant's briefcase. Actually, I'm not sure 'brainwave' is exactly the right word . . . We giggled about it for a bit, and fairly quickly went back to being bored and waiting for our turn. Eventually, the sound men arrived, mic'd us up, and we got ready to do our bit. Chris had finished his speech, made his way back upstairs and was now shooting the breeze with Sir Trevor and Des, who'd also finished. We were just leaving the room when we heard the unmistakable tones of Tarrant cry out, 'Who put these muffins in my briefcase?'*

We'll never know if that question was followed by four possible answers 'Was it (a) Des Lynam (b) Sir Trevor McDonald (c) David Jason or (d) Ant and Dec?' We quickly said, 'We're on,' and ran towards the stage. As we were leaving the room, we could hear Chris asking if that was our final answer, but we didn't bother looking back.

*We did a lot of those kind of events for ITV but, at the time, didn't really appear on other TV shows. We figured that we were on air every Saturday for three hours and thought we may be in danger of over-exposure, so we turned down most invitations. One that we did accept, though, was an appearance on TFI Friday on Channel 4. TFI was edgy and cool, and Chris Evans was someone whose work we really admired. Despite our admiration, though, we also had some issues with Chris – when we were making the highly forgettable Ant and Dec Unzipped for Channel 4, he had been critical of the show – so the invitation to appear on TFI Friday left us unsure. We thought maybe he was going to stitch us up.*

We couldn't have been more wrong. As soon as we arrived at the Riverside Studios in Hammersmith, he thanked us for coming and told us to come into his dressing room; he said all the others were crap, and we should share his. And the show itself couldn't have gone better – the crowd gave us a great reception, and Chris was really complimentary about us and *sm:tv*.

As you'd expect with Chris's reputation, we went for a few drinks afterwards, although only a few, as we had a show to do the next morning. When we left him in the pub, we invited him to come down to the *sm:tv* studios the next day and, although he said yes, we never thought he'd turn up – I mean, what kind of sicko wants to get up early on a Saturday morning when they don't have to?

The next morning, as good as his word, he turned up. He watched the show from the studio floor and even made a brief cameo appearance in *Chums*. We couldn't believe he'd done that just for us – his new best mates. And, of course, he hadn't. Nobody knew it at the time, but Chris was going out with Geri Halliwell, who was on *sm:tv* that morning, and he'd come down to see her.

*After the show had finished, he jumped on his moped and went to host his football show on Virgin Radio, 'Rock 'n' Roll Football'. We were up in the bar at the London Studios and had already had a couple of pints when he rang and invited us to come over and be on the show. Thanks to a combination of Chris being so persuasive and the pints, we did it. When we arrived, it was obvious Chris had had a drink too – there was an open bottle of champagne in the studio and he was wearing a pair of jeans, no top and a belt round his neck. Oh, and he was sporting one other rather fetching little accessory – Cat Deeley, who was sitting on his lap. Cat had gone ahead and, the next thing we knew, we were drinking champagne and reading out the football results – Dec did the Scottish Premier League and I did the third division, in case you were wondering.*

*After that, we went to the pub and ended up back at Chris's house. By the time we got there, we'd been going all day – there was me, Lisa, Dec, Cat and a few other waifs and strays we'd picked up along the way. It was starting to become a very surreal evening, typified by the moment I returned from the toilet to see TV presenter Andrea Boardman doing the splits in the middle of the living-room floor. We were all in the front room, watching Queen: Live At Wembley on what is still the biggest TV I've ever seen in my life, when Geri turned up. She'd been performing on the National Lottery and shortly after her arrival, she and Chris disappeared together. That was the moment we worked out that there just might be something going on between Chris and Geri.*

I remember suddenly having one of those drunken moments of clarity when I just thought, 'I'm hammered, I've got to get out of here. I'd also just been sick in Chris's downstairs toilet. In my defence, I blame Chris's bathroom. He had this wallpaper that looked like bookshelves, and it messed with my mind – I was trying to take books off the shelves for a good ten minutes before I realized.

*Once we'd decided to leave, I took it upon myself to go and tell Chris – it would've been rude to leave without saying goodbye. I was walking around his massive house, very drunk, shouting, 'Chris, Chris, Chris,' trying to find him, when eventually I did – and immediately I wished I hadn't. Let's just say I found him and Geri at the same time and leave it there.*

*Saturday nights were often messy, but we really tried hard to keep our Friday evenings uneventful. We couldn't have done sm:tv with a hangover, it was so frantic and there was so much to remember that it would have been impossible. We would have ended up looking sloppy, disorganized and as if we were making it all up as we went along. What do you mean, 'No one would have noticed the difference'?*

Although there was one notable exception – the millennium was fast approaching, the first of January was a Saturday, and ITV were keen for us to do a show on New Year's Day. They said they wanted us to be the first live show of the twenty-first century although, looking back, I assume that, very wisely, all of their big stars were refusing to work on New Year's Day, so they came to us. In many ways, it was a huge honour and one we greeted with the words, 'What, us? New Year's Day? No chance,' but ITV were – and still are – our bosses, so we were told we thought it was a great idea and that we'd love to do it.

There was just one problem: by the time we agreed, we'd both made plans to spend New Year's Eve in Newcastle and party like it was 1999. So, like the stubborn gits we are, we decided to stick to those plans. We'd have New Year's Eve at home, then get driven through the night to London and do the show that morning. We saw in the new millennium, had a drink or six, then got in the car to be taken to work. It might have been a long journey, but we weren't stupid – we made sure the car was filled with all the essentials for a long winter's night: two blankets and eight cans of lager.

*We arrived at the studio, had a shower, started to feel a bit more sober and got ready – we were at work now and it was time to settle down, pull ourselves together and be professional. However, all of that went out the window when we got into make-up and saw two things – Cat Deeley and a bottle of champagne. Cat gave us a wink and, next thing we knew, we both had glasses in our hands. We weren't completely irresponsible, though – we mixed the champagne with orange juice and made a Bucks Fizz. We did ITV's first live show of the new millennium from a bed on our set, sipping Bucks Fizz during an episode of Pokémon. It got less fun as our hangovers started to take hold, and let's just say we played a lot of cartoons that morning.*

sm:tv had established itself as *the* Saturday-morning show of choice. We were having the time of our lives, but had one eye on our next move, a move that would develop our careers, change our lives and move us forward by a whole seven hours.

*It was time for a crack at Saturday-night telly.*

# Chapter 21

*With* sm:tv *flying high, there'd been interest in us from our old friends the British Broadcasting Corporation. We'd had a few meetings about doing prime-time shows, and we were hoping that, if things worked out, we might get a chance to achieve what had become one of our biggest and most important ambitions – a lie-in on Saturday morning. In the summer of 1999, during our four-week summer break from* sm:tv, *we'd made a pilot of a Saturday-night gameshow for BBC1 called* Friends Like These.

*The show was devised and produced by the then head of light entertainment, a very talented man called David Young, which meant we'd gone from making a show on Saturday mornings for young people to a show on Saturday nights made by a Young person. The basic idea was that two groups of five mates played against each other to win the 'holiday of a lifetime'. Of course, every holiday described on TV is the 'holiday of a lifetime', but it was worth saying anyway. At the time, there was a lot of talk about friends being the new family, and as best mates, we were seen as the perfect people to host the show. Plus, the Chuckle Brothers were busy.*

The show was very different to what we were doing on Saturday mornings. *Friends Like These* had a studio audience, it was pre-recorded and it was very heavily formatted – there was no room for comedy, or dressing up, and there were no witches in their teens, or donkeys that were wonkey. It was all about tension, jeopardy and other words you only ever hear on gameshows. Basically, everything about it was very rigid, which frankly meant any two idiots could've hosted it. And any two idiots did host it.

Returning to the BBC was a proud moment. It's a phenomenal institution, BBC TV Centre, and after *The Ant and Dec Show*, we'd left under a bit of a cloud, so it felt good to be going back. We saw the BBC as our spiritual home. At that point, we honestly thought we'd do a series and, if it went well, we could be at the BBC for twenty years. Don't get me wrong, we'd go back to our houses in Chiswick in between shows, I just meant we hoped we'd have a long career there. At the time, Noel Edmonds was coming towards the end of his stint on *House Party*, and we hoped we might be able to fill that slot and do a big Saturday-night show of our own. We were even prepared to grow goatee beards and get blond highlights if that's what it took.

*Working on* Friends Like These *was also, appropriately enough, where we met one of our best friends. Alan Conley was the floor manager on the show. In case you're wondering, a floor manager is the one who wears the headphones, shouts out what's happening and is in charge of everything that happens on the studio floor, whether it's props coming on, getting the audience to applaud or getting presenters to pay attention (he had a lot of practice on the last one with us two). It's a job that needs someone who's organized, on the ball and very reliable. When he's at work, Alan has all those qualities in abundance. What's so funny is that, when he's at home, he's a complete shambles. His poor wife, Jo, has to put up with all sorts of calamities – he constantly leaves his key in the door, and regularly goes away for the weekend and leaves the hob on. Anyway, we bonded immediately and have been mates ever since. And if you're reading this, Alan, just check your keys are in your pocket, will you?*

Each episode of *Friends Like These* took about four hours to record. We were used to live stuff that was over and done with quickly, but this was the complete opposite. It meant we learnt patience, understanding and the importance of outside catering. *Friends Like These* did pretty well in the ratings, and we went back to our Saturday-morning programmes after the summer expecting to do more with the BBC, but before we could think about doing any other shows with them, we had the small matter of fifty-two weeks of *sm:tv* and *cd:uk* to deal with. I don't mind telling you, it was hard work keeping up a relationship with two channels at the same time.

*Going back to Saturday mornings also meant going back to something else very familiar – getting into trouble with the TV watchdogs. Ever since Beat the Barber, we'd enjoyed pushing our luck, and on sm:tv we pushed that luck as far as we could. We'd litter the show with double entendres. For instance, Ant played a camp superhero called Captain Justice, who always 'disappeared with a puff' and, on the wedding episode of Chums, Dec went to some themed bars for painters, rugby players and people from Lapland, where he met some 'strippers, hookers and lapdancers'.*

*The thing that got us into trouble was actually a practical joke. In 2000, April Fool's Day fell on a Saturday but, somehow, neither of us two, Cat, or anyone in the team realized until the day before, so there was a mad scramble to try and think of something we could do the next day.*

Then I had an idea: what if I fainted on air? I could pretend to pass out in the middle of the show. Like most of my ideas, I thought it was brilliant.

*And like most of Dec's ideas, it wasn't.*

We decided we'd call the nurse in, cut to a black screen, then go into some cartoons, so everyone thought it was a real emergency. After the cartoon, we'd come back to me and say, 'Ha, ha April Fool!' Understandably, there was a bit of resistance from the producers, but we managed to talk them round with that cunning and sophisticated argument, 'Come on, what's the matter with you? It's only a joke.'

On the day, we came to the part of the show where we read out viewers' letters, and to signal the arrival of the postbag, me, Ant and Cat do a dance to 'Wait a Minute, Mr Postman'. We'd decided that I would faint during this, so just before the music got going, I started to try and look a bit under the weather and, as the three of us got up to do the dance, I keeled over.

*That's not quite the whole story – he milked it much, much more than anyone expected. If you watch it back, he's puffing out his cheeks and saying how queasy he feels, hamming it up like, well, like only Declan can.*

Thank you.

*That wasn't a compliment.*

As the camera panned round the studio, Cat said, 'Oh my god, get the nurse,' and the TV picture went to the test card. And that's when the trouble started. During the cartoon, the phone lines went crazy. Kids and their parents were phoning in saying, 'Is Dec dead, is Dec dead?' My initial reaction was 'Brilliant – this is going to be hilarious,' but as everyone around me began to panic, I realized that the whole thing had gone badly wrong. One of the big bosses at ITV rang up to find out what the hell was going on, and ITV told us the whole thing was in bad taste. Just like the producers had done when we first came up with the idea. Oops.

*The thing is, we're not egomaniacs who spend half our life sitting around thinking about how much the audience love us.*

Aren't we? I mean, yeah, you're right, we're not.

*So when we did something like the April Fool, we didn't really think it would upset kids who were watching at home. We certainly didn't anticipate the backlash, and the whole thing got quite a lot of press coverage.*

I was flying to Newcastle the next day to see my family, and when I got to the airport I saw the local paper. On the *Sunday Sun*'s front page, there was a picture from the show and a headline that said: 'We thought Dec was dead.'

*Your mother must have been so proud.*
   *Even if Dec thought he was a great actor – which he wasn't – there were people we worked with on Saturday mornings who showed us up from time to time. One of the finest, most professional and downright beautiful people we ever had on sm:tv was Ms Kylie Minogue. As well as coming on to perform on cd:uk, and of course appearing in Chums, she also stood in*

*as a guest host. Cat had a few weeks off and Kylie was kind enough to step in. She must have been well paid. I remember the first time it happened very clearly. We'd always rehearse the whole show in Brixton on a Wednesday morning and, although we'd be in the office earlier in the week, that would be the first time we'd see the whole script. Unbeknown to us, in her role as our stand-in co-host, Kylie had asked if she could see a copy of the script the night before. I should tell you at this point that the script for* sm:tv *and* cd:uk *was an absolute monster — the show lasted for three hours, so the script was about seventy pages long. Anyway, we turn up for rehearsal on Wednesday morning with a bacon sandwich in our hands and a tabloid paper under our arms, ready to try and get our heads round that week's script.*

*We said hello to Kylie — which isn't a bad way for anyone to start their working day — and after a quick chat, started rehearsing. It quickly became apparent that Kylie had learnt the* whole script *off by heart. Every single word. She was word perfect before we'd even seen our scripts. You might think that, after being shown up like that, when it came to the following Wednesday, we'd have followed her lead and learnt the whole script before rehearsals.*

## She should be so lucky.

*We had much better things to do with our time than to spend it learning scripts. We had important stuff to deal with — like arguing over a board game. Yes, that's right, a board game. This was the time when we had the second and, so far, only other fight of our twenty years together. It was over the* Who Wants to be a Millionaire? *board game.*

## It was ridiculous.

*I'm glad you admit that now.*

## No, what you did was ridiculous.

*We'll let the readers be the judge of that, shall we? We were round at my house playing the game, and it was Dec's turn. The question was:*

'The novels of which author are the most-borrowed books from British public libraries?

A: Catherine Cookson

B: Agatha Christie

C: Barbara Cartland

D: Ruth Rendell'

I knew it definitely wasn't Catherine Cookson or Barbara Cartland, so it had to be either Ruth Rendell or Agatha Christie.

*I asked him if he had an answer yet.*

'I think it's between Ruth Rendell and Agatha Christie . . . but I'm not certain,' I said. 'I think I'm going to have to take a 50–50.'

*So, naturally I took away Catherine Cookson and Barbara Cartland, leaving him with Ruth Rendell and Agatha Christie.*

It was a sneaky thing to do – and we quickly got into a heated debate:

'You arsehole.'

*'What? It's a 50–50 – that's what they do on the telly.'*

'You just sat there and heard me say Ruth Rendell or Agatha Christie.'

*'Exactly – that's what they do on the telly.'*

'You arsehole. That's not fair.'

*'It is fair – I'm in control of the board and I decide what the 50–50 is. Christ, Tarrant doesn't have to put up with this shit . . .'*

'And *I* don't have to put up with your shit. It's my board, and I'm going home.'

And with that, I packed up the board and went home. I was furious. I thought – and I still do think for that matter – that Ant was an arsehole and he wasn't playing fair.

*The worst thing about it was that I was his phone a friend, but he couldn't call me 'cos he'd just stormed out of my house with a board game under his arm. We made up the next day but Dec has never managed to forgive and forget.*

No I have not. I think we'd better change the subject before this turns ugly.

*You're right. Let's move on to two very special and memorable moments for sm:tv and cd:uk. The first was that we actually made it to our one hundredth show.*

After the programme's rocky beginnings and low ratings, to have made it to one hundred shows was probably the proudest moment of our career so far. The show was a blockbuster. There was a star-studded episode of *Chums* that was all about the fact that Ant couldn't blink. Don't worry; it was funnier than it sounds. In the episode, I organized a charity single for 'Ant Aid', where we all sang a song called 'Blink For Ant'. There was Victoria Beckham, Martine McCutcheon, Mel C, 5ive, Atomic Kitten and Billie Piper, all trying to help Ant blink. It was one of the biggest things we ever did. Plus, I managed not to faint, which was a bonus.

*Standing in the studio that morning, I thought to myself, 'Look at this, look at what we've created, all from an idea we had in the flat in Fulham three years ago.' At moments like that, I feel really lucky to do what I do, and I think it's important to stop and savour them every now and then. I snapped out of it, though, put on some comedy eyes on springs and went to work.*

The second memorable moment came in *cd:uk* and a section of the show called the People's Choice. This was where viewers could vote for which one of three tracks they wanted played at the end of that morning's show. After much persuasion, long discussions and a bit of blackmail, the producers talked us into making one of the three tracks a live performance of 'Let's Get

Ready to Rhumble'. Despite the fact we hadn't performed the track for at least three years, we weren't too worried. The other two tracks in the vote were by Steps and Mel C – two of the most popular acts on *cd:uk* that week, so we thought it was pretty unlikely we'd have to dust down the old dance moves. Then David Staite and Phil Mount took us to one side and said, 'It's your show, and you're being very foolish if you don't think they'll vote for you.' We still didn't believe them – after all, it was Steps' 'When I Said Goodbye' and Mel C's 'I Turn to You' versus a track that had got to number nine six years ago.

*We got 86 per cent of the vote.*

It looked like we would be wrecking the mics after all.

We'd gone through a period of being embarrassed and ashamed of our pop-star past. But this was a bit of a watershed for us: it was the first time we'd publicly had a laugh about it, even though everyone else had been doing that for years. When it came to doing the track on *cd:uk*, it was actually really good fun, and it was amazing how quickly the dance moves and the lyrics came flooding back.

*Even now, at every end-of-a-series wrap party for every TV show we do, the DJ plays it, and everyone tries to get us to do it. We did it for Phil Mount's wedding a couple of years ago, and we once did it at a Saturday Night Takeaway party, but generally we try and leave it alone. So if you're a DJ reading this and you ever play at any party we're at, please don't bring it. Trust us, it's best for everyone.*

So, with a hundred shows under our belts, the first year of a new century ended with one of the biggest decisions we'd ever had to take. It was a straight choice between two of the biggest and best-known institutions in Britain.

*Would we have lunch in Burger King, or McDonald's?*

And after we'd worked that one out, we had to choose between ITV and the BBC – neither channel was happy with us making shows for the other one, and they both wanted to offer us an exclusive deal, so it was decision time.

# Chapter 22

Relationships are difficult things at the best of times – and keeping two of them going at once is very tricky.

*You've used that line before, haven't you?*

Despite the fact we were doing some of our very best messing about on ITV on Saturday mornings, we'd also done a second series of *Friends Like These*, and were still talking to the BBC about other ideas. We were very keen to do a 'zoo' show on Saturday nights – that's not a show set in a zoo, by the way, although that's not a bad idea. Stick it on the list, will you, Ant?

*I like it – keep an eye out for that one next year, readers. This particular show consisted of lots of different items – games, sketches, challenges. I think that type of programme is called a zoo show because there are so many different things to see. Anyway, we really wanted to do one, and the BBC weren't opposed to the idea, but they said we should sign an exclusive contract with them, bide our time and do more* Friends Like These, *and then maybe we could do our zoo show. 'Maybe' didn't really do it for us and we had our reservations. We thought there were only so many friends, so many games and so many four-hour recordings we could put up with. The two of us and the BBC wanted different things in the immediate future, which meant we reached a stalemate.*

We asked them for some time to think about it, left Television Centre, got in the car with Paul, our manager, and rang ITV. One hour later we were sat in a room at the Hempel Hotel in Central London with David Liddiment, the ITV Director of Programmes, and Claudia Rosencrantz, the Controller of

Entertainment. We told them the BBC had offered us an exclusive deal that would mean leaving Saturday mornings, but it wasn't to make the kind of shows we wanted to make. Right there and then, they offered us an exclusive deal. We would only make shows for ITV, we could keep doing *sm:tv* and test out stuff, including a Saturday-night zoo show, in prime time.

*This was a dilemma – we had a successful Saturday-morning show on ITV and a successful Saturday-night show on the BBC, and we were going to have to give one of them up. We needed some time to think about it. We were still weighing up our options when Claudia used an expression I'll never forget. In an effort to try and get a decision out of us, she said, 'Well, boys, it's time to shit or get off the pot.' And I'm proud to say we took a big shit in the ITV pot and, metaphorically, we've both been sat there with our trousers round our ankles ever since.*

As is the case with so many relationships, a few hours in a hotel room had taken things to the next level. We've never flirted with another channel since. Like most decisions we've made in our career, it wasn't a grand plan we'd had from the beginning, we just dealt with it as and when it came along. The thing that was most unusual, though, was that there were no staircases involved. Although we did go and stand on the steps of the hotel fire escape for a bit, just for old times' sake, before we gave them our verdict.

When it came to actually signing the ITV deal, we almost didn't have time to put pen to paper. It was a Friday, and we were in the studio rehearsing a particularly hectic episode of *sm:tv*. Our schedule that day was so busy that we only had a fifteen-minute break for lunch. We got a call from Paul asking us when we could pop out of rehearsals and sign and we agreed to do it in our lunchbreak. He arrived with Darren, our other manager, and Ali. We needed somewhere private we could sign the most important piece of paper in our career, so we went into the back seat of Paul's car and drove round the corner next to a newsagents. It was so glamorous.

After we'd signed the contract, Darren produced a bottle of champagne and we had a plastic cup full of bubbly to celebrate – we were over the moon, convinced we'd made the right decision and, at the time, even though the five of us were cramped into a car next to a newsagents, we knew it was a defining moment in our career.

*By now, Saturday mornings were going from strength to strength, we'd established the new items in the show, we were the undisputed number-one show in the slot, and we started winning awards, including one from* Loaded, *who crowned us Best Double Act, and a very prestigious BAFTA for Best Entertainment Programme.*

*In the run-up to Christmas 2000, we recorded a special extended Christmas episode of* Chums. *It got a very respectable three and a half million viewers which was more than some episodes of* Friends, *meaning somehow we'd beaten the thing we'd started off parodying. Pre-recording the show also meant we could be on Christmas telly without leaving our front rooms, and that our families were forced to watch us, for once.*

Now that we had an exclusive deal with ITV, they gave us our first big event to host – The BRIT Awards. Hosting the BRITs is a strange job – the hosts are only ever really remembered if they make a pig's ear of it. Everyone is there to see the bands and, if the hosts do a competent job, they can end up being slightly pushed to one side, so either way you lose.

The BRITs has three different audiences – a mosh pit of schoolkids and a load of record-company executives sat at tables in the actual venue, and the viewers at home. We decided to just talk to the viewers at home – mainly because neither of the other two audiences seemed particularly interested in anything we had to say. For some reason, they were more concerned with the multi-million-selling superstars of the music world. We hadn't been back to the BRITs since we were so cruelly robbed of our 1995 Best Newcomer Award by those one-hit wonders Oasis, and this was another tough night. Although, when it came to the travel arrangements, we insisted on getting there by car, rather than in an ice-cream van.

*On the plus side, we got to meet Coldplay, which was an honour and a real buzz . . . for Coldplay. I'm joking – we were big fans, and when they told us they watched* sm:tv, *we were amazed. We couldn't believe rock bands were awake on a Saturday morning. Surely they should have been asleep, or busy throwing tellies out of windows – especially if we were on. One of the other big stars we met that night was Eminem and, when he came on stage to receive an award, he gave me a kind of hip-hop man hug. What he was really trying to say to me with that hug was 'Respect to the original white rapper.' He didn't actually say it out loud, but I knew that was what he meant. On the whole, though, the BRITs wasn't our favourite job – we'd have enjoyed it much more if we'd watched it down the pub.*

But our next gig was one of the most surreal, ridiculous and downright brilliant things that's ever happened to us.

In the summer, me, Ant and Cat were due to host a concert called Party in the Park, which was celebrating twenty-five years of the Prince's Trust, a charity started by Prince Charles to help disadvantaged young people all over the UK. A few months before the concert, something very strange happened. Ten years earlier, the Trust had celebrated its fifteenth birthday – I know, my arithmetic's pretty sharp, isn't it? – and Prince Charles had done a TV interview to publicize the event, but it had got too personal and ended up detracting from the work the Trust was doing. He wanted to avoid a repeat of that, and he thought the way to do that was not to be interviewed by a political journalist but to talk to a couple of Geordies who spent their Saturday mornings dressing up and making children cry.

*Prince Charles asked us to interview him, that's what he's trying to say.*

*I'm just going to write that again, to make sure you realize how insane it is. Prince Charles asked us, Ant and Dec, two lads from the west end of Newcastle, to interview him. On telly.*

*It must be the first – and last – time in TV history that the candidates for a job were Sir Trevor McDonald, the Dimblebys and Ant and Dec.*

After we'd got over the shock of being asked, we leapt at the chance. The whole thing took months to organize – it takes that long to clear the diary of one of the most busy and important men in the world, or Ant, as he's known to you and me. The day of the interview finally arrived and myself, Ant and a TV crew – including Conor, our faithful executive producer, made our way down to Prince Charles's residence, Highgrove, in a state of great excitement.

As we approached the estate, I turned to Ant and said, 'This isn't just one for the book, this is a belter for the book.' Before we started, we met Prince Charles off camera, which gave us an opportunity to get the protocol out of the way. For a start, you have to call him 'Your Royal Highness' the first time you address him, and then 'Sir' every time after that, and going through all that kind of stuff was really important. We'd planned on just calling him Chas, but in hindsight, that probably wouldn't have gone down well. He was warm and genuine, which really put us at ease because, understandably, we were both incredibly nervous. Once we'd relaxed a bit, we started interviewing him properly, and we treated him, well, I'd like to think we treated him like royalty.

He told us about how the Trust came about and what it had achieved, and he also told us about Duchy Originals, his organic-food company, which has a giftshop on the grounds of Highgrove. We shot the interview in the gardens next to an incredible treehouse. When we first sat down by the treehouse, he told us he'd built it years earlier for William and Harry and that 'they never bloody played in it.'

*It was bigger than the house I grew up in.*

We asked our carefully prepared questions, his answers were witty and charming, and he even asked us to be ambassadors for the trust, which was a massive honour. Throughout the whole thing, he was very easy to talk to, and he didn't mention carting us off to the Tower or chopping off our heads at any point, so we thought it must have gone okay. After we'd finished the interview itself, the three of us did some shots together. Maybe I should rephrase that – it made it sound like we were downing tequilas with the Prince of Wales. We had to record some extra footage of the three of us talking to each other – there was no alcohol involved. These shots were done of us walking around the grounds – he's really proud of his gardens, and he was telling us about bushes that had been planted by the Dalai Lama and amazing things like that. I had a pot plant my mam had given me in my bedroom, but this was a whole new ballgame.

*Once the director had everything he needed, he called a wrap, Prince Charles shook our hands, did the same with the crew, including Conor, and walked off back to, well, back to whatever princes do with their days. We both immediately breathed a huge sigh of relief: we'd done it and we hadn't ballsed it up. The whole experience had been fascinating but, at the same time, there's a part of you that's glad when something like that's over, because you're relieved not to have made a mess of it. Then, suddenly, we heard this huge bellowing Irish voice, shouting out:*
   *'Your Royal Highness!*
   *Your Royal Highness!*
   *Your Royal Highness!'*
   *We spun round, and it was Conor, calling out at the top of his gruff Irish voice. I was thinking, 'What's he doing? He's going to make us sit down and do another take of something. Don't do that, let's quit while we're ahead – it went really well.' Prince Charles heard him and turned round. With all the crew looking on, and Prince Charles giving him his undivided attention, Conor looked straight at him and said,*
   *'Your Royal Highness, one more question: what time does the giftshop open? My wife loves your jam.'*

I could've died. We're at Highgrove with the future king of England, we've done the biggest interview of our career, pulled it off without any cock-ups, and Conor starts worrying about what his wife's going to put on her toast. Prince Charles was clearly a bit taken aback by the question, but he very politely said, 'I'm not sure. I'll get someone to find out and get a message to you.' But Conor carried on: 'Yeah, she loves the jam – and your fudge as well, and . . .'

I was just thinking, 'Shut up. Just leave it.'

*We were both mortified, but Prince Charles didn't seem to mind too much, and Conor's wife got her jam in the end, so everyone was happy. One of the many lovely things about that day were the pictures that came out of it. We asked Ken McKay, the photographer who's done the publicity shots for almost all our TV shows, to send us prints, and I gave them to my mam and my nanna, who put them straight up on the wall. I even chucked in a couple of jars of jam, but that didn't seem to make the same impact on them as they had on Conor's missus.*

And the nice thing is that, ever since that interview, we've become best mates with Prince Charles – the three of us speak on the phone most days, we're often round at one of his palaces for dinners and DVDs, and the three of us go on holiday together every year.

*You've always got to go too far with some stories, haven't you?*

Sorry.

# Chapter 23

When you're mates with Prince Charles, the world is your oyster and . . .

*I won't tell you again – drop it.*

Okay, in the summer of 2001, it was time for us and ITV to take a trip to the zoo. And by that I mean we finally got to make the big prime-time, Saturday-night zoo we'd been badgering ITV to do. It was called *Slap Bang*, and it was the show we'd been waiting all our presenting lives to make. Unfortunately, it ended up being the show we've spent the rest of our presenting lives trying to forget.

*There were so many things wrong with the show that we could spend a whole book talking about it, but don't worry, we won't. The main one was that the prime-time audience didn't really know who we were. Before you can be a success in the harsh battleground of Saturday-night telly, TV experts have proved that it's important for the audience to actually know your names. We might have been popular with kids, hungover students and some mums and dads on Saturday mornings, but that didn't mean we could just roll up on a Saturday night and take the world by storm. Admittedly,* Friends Like These *had gone down well on Saturday nights, but that was a format, and people tuned in to see the games more than they did to see us. It certainly wasn't an all-singing, all-dancing Ant and Dec show which, come to think of it, was probably one of the main reasons it was relatively successful.*

*The second problem was that the show didn't have what we call 'a spine', a point, a reason to be on telly. As presenters, when you come on at the top of a show, it's important to be able to say, 'Hello and welcome to the show that finds the best talent in Britain' or 'Hello and welcome to the show that finds the famous person who's best at eating a kangaroo's unmentionables,' that kind of thing, and* Slap Bang *just didn't have that.*

It was called *Slap Bang* because it was on a Saturday night, which was supposed to be slap bang in the middle of the weekend, but we quickly discovered that wasn't enough to hang an hour of prime-time entertainment on. The final problem, or at least the final one I'm going to go on about, was that Saturday night is a very unforgiving piece of the TV schedule. On Saturday mornings, you can mess around, dress up, do double entendres and, if things don't work, a lot of people don't notice. But if people are taking the time to sit down and devote an hour of their time to your show on a Saturday night, it's got to be polished and slick – two things our new show definitely wasn't.

It also got us into trouble with the TV watchdogs again. We had an item on the show called *Donnelly*, which was a spoof of *Parkinson*, and every week I would interview a celebrity while Ant kept interrupting. You're starting to work out why the show wasn't a hit, aren't you? One week on *Donnelly*, our guest was Bill Roache, who plays Ken Barlow in *Coronation Street* and, in the sketch, I shot him with a plastic gun. There were hundreds of complaints, divided equally between, 'You shouldn't shoot people on Saturday-night telly' and 'That Ken Barlow sketch was dreadful.'

We knew the whole show was in trouble when, after a couple of weeks, ITV started moving it earlier and earlier in the schedule. We started off at 7.30 on a Saturday night and, by the sixth and final episode, we were on at 5.30 in the afternoon. If they'd shifted us back much further, we'd have been back on Saturday mornings.

*Not long after the series finished, our management team, Pete Powell, Paul Worsley and Darren Worsley, knocked on my door one Wednesday night just as me and Dec were about to head off for our weekly game of football. They told us that ITV had cancelled the show and that* Slap Bang *wouldn't be coming back. It was the first real blip in our career at ITV. We were both, to use a technical TV term, properly gutted. Any other day we would have taken a deep breath, evaluated the decision and then gone and got very, very drunk. But, for once, we didn't, we decided to go and do something else that left us red-faced and sweating – play football. It was the most aggressive, competitive game of our lives – we were like men possessed. Actually, Dec has been known to lose his temper on a football pitch before but, to be honest, that's probably more due to small-man syndrome than anything else.*

Watch it, or you'll get a smack in the mouth.

*I rest my case.*

It felt really good to go out and take some exercise and, when I say exercise, I actually mean running around trying to kick people. Although after that game, we were still, to quote Ant, 'properly gutted'. No one likes to fail, and it felt like we had – spectacularly. Critics and audiences hadn't liked it, and that hurts when you've worked so hard on something. On the way home, we stopped at a well-known Colonel-and-chicken eatery and, as we were coming out of the place, two drunk blokes walked past and said, 'Oi, you two, that show you do on a Saturday night is absolutely shit.'

*It might not have been the most detailed audience research we've ever done, but it was impeccable timing and even more proof that we'd done the wrong show at the wrong time. On the plus side, they hadn't thrown any chairs at us, but the whole thing left a bad taste in our mouths. The incident with the blokes, that is, not the chicken, which was delicious. Slap Bang was the first new thing we'd done as part of our exclusive ITV deal, and it had bombed.*

We did the only thing we could – we went back to Saturday mornings, played general-knowledge quizzes with kids, dressed up as cartoon characters and did sketches about farting.

*After all, we still had our dignity.*

# Chapter 24

After the gun-toting nightmare of *Slap Bang*, going back to Saturday mornings was like slipping on a comfy pair of old shoes. *sm:tv* and *cd:uk* were familiar by now, plus they had an audience who not only knew who we were, but were also on the same intellectual level.

*That's not fair.*

You're right – some of those kids were much brighter than you, as Challenge Ant proved on a regular basis. By now, we were getting some pretty amazing music guests on *cd:uk*. It seemed like we had a different musical idol of ours on every week. There was the band we'd seen at the Newcastle Riverside all those years ago, Jamiroquai, one Saturday; we had REM another Saturday; and then one week there was a little band that Ant in particular got very excited about – Blur.

*They're my favourite band of all time, and Dec let me interview them on my own. I can still remember the first three questions I asked Blur: 'What was the inspiration for your new single?'; 'Can I have your autograph?'; and 'Why do I have to stop cuddling you?' Graham Coxon said he loved the show, which was a massive buzz.*

*We even had Paul McCartney on. You might not know this, because you haven't worked in the music industry like us two but, before his solo success, he was in a band called The Beatles. When we met him, we were both so starstruck, so worried about saying something stupid to him, that we hardly uttered a word. Fortunately, Conor broke the silence by asking if Macca knew where to get any decent jam.*

*Then you had some American singers, who would make ridiculous demands – asking for fourteen dressing rooms and Evian water at room temperature. Frankly, it was absurd, we were the hosts of the show and we didn't even behave like that.*

Too right – we only had ten dressing rooms each and didn't even mind if our water was a bit cold.

*One of my favourite guests ever has to be the American singer Jessica Simpson. I don't like her music; she was just part of something very funny that happened off camera. As was always the case on a show day, we had loads of kids milling around on the studio floor – some from the audience and some of them the children of guests or people who worked on the show. During an ad break, Jessica was standing on the studio floor, when I spotted a little boy about five feet away from her. He was looking at her and jumping up and down on the spot, clearly very nervous and excited. It was pretty obvious he was a big fan. I pointed him out to Cat, and, being good with kids, she went over to the little boy, took him by the hand, walked him over to Jessica and introduced him to the American pop princess.*

*'Hello,' said Jessica. The kid took one look at her and wet himself on the spot. Literally. Jessica's feet were soaking. We later found out that the boy didn't give a toss about Jessica; he'd been jumping up and down on the spot because he was desperate for the toilet. I don't think Jessica ever came back.*

*There was one other set of guests who nearly caused people to wet themselves – U2. They're a band we've both loved for decades, and we couldn't believe they'd agreed to come on cd:uk – they even asked us to pop into their dressing room and say hello.*

*As you can imagine, we were just the tiniest bit nervous when we knocked on their door. When we walked in, the first thing they said, after, 'You two look much bigger on the telly' was 'Thanks for having us on the show.' That's right: U2, the biggest band in the world, thanked us for having them on our little old Saturday-morning programme. They said we were introducing them to a new generation, and that they were actually fans of the show. I was expecting Jeremy Beadle to jump out of The Edge's guitar case at any moment.*

They were so lovely that it seemed to prove that old rhyming showbiz theory, 'The bigger the star, the nicer they are.' They did a special session of four songs that would go out over the following few weeks, and it was recorded after *cd:uk* had come off air. We just got a couple of beers in, stood at the back of the studio and took it all in. It was amazing. A year earlier, U2 had released 'Beautiful Day', which was also being used on ITV's coverage of the Premiership football. Their music was everywhere, and it felt like they were really on top form.

*A week later, we ran a U2 competition on* cd:uk, *and the prize was tickets to one of their gigs at Slane Castle, with flights to Dublin and accommodation at their hotel, the Clarence, included and, for a laugh, I added, 'And isn't it nice, Bono's said we can go too.'*

And I said, 'Is that right? He's a lovely fella that Bono, isn't he?' Obviously, we were just messing about, we never imagined Bono would be watching. He rang up after the show, called us a couple of cheeky buggers and told us he supposed he'd have to invite us to the gig now. It was weird to think that, just because we'd said something on telly, Bono had to do it (we started the following week's show by saying, 'Hello, welcome to *cd:uk*, Bono said he'd buy us some cars made of gold,' but he didn't fall for it twice). He paid for me, Ant, Clare, Lisa, Cat, Phil Mount and his girlfriend to fly over, go to the gig and then attend the after-show party at the Clarence.

*It came to the weekend of the gig, and it was unbelievable. We flew over to Dublin in time to watch the Republic of Ireland beat Holland in a pub, then saw England's 5–1 demolition of Germany, and then sat next to Bob Geldof in the backstage area of Slane Castle. Bob Geldof gave me some good advice: 'Never drop names,' he said – or was that Bono? Or Prince Charles? I can never remember . . .*

*You won't be surprised to hear that, by the end of the gig, me, Dec, Cat, Phil, Lisa and Clare were all in 'good spirits', mainly because we'd spent most of the day drinking good spirits. By the time we arrived at the after-show party, we were plastered. When Bono came over to say hello, we just stood there, in a drunken haze, starstruck all over again and thinking,*

*'It's Bono, it's Bono, and he's talking to us.'* Phil, our producer, was particularly dumbstruck; he's the world's biggest U2 fan. He finally managed to open his mouth and say to Bono, *'I can't thank you enough for inviting us — the football was amazing, the gig was incredible and, all in all, it's been, it's been . . .'*

*We all looked at him expectantly, waiting for the end of this sentence. Finally, after what seemed like an age, Phil, clearly overcome with emotion, looked at Bono and said, 'It's been a beautiful day.'*

He went silent. Bono looked at him. Phil looked at us. We looked at Bono, then Bono smiled and walked away. We all turned to Phil and asked the same thing, 'What did you say that for? You can't say, "It's been a beautiful day," to Bono. "Beautiful Day" is one of U2's most famous songs!' Phil was gutted, he hadn't meant it and had just got tongue-tied. I still can't believe that, of all the things he could've said, he went for that. He may as well have gone up to Bono and said 'I'm dying for a pee and I don't know where the toilet is. "I Still Haven't Found What I'm Looking For", but I'm going "With or Without You".'

*We haven't seen Bono since. Thanks, Phil.*

# Chapter 25

*We were loving Saturday mornings but, now that we had an exclusive deal with ITV, we still had ambitions to host a show in prime time. Slap Bang hadn't worked, so we needed to find something that did. We went to a meeting with the same ITV big cheeses who'd wooed us at the Hempel Hotel, David Liddiment and Claudia Rosencrantz.*

*Even though the meeting turned out to be a bit of a milestone, we almost didn't get into their offices that day. We arrived at ITV Network Centre with Paul, and Dec and I sat in reception while he went up to the receptionist, gave her his name and told her that he was there with Ant and Dec. When our visitor passes were ready, there were only two of them – one for Paul and one that said 'Anton Dec'. I know people sometimes say we're joined at the hip, but we definitely are two different people. After some confusion and explanation, they made us up separate passes and let us in. As we headed for the lift, though, I could've sworn I heard the woman on reception say, 'It's the third floor, Anton.'*

We finally got into the meeting, and David and Claudia kicked off by reminding us of a show called *Popstars,* which had been broadcast to great success on the channel. On the show, people from all over the country auditioned to be – you've guessed it – pop stars, and a panel of judges chose the five best singers to be part of a band, which was called *Hearsay.* They told us they had a new twist on the format which, incidentally, is a phrase you hear a lot in telly. Normally, 'a new twist on the format' means 'We're going to make a rubbish version of something that's already a hit,' but not this time – this was a genuinely fresh and new idea. They wanted to find a solo artist rather than a band, and the big twist was the public would decide who that was. The show was called *Pop Idol,* and they wanted to know if we were interested in hosting it.

*Normally, in a meeting like that, we'd listen to everything the big cheeses had to say, then go away and talk it over with each other and our management but, on this occasion, we took one look at each other, and said, 'We'll do it.' We'd been huge fans of* Popstars, *and this sounded like a great opportunity for us. Unlike* Slap Bang, *this was a format, which meant we were part of the show, rather than the whole show, so it would introduce us to the prime-time family audience more gradually. By now, we'd learnt not to rush our relationship with viewers – we just hoped they'd take us into their hearts and their front rooms when they were good and ready.*

*With* Pop Idol, *we'd found what we called our 'bridge' show, not because it stopped us getting into deep water – which it also did – but because it would be a bridge between Saturday mornings and prime time. We were also genuinely intrigued by it – could it actually find a genuine pop star? Who would the public choose? And what kind of clothing budget were we going to get? We'd had a music career ourselves, and we knew how tough it could be, so we were fascinated to see how the selection process would play out in the public eye. The whole thing would be an emotional rollercoaster that would require sensitivity from everyone involved. I think our exact words were, 'This should be a right laugh – hope there's plenty of crap singers.'*

It's hard to imagine telly without phone votes, evictions or winners and losers now but, back then, things were really quite different. I know I sound like an old man, but I also know I'm right – I've checked. *Big Brother* was still brand-new, and there weren't really any other shows on TV where the viewers controlled what happened. *Pop Idol* was certainly the first talent show to let the public choose the winner by phone voting, and that was a very bold idea.

*The first thing we did was go to the auditions, where we met the judges – Pete Waterman, Nicki Chapman, Neil 'Dr Fox' Fox and a bloke called Simon Cowell. We had met Simon once before, in the early days of sm:tv, and we liked him. He was honest, straightforward and very cutting, by which I mean very horrible about various pop groups. If there's one thing you can rely on Simon for, it's having an opinion – and, nine times out of ten, it's an opinion that's horrible and entertaining. Having known Simon for ten years now, I can honestly say that fame hasn't changed him one bit.*

That's absolutely right – he's always been arrogant, conceited and self-centred, whether there's a camera there or not.

*Generally, the judges were lovely, apart from Simon, who was arrogant, conceited and self-centred – did we mention that already? Nicki was very sympathetic towards the acts, Pete was like a mad uncle, and Foxy (as we'll call Dr Fox from now on) was always searching for a funny one-liner about the contestants. After people had auditioned, he'd say things like, 'I wanted a Ferrari, and you gave me a Mini.' And as you can tell from that sentence, he never did find those funny one-liners . . .*

It was never our intention to go to all the auditions. Nigel Lythgoe, who was the executive producer (and had also been a judge on *Popstars*, where he was christened 'Nasty Nigel'), said, as hosts, we should come down and, frankly, we couldn't believe what we saw – so many of the singers were talentless, tone deaf and deluded. It was brilliant. We sat in the audition room and had to hide our faces behind sheets of paper because we were laughing so much.

As well as giving us a good laugh, hanging round the auditions also helped us work out what the hell our role on the show was. Yes, we were the hosts, but we wanted to be as involved as possible and, short of getting lunch for the judges, we didn't know what to do, so we did what we've always done and made it up as we went along. We spent a few hours sitting in the audition rooms, watching the contestants, and then, in the afternoon, we took a big decision, a decision that instigated a drastic shift in our role on the show – we went and stood *outside* the audition rooms. That meant we could talk to the contestants when they came out. They would hug us when they were upset, or hug us if they were ecstatic – it was basically wall-to-wall hugs. These days, it's an established convention of telly, the post-audition hug, but then it was something that just developed organically – it wasn't as if we had a director standing behind us shouting, 'And cue the hug.' We wanted to hug these people because we knew what most of the contestants were going through – we'd had a music career and, as actors, we'd been to auditions, so we felt qualified to help them through the terror that is singing in front of the Prince of Darkness himself, Simon Cowell.

*The auditions tour went all over the country, which was all you could ask of it really – it wouldn't have been much of a tour if it had just stayed in one place – and a real team spirit developed between everyone who worked on the show. The whole crew wore* Pop Idol *T-shirts, (except us – that would have looked weird), and there were so many different things to enjoy about travelling around the country. It was full of variety and every day was different. For instance, sometimes we'd drink wine in the hotel bar, sometimes we'd drink beer, and when we were in Scotland, we drank whisky. It was also great to work outside of London. Because the TV industry is based in London, a lot of TV professionals often lose touch with real people and real life. In fact, we were saying that to our chauffeurs and butlers only the other day.*

Apart from a job on prime-time telly, one of the most important things *Pop Idol* gave us was something that we later developed on *I'm a Celebrity . . .* and *Britain's Got Talent*, the idea that our role was to be the voice of the audience. What I mean by that is that it was our job to react to what was happening in the same way the audience would – so, if we felt sorry for an act, we'd commiserate with them and, if they'd had a great audition, we'd congratulate them. Similarly, on *I'm a Celebrity . . .*, when one of them does something stupid, we laugh at it, just the same way you all do when you're sat on your sofa at home.

*That's as far as it goes, mind. We're not copying other stuff you do at home. What you get up to behind closed doors is none of our business.*

After seeing the auditions, which included the good, the bad and the truly appalling, we started to think that maybe, just maybe, *Pop Idol* would be a hit. Some of the contestants were so funny that, even if we didn't find the next superstar, we were pretty sure *Pop Idol* would be entertaining telly. Even now, I can still remember some of the amazingly awful contestants. There was the 'YMCA girl', for example, who turned up without knowing it was a singing show, forgot the words to 'YMCA' halfway through and ended up being one of the cult hits of the series. She even got a part in panto but, as we'd proved at the Sunderland Empire, they really will let anyone perform in those things.

*But there were great singers too – like the kid who could hardly say his own name because of his terrible stutter, and then, when he sang, had the voice of an angel. That was Gareth Gates.*

*The very last auditionee, who later ended up arguing with Simon Cowell, was Will Young, and Will eventually went on to become the Pop Idol we were looking for.*

*We also worked with some people, who – especially if they're reading this – are extremely talented professionals. There was Clare Horton, the producer, Andrew Llinares, a producer/director who now runs* Britain's Got Talent, *Richard Holloway, the executive producer, and Jo Brock, who was one of the associate producers and is still one of our best friends. Jo's married to Alan Conley – our best mate who leaves his keys in the door and the hob on. She's a very patient woman. We also did a lot of work with Charles Boyd, a writer/director/producer (he was quite greedy when it came to jobs), who went on to run* American Idol *in Los Angeles. We still see a lot of those people regularly. After all, that's the easiest way to collect the cash-for-compliments fee we charge for favourable mentions in this book.*

The *Pop Idol* audition tour had been a roaring success and, by the time it came to the autumn, when the first episode went out, we knew we had a hit show on our hands. We'd also realized two things: 1) we weren't the worst singers in the world and 2) it was time to leave *sm:tv*. We'd spent more than three years on TV on Saturday mornings, and had real mixed feelings about leaving it behind, but we decided that our last show would be 1 December 2001. It was one of the hardest, most emotional things we've ever done on TV – and yes, that includes Ant being blinded by a paintball. After more than 150 episodes, and countless accolades, including by now several awards from the BAFTAs, the Royal Television Society, the Television and Radio Industries Club and even a British Comedy Award where we'd somehow beaten *The Royle Family* and *Da Ali G Show*, it was all coming to an end.

*The biggest of dozens of highlights on that last show was* Chums, *when Dec married Cat. The guestlist included Mariah Carey as one of Cat's bridesmaids. At the time, the press was full of stories about what an eccentric diva Mariah was and, although we were thrilled about having her on the show, we were also worried she might not play along. That worry disappeared when, in the middle of the week, the producer, David Staite, got a phone call:*

*'Hi, David, it's Mariah Carey.'*

*'Er, um . . . hi, Mariah.'*

*'I have a question for you – what colour is the wallpaper on the* Chums *set?'*

*'Pardon?'*

*'What colour is the wallpaper?'*

*'Green, why?'*

*'I'm in Virgin Brides in Manchester, and I want to make sure I rent a bridesmaid's dress that clashes with the wallpaper – it'll look funnier then, won't it?'*

*'Er, yeah, it will, yeah.'*

*'Great – I'll get a blue one – see you Saturday!'*

On the day of the show, when Mariah turned up, some people were still worried that she'd be a total diva and expect to have rose petals sprinkled wherever she walked and freshly born puppies in her dressing room, but the moment she walked in, we knew that wouldn't happen. There was a good reason for that – she was carrying a plastic bag from Virgin Brides. She'd got the dress and she was great on the show.

The other memorable thing about the wedding was that, finally, after three years of me and Cat trying to get it together in every episode of *Chums*, I got to kiss her. Before the show, I told the producer that we would lock lips for exactly ten seconds, to give the moment maximum drama and romance. As you'll know, ever since I nicked Ant's lass on *Byker Grove*, I've always been a very professional screen kisser. When it came to the big moment, we started the kiss, and all I could hear in my earpiece was the whole gallery counting down, '10–9–8–7–6–5–4–3–2–1!' It all went in slow motion, and I never wanted that kiss to end – not just because it was Cat and she's lush, although that was a small part of it, but primarily because I knew the moment it did, me and Ant were going to walk off the set and that would be the end of our last ever *Chums*.

There were all sorts of surprises on that last show. We had goodbye messages from everyone – Bono, the late great Sir Bobby Robson, Alan Shearer, Kylie Minogue, Paul McCartney, David Beckham and Sting, to name but seven – and even though I'd promised myself I wasn't going to cry on telly, we were both filling up on the last link of the show. What made it harder was that, all around us, off camera – the people holding the cue cards, the researchers – the whole production team was in tears, which only made us two more emotional.

*In a way, one of the only things I can liken that last Saturday morning to is my wedding day. Obviously, my wedding day was much more important, and had fewer members of Steps there, but what they both have in common is that, even though you're right in the middle of it, it doesn't feel real. It's like you're not really there. I was there, at both of them, by the way.*

*I don't want to sound like I've just been kicked out of* The X–Factor, *but it was the end of something really special and one of the most emotional experiences of my life. It might sound silly to say that about a Saturday-morning kids' show, but leaving a job you love, with people you love, on a show you love is a very, very difficult thing*

I feel the same. I still miss it dearly. It was glorified messing about for three hours every week and it was a once-in-a-life-time job.

*When we left sm:tv, we also left behind something very special, and something that always made us both smile on a Saturday morning. That was Cat, and she stayed on while we flew the nest to spend more time with potential Pop Idols. For the whole time we'd done sm:tv and cd:uk, Cat had been there – as our co-pilot, friend and 'that lass who wears the goofy teeth and the funny wigs'. We've never worked with anyone else so closely – before or since – and she was an absolute joy from start to finish. She also made me write all that. So, for the memories, the laughs and this whole paragraph – thanks, Cat.*

No matter how much fun it was, though, and no matter how hard it was to leave, we knew the time had come to move on. *Pop Idol* had given us the chance to do that and, although we didn't know it yet, 2002 would be a year unlike any other.

*For a start, we had our first Saturday lie-in of the twentieth century.*

Why do you always have to spoil my end-of-chapter statements? Keep it zipped when we get to the end of the next one.

*Okay, I'm sorry.*

# Chapter 26

By the time Christmas came around, even though there were still eight contestants on *Pop Idol*, there was only one question on everyone's lips: 'Will or Gareth?' It was great to be doing a show that had captured the public's imagination, but it was such an intense experience that there was also a part of me that was relieved to be back home for Christmas, in the bosom of my family. Here was an opportunity to forget all about *Pop Idol* for a while. Or so I thought – the whole country was talking about it, and I was naïve to think my family would be any different. Round the Christmas dinner table, all I heard was *Pop Idol* this and *Pop Idol* that, and then, I got the update that really mattered – the votes were in from the Donnellys. 'Four of us have voted for Will and four of us have voted for Gareth.' I pointed out that those eight votes would cancel each other out, but no one cared. By the time we got to the Christmas pudding, I had to politely ask them all to change the subject and, when that didn't work, I went with: 'Can we have five minutes without talking about *Pop* bloody *Idol*?'

*Despite the fact it almost ruined Dec's Christmas, the show was great fun to work on. Charles Boyd and us two would come up with little sketches about the judges every week; Dec would play Simon and Nicki, and I'd play Pete and Foxy, and that was where the whole 'Simon Cowell wears high trousers' thing started. And, for the record, back then, those trousers were very, very high – he could touch his ears with his belt on a good day.*

By the time it came to the last few weeks, the hype around the show was enormous, and Gareth had emerged as a clear favourite with the public. Privately, we always wanted Will to win – we'd loved his cover of The Doors' 'Light My Fire', even if it wasn't a patch on the version we'd done in the log cabin with Rory.

Obviously we had to keep our preference for Will a secret and remain impartial – it wouldn't have been very professional if we'd gone, 'Hi, welcome to *Pop Idol* – Vote Will!' Despite our preferences, Gareth became the bookies' favourite. He was very popular with teenage girls, which is obviously a vital section of the audience in any talent show: they do a lot of voting, they buy records and, most importantly, they scream at pop stars. I don't know what the music industry would do without them. Gareth was also a good singer, and had a great story – he was the kid who was overcoming his stutter to win the nation's hearts.

Understandably, Gareth had a lot of trouble with his stutter when we'd talk to him live in the studio – it was nerve-wracking for any contestant being on telly with millions of people watching, but for him it was even harder, and he often struggled in our interviews with him. To try and makes things easier, we would get him into my dressing room before the show and run through the questions with him; it meant he stuttered less, and it also meant we could get his autograph for our nieces and nephews, which made it a win–win situation.

*In the week leading up to the final, the whole country went even more* Pop Idol *crazy. Will and Gareth both had election buses and toured the country, like politicians, drumming up votes. I'm telling you, Gordon Brown could take a few tips from those boys when it came to winning votes.*

Finally, the big night arrived and, for the two of us, just knowing we'd be hosting it and announcing the result was such a mouth-watering prospect – we couldn't wait to find out who the public would choose. We were later told that more than eight million votes were cast, which was more than the Liberal Democrats had received in the previous year's general election. I'm no political expert, but it struck me that if the Lib Dems had stuck on some hair gel and banged out a version of 'Light My Fire', they could've won that election. The whole thing was an incredible phenomenon. When it came to actually announcing the big result, the moment of truth, the climax of months of hard work, the winner of *Pop Idol* . . .

*I did it! It was just one word – 'Will', and I got to say it.*

I was fine with it.

*That's not what you said at the time.*

Come on, there's no need to rake up the past.

*Pop Idol* really did change everything – the prime-time audience finally knew who we were, and it seemed like maybe, just maybe, we'd managed to successfully leap forward seven hours from Saturday mornings to Saturday evenings. It was now twelve years since we'd met at the Mitre and, in all of that time, no one had noticed we were pretty much making it all up as we went along.

Without even realizing it, after *Pop Idol*, we returned to our first two jobs.

*Paperboy and Irish dancing busker?*

No, acting and singing. Look, you've interrupted my big end-of-chapter statement again.

*Oh yeah, sorry.*

# Chapter 27

*The success of* Pop Idol *led to us being offered all sorts of other projects. We returned to acting when we filmed a one-off sitcom for ITV – A Tribute to the Likely Lads. It was a remake of an episode of one of our favourite ever sitcoms,* Whatever Happened to the Likely Lads? *We had to trim the title of our remake a bit, though, otherwise it would have been* A Tribute to Whatever Happened to the Likely Lads?*, and that's just too long for the* Radio Times. *The original show starred James Bolam and Rodney Bewes and was written by Dick Clement and Ian La Frenais. It was brilliant. It's the story of two best mates who are from Newcastle and live in Newcastle – ringing any bells?*

To put it mildly, *The Likely Lads* is an institution in Newcastle and, when we announced we were doing it, the reaction from our fellow Geordies was simple and straightforward: they all said, 'We can't think of two better lads to do it but, whatever you do, make sure you don't mess it up.' Well, 'mess it up' wasn't exactly the phrase they used, but you get the drift.

The two main characters, Bob and Terry, are very different – Bob is excitable and optimistic, while Terry is grumpy and disillusioned with the world. Can you guess who played who?

*Will you stop saying that sort of thing, Declan? I'm really not that grumpy.*

Careful – you sounded a bit grumpy there.

It co-starred John Thomson and was directed by the legendary comedy director Bob Spiers. We shot the episode on location in Newcastle and in a studio in London and it received mixed reviews, but the people who really mattered to us – the people of Newcastle – said nice things. And as long as our fellow Geordies were happy, then we could rest easy.

*Another unexpected offer that came our way was from Sony Records, who approached us to make the official England World Cup single, for, well, for the World Cup, which that year was happening in Japan and South Korea. Our first reaction was very simple: 'Didn't you hear any of our music?' But Sony weren't joking; they genuinely wanted us to do it. Once we'd stopped laughing, we assumed they'd put us with 'proper' songwriters, the way Frank Skinner and David Baddiel had been paired with the Lightning Seeds, or the England Squad had worked with New Order in 1990, but Sony said, 'No, we just want you two, and we've already chosen the song.' It was an old terrace chant from the 1970s called 'We're on the Ball'. That was one less headache – we were worried for a minute that they might actually want us to write and compose the whole track.*

We weren't getting off lightly, though, we still had to write some new 2002 World Cup-inspired lyrics, but we were incredibly busy, and there appeared to be no free time in our diary to actually write the song. Eventually, we managed to clear a couple of hours one afternoon after a Variety Club lunch . . .

*That is the most old-school-showbiz thing I've ever heard you say.*

Thank you. So, there we were – Ant and I had a couple of hours to spare, an instrumental version of the track, a pen, some paper, and there was no point in putting it off any longer: it was time to get serious. To write the lyrics, we decided to go to a place that was quiet, disused and had been deserted for years – my kitchen. Once we were in there, the songwriting magic came flooding back, and inspiration immediately struck.

*What he means is, we wrote down a list of footballing clichés, picked out the ones that rhymed, then chucked in a verse about the players, and we were done.*

221

What can I say? Some people are just born songwriters. And us two definitely aren't some of those people. After spending literally minutes on the lyrics, it was time for the next big part of the project: shooting the video. The story, and I use that word in the loosest possible sense, was that we were trying to blag our way to the World Cup in Japan by kidnapping the England manager Sven Goran Eriksson and his assistant Tord Grip and posing as impostors.

The FA had promised us access to the players – we could do some filming with David Beckham, Michael Owen, Steven Gerrard and the rest of the squad. That turned out to be the exact opposite of the truth. We never got any access to the players, and we ended up sat in a minibus outside Elland Road, in Leeds, where the whole squad were training, and didn't get so much as a picture with them.

It wasn't all bad news though – we got to work with Mike Hedges, who'd produced albums by the likes of Radiohead and U2. And now, to that list, he could finally add the artists formally known as PJ and Duncan – all that time messing about with nobodies like them must have been worth it when he got to work with us.

As part of the promotion, 'the record company thought it was a good idea' to perform live on *cd:uk*. 'We're on the Ball' had a brass section on it, and we'd asked Phil Mount, our close friend and the show's producer, to book a brass band to have on stage with us. He said no. That would cost money, and he wasn't prepared to spend cash on a backing band for a couple of presenters who six months earlier had been hosting the show themselves. 'Charming,' we thought, although we did come up with an ingenious plan. Si Hargreaves, our press officer, came down with a bunch of guys from the office, and they all pretended they knew how to play trumpets. It turned out that what they actually knew how to do was drink a lot before the show and then mime badly on the telly. In their defence, they did at least get drunk on Becks, and with David Beckham as England captain, I thought that was very patriotic of them.

*Once we'd recorded the track, shot the video and done the bare minimum of promotion, there was just one thing left to worry about – the singles chart. It felt strange to be back in the world of record sales and chart positions, but we quickly got swept up in the excitement of the whole thing. Before we go on, a quick quiz question to see if you've been paying attention: can you remember what our highest chart position was as pop stars? And for a bonus point, which track was it? You give up, don't you? It was 'Rhumble' and it was number nine.*

*As 'We're on the Ball' got more airplay and more press, we started to think we might eclipse our number-nine smash. Our imagination quickly ran away with us and we started to dream about having our first ever number one. We figured that it would sell plenty through sheer patriotism – after all, it was the official World Cup single, everyone had flags on their cars and in their windows, and football hysteria was sweeping the nation. Maybe, just maybe, that hysteria would have one other side effect: people wouldn't be able to tell awful music from good music – and they'd buy our single.*

We were so convinced we'd top the chart that we both started planning to buy *Music Week*, the industry's trade paper, and have it framed. The whole thing was very exciting. And then the news came through.

*Will Young, the winner of* Pop Idol, *and one of the most popular artists in the country, was releasing his second single, that cover of 'Light My Fire' that had done so much to win him the show. It was a dead cert to be number one and, in that moment, our dreams went up in smoke. Smoke that came from Will Young lighting his fire.*

We ended up charting at number three, with Will Young at number one and Ant's old friend from the Brits, Eminem, at number two. We'd tried acting and we'd tried singing, and the results were clear – get back to doing what we did best. It was time for some more messing about.

# Chapter 28

*Our next project can be summed up in three words, three words that in 2002 were very unfashionable.*

**'Turquoise shell suit'?**

*Saturday-night telly. Back then, in the olden days of the early twenty-first century, there was a lot of talk about Saturday-night telly — and that talk was about it becoming extinct — like dodos, or white dog poo. Admittedly, Pop Idol had been a big hit, but that was the exception that proved the rule. A lot of people thought that the internet, multichannel TV and DVDs meant there was no place for big entertainment shows. They thought it was no longer possible to make a big, ambitious Saturday-night show that the whole family would sit around and watch together, so we did the obvious thing — we made a big Saturday-night show for the whole family to sit around and watch together. Or at least we hoped they would.*

When it came to developing a new show — 'developing', incidentally, is another one of those fancy TV terms, this time for 'coming up with a whole load of ideas in the hope that one of them sticks' — by far the best idea was something that came from Granada Entertainment. When we heard it, we knew straight away that this was the programme we wanted to do. The main strand of the show was that we would give away the products that featured in adverts. It's very simple, and it had never been done before — people play a gameshow to win the stuff that's advertised on the telly.

*It was also — and this is always a bonus for anything on ITV — the show the BBC couldn't make because, as the TV experts among you will have noted, the BBC don't show any adverts.*

*In case you hadn't guessed by now, this was the show that became* Ant and Dec's Saturday Night Takeaway, *which has gone on to run, at the last count, for nine series. It's amazing, isn't it? Nine series, and we still haven't collapsed from a heart attack with all the running around we do on set.*

We took this idea and, with the help of some key personnel, or clever telly people, built a show round it. This was the zoo show we'd been waiting years to make, and me and Ant worked so hard to get it right. Along with Duncan Gray, the show's executive producer, Nigel Hall, the producer of the first series, Siobhan Greene, the development producer who helped put the show together, and Leon Wilde, who was part development and part producer, we came up with a collection of mini-formats that formed the basis of *Saturday Night Takeaway.*

We also brought in a director who has been stuck with us ever since – Chris Power. As well as directing *Takeaway*, he also does *I'm a Celebrity . . .* Our relationship with Chris is probably best summed up by us two, about five minutes before a live TV show, saying to him, 'Can we just change this massive thing that's really complicated into another massive thing that's even more complicated?' and him, miraculously, saying, 'Yeah, all right,' no matter what it is. Those kind of skills means he's the perfect director for a show like *Takeaway* because, from the first script on a Tuesday to the actual show on a Saturday, it's like Madonna – it never stops changing.

*We wanted to make each show an 'event', a special piece of live telly, and along with the production team, we worked very hard to put as much different stuff into the show as possible. This meant that as well as Win the Ads, there were also items like Jim Didn't Fix It, where we'd surprise someone in our audience who'd written a letter to Jimmy Saville as a child and then help them realize their ambitions as an adult. For this poor member of the audience, the whole thing could be very embarrassing. It's one thing wanting to dance with overweight dance troupe the Roly Polys when you're a kid in the eighties, but doing it twenty years later as an adult on live TV is a very different kettle of fish.*

*This was also the beginning of a fundamental element of* Takeaway *— surprising members of the audience. And, let me assure you, these surprises are planned with military precision, by a brilliant and very dedicated team. They know everything about the people in our audience. Put it this way, if Bin Laden had written to* Jim'll Fix It, *they'd find out, track him down and, before he knew what had hit him, he'd be singing wth Chas 'n' Dave live in the studio. We also littered the show with sketches, monologues, star guests, prize giveaways and something called Banged up with Beadle, which was a mini reality show where, every week, a member of the public would spend seven days living in a naval fort just off the coast off Portsmouth with the late, great TV prankster, Jeremy Beadle.*

Hosting an episode of *Saturday Night Takeaway* is the biggest buzz on telly. There are so many different things going on in the show, so much to remember and so many different roles for us to play, it's like a rollercoaster – it's a huge thrill and, once it starts, you can't get off. We're live on air for seventy-five minutes, so you have to see the journey through, no matter what twists and turns it takes.

Takeaway *could also be described as a circus show, because it's got all the elements you'd find under the big top: excitement, jeopardy, danger and comedy. At least I think that's why it's called a circus show – either that or it's because it's got a pair of clowns hosting it.*

Every show starts with us two at the top of the studio stairs, surrounded by the audience within the studio, then we run down those stairs and on to the stage. Even the way we handle that tells you a lot about us. We might be about to do a live TV show, but I like to shake hands with everyone on the way down the stairs – it's a lovely thing to do with the wonderful people who've made the effort to come and be there.

*Once a show-off, always a show-off. He milks every single second of it – he's practically kissing babies on the way down those stairs. I, on the other hand, don't really shake anyone's hand – I'm deep in concentration and firmly focused on one thing and one thing only.*

**Not tripping over and falling down the stairs?**

*Exactly. When you're as clumsy as I am, you could lose your footing at any minute. So if you do ever find yourself in the audience for Takeaway and I don't stop on the way down the stairs, don't take it personally, I'm just trying not to break my neck.*

It's live, exciting, seat-of-the-pants telly, and that's why we love doing it. We love doing the other programmes too, but *Takeaway* is our baby. And I'm not just saying that because it requires constant attention, keeps us awake at night and often makes a mess of our clothes, it's the show we love doing the most, because it's constantly challenged us as performers, from stitching up Simon Cowell to working with two eight-year-old children that we christened Little Ant and Dec.

*We'd completed the first series, but ITV had another show they wanted us to do – it would be live on air less than a month after we'd finished giving away the adverts, and it was the most insane TV show we'd ever been pitched.*

# Chapter 29

*Tony Blackburn, Tara Palmer-Tomkinson, Christine Hamilton, Nell McAndrew, Rhona Cameron, Darren Day, Nigel Benn and Uri Geller.*

I'm a Celebrity . . . Get Me out of Here!, *or the 'new show that's set in the jungle', was the latest part of our golden-handcuffs deal with ITV, and it was pitched to us at the James Grant offices by Richard Cowles and Natalka Znak, the executive producers. From the moment they arrived, you could tell they meant business, because they brought pictures of rainforests with them. Even as they were explaining the show, I couldn't stop thinking about the title and how long and strange it sounded.*

We listened intently to the idea, and shot each other a few sideways glances as they explained how eight celebrities would live together in a tiny camp in the middle of a rainforest for two weeks. We would broadcast a show every morning, live from Australia, at around 7 a.m., and the public would control what happened with phone-voting. The celebrities would have to win their own food, wash their own clothes, and there were cameras there to capture their every move. After the meeting, I was slightly keener than Ant, although we were both very interested. I just remember saying to him, 'We've got to do this because, if it works, it'll be brilliant and, if someone else does it and it's a big hit, we'll be gutted.'

*But I just kept thinking, 'It sounds stupid – and that title's far too long.'*

Eventually, we signed the contract, which was really long – mainly because it kept mentioning the title of the show – and flew out for the first series to Mission Beach, Queensland, with Ali Astall, our artist manager. We didn't have a clue what to expect. We were picked up from the airport by an

Australian driver who spent the entire journey to the hotel telling us about spiders the size of dinner plates, deadly snakes and generally trying to scare the pants off us. Over the years, we've realized that scaring the English is a national pastime for the Australians, and this driver seemed to be some sort of national champion.

*It wasn't hard either, because I hate spiders, absolutely hate them.*

We made it to Mission Beach to find a lovely big hotel that all the crew were staying in and, after a long flight, we were looking forward to checking in and chilling out. But we were informed that our accommodation was three miles down the road; we'd been booked to stay in a smaller, more private and intimate location. It was a small eco-hotel that was run by a gay couple called 'Gary and Barry' – at least, we think that was their names: it's what we christened them anyway.

*As we wandered from room to room, I couldn't help but notice there were what I'll politely call 'erotic statues' everywhere, the showers were outside and, most terrifyingly of all, there was no telly in any of the rooms. The whole place was like a hippy, sexy haven and two things we aren't is hippies or sexy. Natalka, the executive producer and general all-round guvnor of I'm a Celebrity . . ., turned up at Gary and Barry's to say hello, and when she asked us if there was anything we needed, we said, 'Yes – a new hotel.' We agreed to move to the crew hotel, climbed into the car and were just pulling away from the front door when I realized something important was missing. Dec.*

I'd nipped to the loo and, when I got back, the place was deserted – apart from Gary and Barry, who were enjoying a pot of herbal tea while polishing their sex statues. And no, that wasn't a euphemism, before you ask.

*When we arrived at the big hotel, we had the first of several thousand surreal experiences we'd face over the next few weeks. We bumped into Keith*

*'Cheggers Plays Pop' Chegwin. Every year on I'm a Celebrity . . . , they fly stand-ins out in case any of the cast get ill or realize what they're getting themselves into and, in series one, Cheggers was that stand-in. One thing about Cheggers is that he's a very heavy smoker and, when we ran into him, he'd just got off the twenty-four-hour flight from London. To combat his cigarette cravings on the plane, he'd come up with a carefully thought-out plan – he would wear nicotine patches, chew nicotine gum and drink copious amounts of Coke.*

### 'Cheggers drinks pop' – ha!

*All of this meant that, when we saw him, he was completely wired. He was also keen on showing us some of the home-video footage he'd already taken around the hotel. A lot of animals would wander freely around the grounds because, well, because they could, and because that's the sort of stuff that goes on in Australia. One of the most notorious animals that did this was the cassowary – a kind of giant ostrich-meets-emu-meets-turkey thing that featured heavily in Cheggers' home video.*

*The Aussies had already put the fear of God into us about these deadly birds, warning us that, given half the chance, they'd 'rip your gizzards out'. We couldn't believe they would just walk around the hotel – I think one of them even tried to check in at one point. Apparently, they'd just come down from Gary and Barry's and weren't too keen on the sex statues. The thing about these birds, though, is that they're incredibly stupid. So stupid, in fact, they will attack their own reflection. When we bumped into Cheggers, he had just finished filming a cassowary attacking its own reflection in a car door. So there we were, jetlagged, standing in our second hotel of the day with wired Children's TV legend Keith Chegwin showing us home-video footage of a giant bird attacking its own reflection.*

### And after that, things just got weirder.

There was so much wildlife in that hotel; it was as if we really *were* doing a zoo show. There were birds, snakes – Ant even found a spider in his shower.

*I didn't shower for two days. I'm not ashamed to admit it.*

We also both found small, brown lizards in our rooms. We were reliably informed that they were called gekkos. On one hand, they were good, because they ate the mosquitoes, but the down side is they let out giant, bloodcurdling shrieks in the middle of the night, which as you can imagine, can be ever so slightly inconvenient, especially when you've got a large dose of jet lag. Fortunately, the lizard I was sharing my room with disappeared after a day or so.

*I didn't have such good luck – mine stayed in my room for a whole week. I christened him Michael – Michael Gekko – get it? It's a kind of lizard-meets-Beppe from EastEnders pun . . . we've all done them, haven't we? Every morning, conversations between me and Dec would go like this:*

*'Morning.'*
'Morning. How's Michael Gekko? Did he sleep all right?'
*'Not so good – he had a bit of a rough night.'*
'Oh well, give him my love.'

*It was hilarious, but that might have been the jet lag.*

After days of reptile-based comedy, the show actually started. Getting it on air was a miracle in itself – the format, the trials and the scripts were all constantly changing as we, and the production team, found our feet. We made sure we had a lot of input into the scripts and the overall feel of the show, after hosting *Friends Like These* and *Pop Idol*, we knew how important it was for the show to have its own language – and we thought it would benefit from having catchphrases. The long and ridiculous title of the show somehow stuck, and became one of those catchphrases. Screaming *I'm a Celebrity . . . Get Me out of Heeeeerreeee!'* from the bridge at the beginning was an idea we had during rehearsals, and it helped give the whole show a bit of an identity. It also meant we got a lovely view of the rainforest first thing in the morning. Which was nice.

*And, by the way, for your handy cut-out-and-keep guide to a typical day in the life for Dec and me on* I'm a Celebrity . . ., *you can turn to that nice glossy photo section.*

Before the first series aired, the press had been scathing, calling it '*I'm a Z-Lister . . . Get Me out of Here!*', and other hilarious headlines. Some people were even speculating that the whole thing was fake and we weren't in Australia at all. My sister Moyra heard a phone-in on a radio show where a caller said, 'I've just seen Dec driving down the M1 in his Porsche.' It was absolute rubbish. I haven't got a Porsche.

*That first week was a real struggle. The ratings were nothing to write home about and we were finding it hard to define our role. Aside from giving out phone numbers and going into camp to announce the results, it felt like we were just there to say, 'This is what's just happened, here's what happened next.' We didn't know whether to play it for laughs or be straight. It seems a funny thing to say now, because the show is ridiculous (in a brilliant way, obviously), but it was all new back then and we didn't know if trying to be funny was the right thing to do.'*

*In the second week, things started happening. Darren Day and Tara Palmer-Tomkinson had got stuck into their crazy fight/relationship/hatred thing, and Rhona Cameron had gone off on a rant about every single person in there. Suddenly, there was a buzz about the show. The papers started to talk about it, GM:TV started covering it, word of mouth took over and ratings went up. It became a real-life Australian soap opera – and people loved it. It also started to do something it does every year – it gave the celebrities the chance to shatter the public's perception of them.*

The person who did that best was Tara, who showed, for the first time, that she was a real person. Everyone thought of her as this 'It girl' – a rich, spoilt socialite, but she proved she was funny, vulnerable, likable and, of course, slightly nuts. The public chose Tara to face the first ever Bushtucker Trial, and she had to stand under a tree while bugs and critters were dropped on her. Back in series one, not all of the trials were the kind of gruesome, vomit-inducing brand of light entertainment we've come to know and love. Christine Hamilton had to catch a pig. Nell McAndrew had to ride a bucking bronco. In a bikini. Nigel Benn had to sit under a tree in the dark for a few hours. Boy, those trials have progressed since then.

*The scariest trial involved shutting Rhona Cameron in an underground coffin for ten minutes. We were all thinking, 'This is too much . . . is this too much?' There was a lot of debate with the producers about whether it was inhumane whereas, these days, we suspend the coffin hundreds of feet in the air and fill it with rats. It's nice when you can see how a concept has progressed like that. I think we should all be very proud.*

Halfway through the series, Clare and Lisa came to stay. They'd been given the full 'scare the Pommies' routine from the driver on the way from the airport and were prepared to spend the next week locked in our rooms. We managed to calm their fears and turn their attention to what really mattered – sitting around the pool with a tipple or two and having a lovely time. Of course, we would have to get up at 1 a.m., so we'd leave them down at the bar every evening when we went to sleep.

*On the plus side, it meant I got some quality time with Michael Gekko.*

One night, we got up for work and Clare and Lisa were still in the bar – we went round to tell them off, shocked that people could spend all night drinking like that. The moment we set eyes on them, we could tell it'd been a pretty heavy session. They were trying to hide from us by pretending to be lamps. It didn't work.

*The celebrities also had loved ones staying in the hotel and, to be honest, it could get a bit awkward. Over breakfast one morning, before the series had actually started we were treated to the sight of Christine Hamilton's husband and former Conservative MP for Tatton Neil Hamilton doing press-ups round the pool in very – and I do mean very – skimpy swimming* trunks. Suddenly my sausages didn't seem so appetizing. On another night, while they were enjoying a cigarette and a glass of wine or three, Lisa and Clare were approached by Uri Geller's wife, who told them off for drinking and smoking. Like a lot of Uri's best patter, it didn't really have an effect.

Back in camp, the inevitable was happening – the celebs were starting to go feral, which is a polite way of saying that, amongst other things, they started to develop a certain aroma. Just be glad it's not smell-o-vision, that's all I'm saying. On the show, every day, we go into camp to reveal the result of the viewer vote. On about the fifth day, Tara came running over to sniff us, shouting, 'You guys smell amazing.' We were only wearing deodorant – and clothes, of course – but being in camp and away from the smells and sounds of everyday life had heightened Tara's senses, and the smell of anything that wasn't a campfire or a smelly celeb drove her wild.

In series one, after we'd announced the results of the phone votes for the Bushtucker Trial, we used to stay in camp until the end of the episode, rather than leave, like we do these days. After one show, Dec had Tara sniffing at him like some sort of Lynx-addicted maniac, asking, 'Is anyone watching at home? Do they like me?', while I had Uri Geller asking me about the football scores. At the time, Uri was a director of Exeter City, they were playing a big game and he was absolutely desperate to know how they were doing. All of which led to the following conversation:

'Come on, you're a football fan, you understand. Tell me how Exeter got on in the FA Cup.'

'I can't, Uri. You know I'm not allowed to tell you anything about the outside world.'

'Okay, you don't have to tell me. Just look into my eyes. Look deep into my eyes. I will read your mind and discover the football score.'

He put his hands on my shoulders, pulled me in close and stared into my eyes.

**I half expected his belt buckle to bend and his trousers to fall down.**

*Finally, he pulled away, his face filled with glee, and exclaimed, Yes! They won! They won! Thank you! Thank you!'*

Exeter lost, didn't they?

*Yep — 2–1.*

The biggest difference between that first series and the subsequent ones, apart from not seeing Gary and Barry again, was that, while they were in there, the celebrities had no idea if anyone back home was even watching, cared about them, or had any interest in the whole programme. Tony Blackburn went on to win but, arguably, Tara was the star. When she finally left camp, she couldn't believe that her and Darren had been the talk of the tabloids. Everyone who goes in now — apart, maybe, from some Americans — has seen the show and knows how much coverage it's going to get.

*The series finished and, after two weeks of solid night shifts, we were knackered. Although the show had developed into a hit, it had been a hard slog. We still felt we hadn't really got into our stride and, when we left Australia, we weren't convinced we'd be doing the second series.*

We got home and got a sense of how much everybody had enjoyed that 'Z-list jungle show'. The public had watched in their millions, the press had changed their tune and so had we. We also realized one other thing — doing more series would mean a month in Australia in the middle of the British winter every year.

*We couldn't sign that contract fast enough.*

# Chapter 30

*When you look back at* sm:tv, Pop Idol *and* Takeaway, *it seems we've always had a Saturday job. And we were about to do the longest shift of our career. The second series of* Saturday Night Takeaway *started in January 2003 and had been commissioned for a mammoth run of eleven episodes. We had a new producer, James Sunderland. Obviously, being Newcastle United fans, we weren't too keen on his surname but, when we got to know him, we found out he shared our love of big entertainment shows like* Beadle's About, Noel's House Party *and* Game for a Laugh *and that he didn't mind working Saturdays which, as producer of* Saturday Night Take-away, *was essential. One of the other new faces was an assistant producer called Georgie Hurford-Jones. Georgie had worked on* So Graham Norton *for Channel 4, and she became Little Ant and Dec's TV mum.*

With eleven episodes to fill, we needed a bucketload of new ideas – if you can imagine ideas coming in buckets. One of them was a feature called What's Next?, where we'd both take out our earpieces, turn off the autocue and basically put ourselves in the hands of the producers for about eight minutes and potentially let them embarrass us on a weekly basis. By now, we'd done so much live telly that something like that wasn't too scary; instead, it felt new, exciting and different. The other good thing was that we couldn't do any rehearsals for that section on show day, and we loved that, because it meant a longer lunch break.

The idea was bold and ambitious but, when all's said and done, a lot of it was about the producers making us two look like idiots. For some reason, they always said it was their favourite part of the show. And we did some great stuff: we learned how to be Bavarian bottom-slappers, played Count-down with Carol Vorderman and Richard Whiteley – but the one that sticks in my mind was when they put us in a cage with a pair of gorillas.

*The challenge would always be revealed to us just before the ad break so, while you were at home putting the kettle on or paying for your curry, we'd get fully briefed on what was about to happen. During this particular ad break, we were told we'd be sharing a cage with two gorillas and were introduced to the gorilla expert from London Zoo. He told us that, if the gorillas attacked, he would be there to step in. That was when I started shaking. He told us not to look in their eyes in case it made them angry and, by the time he'd finished with us, I was scared witless. Two dumb animals were about to be locked in a cage . . . with two gorillas. We both kept saying, 'You will look after us, won't you?' He gave a few unconvincing mumbles, but it seemed like he was more concerned with the gorillas than us two. As we were talking to him, we could hear Andy Collins, our warm-up man, telling the audience to be very quiet because we'd be having live animals in the studio. The whole studio was filled with the authentic smell of primates from the hay that was in the gorillas' cage. We were so scared, we contributed with a few smells of our own.*

Our task was to interact with the gorillas, feed them and mimic their behaviour. We stepped into the cage hesitantly. One of them was sat in the corner with a banana, and the gorilla expert, who was now on stage and talking us through the ordeal, told us to communicate with her by making a kind of 'Ooh, aah' monkey noise, which we obediently did. Just as we were growing in confidence and thought we had the gorilla on side, a second one, who was a large silverback male, appeared out of an adjoining pen and into our cage. He seemed to take exception to me tickling his girlfriend's belly and took his frustration out on Ant.

*Wasn't the first time . . .*
*He basically jumped on my back and started thrusting back and forwards. I was disgusted — he hadn't even had the decency to take me for dinner first. The expert continued to advise us on the best way to handle the beasts and*

*told us we should slowly make our way to the exit of the cage, where we could return to safety. We both got out of the cage, to a massive round of applause from the audience, and wiped the sweat from our brows.*

Suddenly the music kicked in. 'King of the Swingers' started playing, and the gorillas broke into a choreographed dance routine.

*It was at this point we realized they weren't real gorillas. They were gifted gorilla mimics. Or, to put it another way, a couple of blokes in monkey suits.*

**You** might have realized. I just thought, 'Wow, those gorillas are great dancers.'

*It turned out the bloke from London Zoo wasn't really from London Zoo – I'm not even sure he was from London. The producers had set us up an absolute treat.*

As well as What's Next?, we introduced another new feature in this series called Undercover. Me and Ant would disguise ourselves with prosthetic make-up – noses, wigs, you name it – and go undercover to try and fool celebrities, while the whole thing was captured on hidden cameras. To make it a success, we needed commitment, dedication and the ability to sit in a make-up chair for four hours at a time. To make it work, we had voice coaches, we did extensive research on the people we were picking on and, most importantly, we had to hide Ant's all too recognizable forehead – hence the hours and hours in make-up. On shows that did hidden-camera stunts in the past – like *Noel's House Party* or *Beadle's About* – the presenter would just come in at the end and reveal the whole thing was a wind-up, but this was the first time the hosts were central to the hit.

*Prosthetic make-up is incredibly time-consuming. Ask any actor or comedian who's done it – Matt Lucas, David Walliams, Harry Enfield, Paul*

Whitehouse or Catherine Tate – and they'll tell you they hate it. And it's not just the time it takes. When you're wearing prosthetics, it's not uncommon for bits of your face to start melting. You could be in the middle of talking to Westlife, disguised as their biggest fan, thinking, 'My cheeks are melting,' or 'My nose is going to fall off.'

I never slept a wink the night before those Undercover shoots They were absolutely terrifying. I was always worried we'd be found out.

Over the course of a few series, we did dozens of Undercovers, but by far the most nerve-wracking, most complicated and most expensive one featured that cheerful little ray of sunshine by the name of Simon Cowell. The plan was that we'd audition for American Idol as Jimmy and Scottie Osterman, two brothers from Denver, Colorado.

The whole shoot took weeks of planning but, when we finally got the go-ahead, everything happened very quickly. The night before we flew out to America, we got a call from Nigel Hall, our executive producer. I thought he was calling to say 'Good luck with the shoot,' but what we got was 'The whole thing's cost about £20,000, so whatever you do, don't cock it up.'

Leon Wilde, who was producing and directing, explained that we would have to do it all for real – we'd have to go and enrol like normal contestants: there was no way to short-cut all of that and get straight to the judges. That meant we had to go and queue up with the rest of the hopefuls. We were scheduled to go in fairly early and we were both incredibly nervous – what if our goatees became unstuck and Simon Cowell recognized us? Then word filtered through to the contestants' holding room that the judges had decided to take an early lunch. If there was one thing we knew from the British Pop Idol, it was that Simon Cowell wouldn't be hurrying back to his seat: he'd keep people waiting in America, just like he did in Britain – he's nothing if not consistent. We were left waiting in the queue alongside all the other contestants. They didn't – and couldn't – know that we were Brits posing as Americans, *so we just 'hung out' with them, chatted and generally felt very awkward and embarrassed.*

Then things got even weirder. *American Idol* was – and is – a phenomenal success in America, and this was the second series, which meant everyone wanted a piece of it. There were crews from every news network there, including one from a show called *Access Hollywood*, which takes you behind the scenes of TV shows and gives you, well, access to Hollywood. They were filming at the *American Idol* auditions and, next thing I knew, I was being interviewed, as Jimmy Osterman. And then Paula Abdul, one of the other judges alongside Simon Cowell, joins the interview, so I'm standing there, on American TV, with Paula Abdul, and all the time, I'm just thinking, 'Is my nose falling off? Are my cheeks melting?'

*I was laughing so much that my nose nearly did fall off. Finally, after the waiting and the interviews, it was showtime. The plan was that Dec would go in first, then say he was too nervous to audition and ask if he could bring his brother in with him. That meant we wouldn't walk into the room as a double act, which hopefully reduced the chances of Simon spotting us.*

It was terrifying – there were twenty thousand reasons to be nervous and I was convinced that Simon was so sharp, switched on and intelligent that he would recognize me straight away. I overestimated him. I arrived in the audition room and glanced up to see the formidable figure of Simon Cowell looking bored. I'd heavily rehearsed answers to every conceivable question they could ask – my name, my age and how I was feeling. Randy Jackson, the third judge, looked at me. I was expecting a 'How you doing?' or a 'What's your name?' but what I got was something I couldn't have predicted:

'Yo dog, what's the deal?'

I was completely stumped. I wasn't a dog, and no one had ever asked me what the deal was – I didn't know if I should tell him the deal was good, or what. In the end I just mumbled, 'How you doing?' or something, while nervously staring at the floor. What it did mean was that I was very convincing at acting nervous. Then, as planned, after a false start to my song, I went out and got my 'brother', Ant. Next thing we knew, it was happening – we were auditioning for *American Idol* in front of Simon Cowell.

*One of our main tactics was to stand the other way round. As the more discerning amongst you will have noticed, normally, when we're on telly, I always stand on the left and Dec's always on the right but, on this occasion, we cunningly switched it around. We launched into 'Opposites Attract', which had been a hit for Paula Abdul in the eighties. It began well, in the sense that it went as badly as we'd hoped. When you're in the middle of a hidden-camera prank like that, all you need is to get to a point where enough's happened that you know you've got a decent story and, after that, everything else is a bonus.*

After a full verse of 'Opposites Attract', we knew we had enough material, and the judges hadn't stopped us yet, so we decided to have a bit of fun.

*Plus, we hadn't learnt the second verse, so we had to do something.*

Ant started beatboxing, I started breakdancing and, eventually, there was a flicker of recognition in Simon's eyes. He'd realized we were the hosts of *Pop Idol*, but it was too late – we'd got Simon Cowell hook, line and sinker. And we hadn't wasted that £20,000.

The last of the big new features we brought to series two involved two little fellas from Newcastle – no, not us two, Little Ant and Dec. Ant and I very rarely go to film premieres, showbiz parties or nightclubs, mainly because, if you go to a premiere, you can't just go and watch the film; part of being invited is to talk to journalists and pose for pictures and, to be honest, I'd rather pay £8 and go to my local Odeon. And as for showbiz parties, well, frankly, I prefer a drink in Chiswick with my mates.

So, the idea was that we'd send miniature versions of ourselves along instead. If only we could've got them to do everything in life we couldn't be bothered with – they could've done our shopping, cleaned our flats and cooked my dinner; but apparently some stupid thing called 'child labour laws' meant we couldn't. That aside, the thought of these two little lads, dressed in identical suits, getting out of limos and meeting celebrities made us laugh – so the next thing to do was find the kids.

*Georgie Hurford-Jones, our new assistant producer, was in charge of the whole thing, and she went up to Newcastle, held auditions and eventually came back with a tape of the two kids she thought would be perfect – James Pallister and Dylan McKenna-Redshaw. We all sat down in the production office and watched the tape of these two kids – who were mates – and we agreed they were just what we were looking for – funny, charismatic and nowhere near as tall as me and Dec. There was only one thing we didn't agree on – which one was which. Georgie and everyone in the office thought James should be Dec and Dylan should be me, whereas Ant and I thought it should be the other way round, so we had a good long chat about it, heard what everyone had to say, and then we got our own way.*

Little Ant and Dec's first assignment was an 'At home with . . .' feature with Neil and Christine Hamilton. Right from the off, the idea just worked: the boys could ask anything they liked – questions that would have seemed rude coming from us were very funny coming from them. So, when they said to Christine, 'How old are you, one hundred?', it was hilarious because, at the time, everyone knew she was only ninety-two.

The lads took a lot of coaching, and Georgie did a fantastic job. They weren't stage-school kids, they weren't experienced at learning scripts, and sometimes they could be nervous, trip over words and get things wrong.

*Like we said, they were exactly like us.*

Before long, the Littles had moved on to even bigger stars than Neil and Christine Hamilton. By the end of the series, they'd interviewed Kylie and asked her some pretty searching questions about her new underwear range (that was one we *did* want to go on), they'd chatted to Jennifer Lopez and, much to the jealousy of the girls in the office, George Clooney. The great thing about the two of them was that you could send them along to interview big stars at 'junkets'. A junket is where the film star sits in a hotel room all day, with a picture of the film they're promoting behind them, and does interviews. They can last anything up to eight hours. So, imagine you're George Clooney . . .

*I do – often.*

. . . you've sat in the same seat for hours on end, answering the same questions over and over again and given your best fake smile to interviewers from every TV show imaginable. Then, in walk two little kids from Newcastle in matching suits holding a plastic bag full of toy props. Chances are, it's going to liven up your day, and you're going to play along with them. Chuck in the fact that they ask some funny questions and then end the interview by tying you to a chair, as they did with Kevin Costner, or dressing you up as a clown, as they did with Ricky Gervais, and they might just be the one reason you end up staying sane.

*In many ways, we were doing those film stars a favour, but don't worry, Clooney, you don't need to thank us.*

We felt very protective towards Little Ant and Dec, and tried to act like responsible adults – which wasn't easy for us two. They would do their interviews and then, on Saturday night, they'd come on the set and tell us all about it. We didn't want them to be phased and, as I say, they weren't stage-school kids, so, during rehearsal, we'd walk them round the studio and say, 'Look at all those empty seats – in a few hours, they'll be full and people will be loud, and you won't be able to hear yourself think.'

*To be honest, I was pretty freaked out myself by the end of it.*

They didn't have the kind of Matthew Robinson figure we'd had on *Byker Grove*, and we wanted to make sure they didn't get too carried away and knew that telly wasn't the be all and end all of everything. We felt it was important they stayed normal, down-to-earth schoolkids, which they did, and didn't turn into attention-seeking fame-hungry egomaniacs.

*After all, that's our job. At the end of the second series, like we always do, we had a party. It usually follows the same pattern – the show finishes, we get drunk with the crew, and the DJ tries (and fails) to get us to perform 'Let's Get Ready to Rhumble' but, being children, Little Ant and Dec couldn't come to these parties, so on the Friday afternoon before the last show of the series, we held our own little party for them. The four of us sat around eating cakes and drinking tea (or, in their case, fizzy pop) and having a lovely time. We felt it was important the show looked after them.*

And everyone knows that the best way to look after kids is to fill them full of E numbers and sugar before you send them back to their parents, right?

# Chapter 31

Once we'd finished eleven weeks of dancing with gorillas, auditioning for Simon Cowell and hanging about with our mini mes, we were ready to do something mature, dignified and civilized: we went to feed bugs to famous people for the second series of *I'm a Celebrity* . . . There were a few changes that year. For a start, the whole operation had moved from one part of Australia, Mission Beach, to another, just north of Murwillumbah, in New South Wales. The cast was bigger and, this time, our victims – I mean contestants – were Sian Lloyd, Daniella Westbrook, Chris Bisson, Catalina Guirado, Toyah Wilcox, Antony Worrall Thompson, Wayne Sleep, Linda Barker, John Fashanu and Phil Tufnell.

*Each and every one of them brought something different to the party. Personally, I was fascinated by Antony Worrall Thompson and his tall stories, like the time he'd run away with a tramp when he was four years old. It just sounded so implausible – what self-respecting tramp would want to run away with Antony Worrall Thompson?*

But by far the biggest and best laugh was John 'Fash' Fashanu – not only was he great value but, without realizing it, he helped us to start doing our links the way we do them today. As we said, series one had been quite a slog and often we weren't sure if we were the right people for the job, but when you've got someone like Fash, it's hard not to have a laugh – and by 'have a laugh', I mean mercilessly ridicule him every night for weeks. We started to relish the opportunity to have fun with the script and our links, and Fash was a gift. He was scared of heights, terrified of the bridges, and of pretty much everything else he encountered. He would endlessly repeat the word 'focus' – and then there was his exercise regime. I've never understood why any of them do any exercise when they're in there – they're exhausted and starving, and exercise just makes it worse. I hardly do any exercise when *I'm* out there – and I'm in a lovely hotel with food coming out of my ears.

*When we weren't at work, we were staying in Coolangatta which, compared to Mission Beach, was like New York. It had shops, hotels and restaurants, and it felt like we were back in civilization. It also had something else we weren't expecting. We were in the restaurant of our hotel, Twin Towns, having dinner one night, and I looked over to a nearby table and thought, 'That bloke looks very like Ian from the Krankies,' then, after a double take, realized it was Ian from the Krankies. We went over to say hello, and it turned out they had a holiday home in Coolangatta. As if that wasn't bizarre enough, he was then joined by his wife Jeanette, who of course is 'Wee Jimmy Krankie'. Seeing the person you'd known on telly as a small Scottish schoolboy dressed as an adult woman was disconcerting, to say the least. We had a quick chat, then went to bed, got up in the middle of the night, went to work and fed witchety grubs to former England cricketer Phil 'Tuffers' Tufnell. It's always nice to have a bit of variety, isn't it?*

*'Tuffers' went on to win and, by the end of that series, we'd decided that* I'm a Celebrity . . . *was a show we loved doing. We were no longer worried about how to play it, or what our role was, because it was simple – we just took the Mickey out of the pampered prima donnas who were miles away from home.*

When we got back, it was time for another tour of the UK's conference rooms and hotels for the second series of *Pop Idol*. After the first series had turned into such a phenomenon, we couldn't wait to get back, but things had changed. We were no longer the only talent show on telly and, thanks to other singing shows like *Fame Academy*, the pool of talent had got smaller, which meant the singers, arguably, weren't as good. Sections of the music industry saw the show as pure evil, plus the contestants had got a lot more savvy about how these shows worked.

*We all worked longer hours, and not just because Simon Cowell kept every-one waiting longer. When Will Young auditioned in series one, we hadn't interviewed him before he went in front of the judges. He'd gone through the auditions almost unnoticed, and we'd missed him, which meant one thing: this time we had to interview everyone. And I mean everyone. At one point, the producers even tried to get us to do a piece with the cleaners, just to be on the safe side.*

Despite the differences on the show, though, one thing stayed the same – there was no shortage of dreadful singers. Incidentally, this is another thing we get asked by people on the street: 'Why do people think they can sing when they can't?' There's a very simple answer to that question: 'How the hell do I know?' I've got no idea what makes someone spend an hour and a half travelling on two trains and a bus, wait to be seen for ten hours, give an awful performance and be publicly humiliated by some know-it-alls. There's no secret to it, these people are just dreadful singers who are completely and utterly convinced they're not dreadful singers.

*The winner of series two was Michelle McManus, and the debate in the media throughout the entire series was about Michelle's weight. It was a big story, and it would be true to say everyone was very conscious of not bring-ing up that kind of thing in front of Michelle, and we did our best to be sensitive to it as well.*

It came to the live studio section of the show, and the audi-ence started voting. Michelle was going great guns and was quickly becoming the favourite to win. Every Saturday after-noon, we and the contestants would rehearse. We'd walk through positions and run through our interview questions and then send them off the set, as we would on the live show. We did this with Michelle, and Ant proved that, not only can he be physically clumsy, he can do it verbally as well.

*Just to put this into context, at the time I happened to be listening to a lot of hip-hop and, in particular, a track called 'Baby Got Back' by Sir Mix-A-Lot. You know what it's like when you listen to a particular song a lot – you find yourself singing it all the time. Well, we did our quick chat with Michelle in rehearsals and, as she walked off, I absent-mindedly started singing a line from the Sir Mix-A-Lot track. Unfortunately, the line in question was this:*
*'I like big butts and I cannot lie.'*
*If that wasn't embarrassing enough, I was wearing a microphone, and the whole sentence boomed out over the PA system across the whole studio.*

'It was a stupid thing to do, but Ant didn't do it on purpose,' I thought, as I frantically pointed to him to make sure everyone knew it wasn't me. Michelle stopped in her tracks, slowly turned to look in our direction and, thankfully for Ant, gave us a cheeky wink.

Michelle deservedly went on to become the winner of *Pop Idol* 2003. A great wrap party followed, but it was the day after that was actually more eventful. As part of the set, there were several giant plasma screens on the studio floor and, the day after the final, two men turned up to collect them. They asked where the plasmas were and were directed towards the studio. They unplugged them all, took them out and put them in their van.

*A couple of hours later, two more blokes turned up at reception saying they'd come to collect the plasmas. The receptionist told them someone had already done it. The first two blokes had walked in there, bold as brass, and stolen the plasma screens.*

And people say crime doesn't pay.

*You can't say that – we're supposed to set an example.*

Sorry, you're right. Crime *doesn't* pay.

*That's better.*

# Chapter 32

The last few months of 2003 were a difficult time for me personally, because Clare and I split up. We'd been together since 1992, and it was very hard for both of us. The whole thing was amicable enough, but for the last couple of years, we hadn't seen each other all that much. She'd be away touring with plays, and I'd be in Australia, or at *Pop Idol* auditions. We were very honest with each other and, after eleven years, decided it wasn't working any more.

We'd had a few trial separations before, as a lot of couples do, but we always got back together. This time, though, we decided this was it. It happened around September 2003, but I think it was around November when it hit the press, and that was one of the hardest things to deal with. Breaking up with someone after eleven years is a painful enough experience without having to cope with newspapers and magazines raking over the whole thing.

Plus, a lot of what was reported was wrong – some said that the reason we'd broken up was because I'd had a fling, but that wasn't the case. During one of our separations, I went to a lapdancing club and ended up having a one-night stand with one of the girls there, but Clare knew about that and we'd got back together afterwards. We were together at least another year after that.

The press was printing all sorts of speculative stories – saying I had a secret flat in Essex, or that me and Clare hadn't slept together for a year, or that we were more like brother and sister. All these things were completely untrue and very hurtful to both of us. I understood that we were in the public eye and, to a degree, 'fair game', but I didn't expect the media to completely fabricate stories. Throughout all of this, me and Clare would speak almost daily, and it was very hard to have to constantly ring her up about any number of ridiculous stories. My management and press officer advised me not to issue denials on all the stories, because it would just fan the flames and make things worse, but it was incredibly difficult advice to follow. Clare also had to deal with journalists knocking on her door, and putting notes through her letterbox. She was offered large sums of money to do stories about us, which of course she turned down. The most important thing throughout it all was that Clare was okay and that we could stay friends, and I'm proud to say we're still good friends today.

The other big consequence was that I was now a single man for the first time since I was seventeen, which felt weird at first – I'd been in a relationship all throughout my twenties and, now, everything had changed. To begin with, it felt like part of me was missing, and it took me a good while to recover and adapt to that. One of the hardest things about being single and in the public eye is that, whenever you do meet a girl, chances are she knows lots about you and has probably already formed an opinion of you, but you don't know anything about her, which tends to put you at a disadvantage.

*Things were very tough for Dec, and I did what any best friend would do and made sure I was always there for him. I told him in no uncertain terms that he could borrow my tin opener for as long as he liked.*

I'll never forget that – you're the best friend a man could have.

*Fortunately, we were so busy that Dec had the chance to throw himself into his work – and there was a big surprise coming our way. We were doing rehearsals for the second series of* Takeaway *one afternoon, when Nigel Hall, the very camp and quintessentially ITV Light Entertainment Producer, came into the studio singing, 'I like to be in America! OK by me in America!' from* West Side Story. *It wasn't unusual for Nigel to belt out show tunes in the middle of the studio, but this time he was doing it for a reason. Fox, one of the big TV networks in America and home of* The Simpsons, The X-Files *and* 24 *had secured the US rights for* Saturday Night Takeaway *and wanted to make a pilot. Nigel told us that, if the pilot went well, they'd do a series and that we'd all move to Hollywood and live happily ever after. On hearing those outlandish claims, we did the only thing we could — we started singing 'I like to be in America! OK by me in America!'*

Once the singing had stopped, and we'd finished all the other stuff we call work, we got on with the American pilot. Fox sent over an executive — let's call her Kimberly-Jane — to oversee the running of the show and be the network's eyes and ears in London. We and the senior members of the production team held a meeting with her and attempted to pick her brains about the direction, the feel and the content for the show. For instance, we knew American one-hour shows are significantly shorter than in the UK because they have more advert breaks, so we wanted to make sure the structure of our show fitted their template and timings. She said we shouldn't worry too much about all that and we should make it as long as we want and put whatever we want in it. At this point, it may be beneficial to know that K-J spent most of the rest of her time in Harvey Nichols, Harrods and Selfridges.

The decision was also taken to shoot the pilot on the existing *Takeaway* set in London. It would be very expensive to build a whole new set in America, so the plan was to record it in our studio, and bring in an audience of Americans who lived in London.

*Bad idea. Very bad idea. Call me old-fashioned, but if you're making a TV show for America, it's a good idea to film it in America. Not doing that meant we lost that American feel that American TV needed. We filmed the pilot and sent it to Fox for their approval. The first thing they said was 'This is far too long.' It had ended up being one hour ten minutes, without ad breaks. In the US, an hour-long show is around forty-three minutes, so we had to lose half an hour of stuff and it left us with a show that didn't make any sense. Unsurprisingly, it never got commissioned although, on the plus side, K-J did get some lovely dresses — and that's the main thing, isn't it?*

So we didn't get the show, although we did get to have one of the most brilliant meetings we've ever had. Before we shot the pilot, we went to LA with Paul Jackson, a very experienced British executive, who was running Granada America at the time, to meet the Fox Network Head of Alternative Programming, Mike Darnell.

*Mike is probably five foot tall. Yes, that's right, he's the only person in telly (apart from Jeanette Krankie) who's smaller than us two. He wears skinny black jeans, cowboy boots and a leather jacket. As well as being a former child-star, he was also a cocktail pianist before he worked in TV. We resisted making a joke about him being a tiny pianist — he was in charge of our show, so we decided that wasn't a good idea. As you'll have gathered by now, Mike is a maverick, but an incredibly successful maverick. For instance, he's the man in charge of* American Idol, *which sort of makes him Simon Cowell's boss.*

We arrived ten minutes early, and just being at Fox Studios was a thrill — there were huge *Simpsons* pictures everywhere, it was a baking-hot Californian day and we walked into the offices, took off our sunglasses and felt good: we were in LA and we were having a meeting about our own TV show.

Behind reception there was a giant Bart Simpson picture, there were *X-Files* and *American Idol* posters on every wall, and glamorous people seemed to be gliding in and out of offices at ten-second intervals. Mike Darnell is notorious for keeping people waiting, and he kept the three of us in reception for forty minutes, which apparently isn't too bad. Plus, we were served chilled water and a fruit platter while we flicked through copies of Hollywood's trade paper *Variety*. This was most definitely LA, baby. Eventually, Mike was ready for us. The moment we walked into his office, he screamed, 'Ant and Dec — I love you guys!' We went to shake hands with him, while, in an effort to make small talk, Paul Jackson said,

'I was just telling Ant and Dec about how you used to play piano in a wine bar before you got into TV.'

*Our hands were still stuck out waiting for a handshake, when Mike turned his back on all three of us and, while we exchanged bemused glances, made his way over to a piano in the corner of his office and started playing it. I didn't have a clue how to react. We were standing there, jackets still on, open-mouthed, while Mike tickled the ivories as if his life depended on it. After a few familiar bars, he stopped suddenly and spun round in his chair.*

*'Do you guys like Elton John?' he enquired.*

*'Er . . . yes . . . of course,' we replied, hoping that was the right answer.*

*'I LOVE Elton John!' he cried, then spun back around, took a deep breath and launched into 'Don't Let the Sun Go Down on Me' at the top of his voice. This was getting seriously weird. Should we laugh? Was it a joke? Should we clap out of respect? Or should we hit him with the dance moves from 'Rhumble'? We were stunned and, at the same time, desperately trying not to laugh. We still hadn't been invited to sit down, so we carried on standing there, dumbstruck.*

I started looking for the hidden cameras. I was convinced Simon Cowell was getting his own back – this had to be a wind-up.

*After what seemed like about four years, Mike finished the first verse, and we all breathed a sigh of relief. We were about to start applauding when Mike pulled out his trump card – the second verse. We waited what seemed like another four years until he'd finished and then burst into applause. Mike said thank you – and, I'm sure, took a bow, but that may just be my memory playing tricks on me. Surely we would grab a seat and start talking business now?*

Wrong. Mike had a test for us. He said, 'Hey guys, what's wrong with my desk?' This was getting ridiculous – first we'd been treated to his live Elton John tribute, and now we were talking furniture.

*We looked at his desk, and all thought the same thing: 'It's had the legs chopped in half.' Mike was so small that he'd had his desk customized. But none of us had the balls to say it, so we all started making guesses we knew were wrong:*

*'Er, is it antique?'*

*'Has it got lots of drawers?'*

*'It's not another piano, is it?'*

*Eventually, after a few more guesses, Mike put us out of our misery. He looked at the three of us.*

*'No man, the f\*\*\*\*\*g legs have been chopped off – I'm only five feet tall!'*

*At exactly the same time, all three of us said, 'Oh yes! So it has!'*

*After that, I think we actually got down to the meeting.*

*One good thing came out of it: the moment we got home, we both sawed down the legs of all our furniture. Try it – it makes you feel like a giant.*

On the subject of home improvements, just before Christmas 2003, I finally won a battle I'd been waging with my mam and dad for years: I bought them a house. When I first suggested it, they'd been very resistant, but I started leaving a few brochures featuring new properties around and, one day, my mam said she'd seen one she liked the look of, and we went to see it. This happened a few times until we found the right house, and I had an offer accepted.

The whole Donnelly family spent every day that Christmas holiday stripping wallpaper, knocking down walls and getting the place ready. My brother Martin, who's a builder, was brilliant, and it was great for me to throw myself into this project and feel like I was helping my family out. Plus, I don't have to fork out for a hotel when I go home.

*You're all heart, aren't you?*

That's me.

# Chapter 33

*Here's a question for you – what connects one of the best-known ex-couples in Britain, a punk icon and a disgraced member of the aristocracy? Yes, you guessed it, I'm a Celebrity . . . Get Me out of Here! If we thought the first two series had been big, then the third instalment of the longest-titled show on TV was absolutely enormous. Of course, I'd like to say that it was all down to a quite brilliant and hilarious performance from us two, but the truth was that it was due to the most intriguing line-up so far.*

The cast of 2004 had something for everyone – there was Kerry (as she was then) McFadden, Lord Brocket, Neil 'Razor' Ruddock, Jenni Bond, John 'Johnny Rotten from the Sex Pistols' Lydon, plus a man called Peter Andre and a lady called Jordan. And they didn't disappoint.

*This series was also when we started working with a writer who's been stuck with us ever since, Andy Milligan. Andy's from Newcastle so, as well as working together, the three of us always spend plenty of time talking about football, but there are happy times too. In fact, Andy's helping us with this very book – say hello to everyone Andy.*

Hi, everyone, I'd just like to say . . .

*Shush, you, that's enough. Keep typing and button it.*

John Lydon was the most exciting booking for us. These days, you might know him as a wildlife presenter and a bloke who advertises butter but, back then, he was just a plain old living legend of punk, and watching him in the jungle was fascinating. Right up until the night before the celebs were due to go in, no one believed John would go through with it. We all thought it would be the ultimate punk gesture to pull out at the last minute – but he surprised us all. Once he got in there, he actually made a lot of friends. Most of them were animals and insects, but he was very popular with those animals and insects.

At the end of every episode, as you know, we always head into camp to announce the results of the viewers' votes. Those moments can be strange at the best of times. We walk across three huge rope bridges, just us two, the floor manager and the cameraman, and then you reach camp and have to go in and deal with a load of starving, angry, smelly celebrities. We always walk in there expecting the unexpected. And with John Lydon in there, you'll understand why we were particularly apprehensive that series. For the whole first week, John was as good as gold – he didn't do anything risqué, and the closest we got to an 'incident' was when former Radio 1 DJ Mike Read and Lord Brocket gave us charcoal moustaches.

But then the atmosphere changed, as it always does. The mood in camp becomes much more about survival and much less about fear of trials.

*We stood there in camp, listening to the countdown in our earpieces, trying to avoid the flies and the smoke from the fire and attempting to concentrate on revealing who the British public would be sending home. As ever, we took turns reading the names and, when it came to me, I wafted some smoke out of my eye, looked at Johnny Rotten and said, 'John, they've decided . . . it's not you.'*

*To which he replied, 'Oh, f\*\*\*\*\*g c\*\*ts!'*

*Right there and then, on live TV, John Lydon used the C word. It's shocking, it's unsuitable and it's not Christopher Biggins. And, to make matters worse, he'd only gone and chucked in an F word before the C word.*

*I couldn't believe it. I'd really enjoyed watching John in that series, and he'd just done the most predictable thing possible for an old punk. There was a deafening silence in our earpieces. I heard myself saying, 'Hey, come on now. Come on, John,' in a tone of voice that we all remember from our childhoods that says, 'I'm not angry, I'm just disappointed.' Then the absurdity of the situation dawned on me: I was standing in the middle of the Australian rainforest at seven in the morning chastising the lead singer of the Sex Pistols for saying a naughty word. Our earpieces suddenly crackled into life, and a voice came through: 'Apologize, APOLOGIZE!' Dec apologized immediately to the viewers and, after we'd finished the rest of the voting announcement, we left the camp. A few days later, John decided to leave the camp too – he walked off the show and went back to the hotel, where he could use all the F, C, W and B words he liked.*

When we weren't at work telling off old punks, we managed to get in a bit of sunbathing, and we both got the worst sunburn of our lives. Most Geordies will tell you they burn easily, and us two got a shocking dose of it on that trip. The back of my legs and my back were absolutely beetroot-red, while Ant scorched his back and his forehead.

*Yeah, I know: there's plenty of it to burn.*

We were in agony, and Claude, our make-up artist, suggested a remedy. 'She's a make-up artist,' we thought. 'She knows about skincare.' She looked at us with a completely straight face and suggested we put sliced tomato on the burnt areas. We burst out laughing, but she was serious – Claude said it worked a treat. We were in agony, so we were prepared to try anything and, five minutes later, we were both lying on our front with sliced tomatoes all over our backs. After that experience, I can offer some great advice to any readers who suffer sunburn in the future: don't put tomato on it; it doesn't do a thing.

*That's not true, it does do one thing – it makes you look like a complete idiot.*

*The series was won by Kerry McFadden who, after a very shaky first few days, really embraced life in the jungle. As we all know, going on 'a journey' is the name of the game on reality TV, and I'm not talking about a first-class flight from Manchester to Brisbane. In a way, though, the real winners were ex-couple Peter and Jordan, or Katie Price, as she's known these days. The thing about* I'm a Celebrity . . . *is that it's impossible to hide your true personality: no one can put on an act all day every day for nearly three weeks.*

*Before Jordan went into the jungle, a lot of people had made up their mind about her. They thought she was just another glamour model, but she turned out to be feisty, opinionated and honest, and people warmed to that – especially feisty, opinionated and honest people. She was also falling in love with the bloke who sang 'Mysterious Girl' and would go on to wow us all with his latest composition, 'Insania'. As you'll remember, almost ten years earlier, we'd lived in the same building as Peter Andre and, while he'd hit the gym every day, we'd be eating Chinese Pete's barbecue ribs. And now, here we were again, only this time, we got to go to the gym every day while he shared a cup of hot water round the campfire with former BBC Royal Correspondent Jenni Bond. Peter was such great value and, alongside his endless renditions of 'Insania' and flirting with Jordan, he would come out with a gem every day which, frankly, made our job a hell of a lot easier.*

I don't think anyone would have put Peter and Jordan together before the series. She had a boyfriend when she went in, and no one had heard from him for years – to most people he was a cheesy nineties pop star (and that can be a very hard label to shake off. We should know). It was the first time two people began a relationship on the show, and it was fascinating to watch. We were so excited, me and Ant even talked about getting hats for their wedding, like Cilla used to on *Blind Date*.

*Series three was fantastic – there were so many intriguing characters and so much going on – and the ratings reflected that. The final was watched by an incredible 15.7 million people, which was the biggest audience we'd ever performed to – and yes, that does include* Slap Bang. *It meant so much because we'd worked so hard with the team to get the tone and the style of the show right. It hadn't been easy but it was well worth all the hard work – the show had become a phenomenon and we were ecstatic.*

*The wrap party for series three had something that no other* I'm a Celebrity . . . *wrap party has had – a VIP area, which meant we got to spend some time with Mike Read and Lord Brocket, who, for some reason, were dressed as women.*

**I think I like it better when there *isn't* a VIP area . . .**

*The other thing I remember from that party is doing shots with Kerry, and Jordan chasing after Dec, who she had propositioned during her departure interview. He managed to avoid her all night, but her mum did corner him a couple of times and try to set him up with her. He wasn't having any of it.*

*At the party, I was really in the mood for a big night. When it finished at around two in the morning, everyone else – Dec, Ali, and Toni and Claude – went back to their rooms and went to sleep. I wanted to keep going and was in a boozy huff that no one wanted to join me. I went back to my room, got my CD player and portable speakers, a few CDs, a couple of beers and headed down to the beach, where I sat watching the sun coming up. I was desperate for some company but, apart from a bloke with a metal detector, who I did have a quick chat with, the beach was deserted, so I texted Ali and said, 'Fancy a swim?'*

*Ali said the moment she got the text, she panicked: she knew I was in a party mood and she was terrified I'd gone for a drunken swim in the hotel pool. She checked my room first. The door was open, but I wasn't there, so then she tried the pool, then finally headed for the beach and found me, sitting cross-legged on the sand listening to music and with a face like thunder – all because no one wanted to party with me. I was in such a bad mood I thought nothing in the world could make me feel more irritated. Then Mother Nature intervened and proved me wrong. A huge wave appeared and washed my CD player and speakers into the sea.*

**What were you listening to? Katrina and the Waves? A bit of Billy Ocean perhaps?**

*Shut up – it still makes me angry to think about it.*

**The Beach Boys?**

*Just leave it.*

As well as providing great drama of its own, *I'm a Celebrity
. . .* was also throwing up people we would soon be seeing
again for Undercover, our hidden camera strand on *Takeaway*.
For our latest series, we went back to the king of the sit-ups,
John 'Fash the Bash' Fashanu.

*All our Undercovers had to be planned with military precision. In Fash's
case, we had a very clear plan to catch him out. ITV had a show called*
Celebrities Under Pressure, *where celebrities went to live with a family
and learnt a skill with them. The plan was that Fash would go and live
with a 'family' from Newcastle and learn the skill of karaoke. However,
this, as they say, was no ordinary family. The dad was Dec, the oldest son
was me, and the rest of them were actors, but of course Fash didn't have a
clue about that.*

*The idea was that at first the family would be excited at Fash's arrival,
then when they realized he was a terrible singer, they'd give up on their
task and try to swap him for another celebrity. As always, that first moment
when we come face to face with our victim was extremely nerve-wracking
but, when he saw us, Fash didn't bat an eyelid. Batting an eyelid, incidentally, was no mean feat for us two – wearing prosthetics meant that we
could barely see two feet in front of us at times, which was a big worry:
what if that made me even clumsier?*

*Over the course of the shoot, we practised karaoke with Fash and then,
as planned, got angry with him and tried to throw him out – it made a
change for us to be laughing at someone else's singing – and that was supposed to be the end of the hit. But he wouldn't go. Fash's response was
'Come on, guys, we're a team – we can do this!' That put a major spanner
in the works.*

We did the only thing we could do and kept going with the
fictional karaoke challenge. It got to the point where we were
standing in the kitchen with Leon Wilde, who was directing
the Undercover but posing as the director of *Celebrities Under
Pressure*, saying to each other, 'What do we do now?' Fash had

fallen for the lot – the family being rude to him, the endless hours of karaoke, sharing a bedroom with one of the kids . . . and he still hadn't sussed us out, so we did something we only ever do in extreme circumstances.

*We sang 'Let's Get Ready to Rhumble'. In the garage of the 'family' home.*

Before that, we'd sung 'If You Don't Know Me by Now', and he still hadn't got it, but we thought once we went into 'Rhumble', he'd rumble us straight away. We were wrong. At the end of the song, when Fash had been giving it his all, and wrecking mics left, right and centre, we asked him if he knew who'd sung the original. He didn't. We told him it was Ant and Dec. Still nothing. In the end, we were forced to remove our false teeth and fake faces and say, 'I'm Dec and he's Ant.'

*Even though by the time we told him who we were, my forehead was starting to melt and Dec's nose was looking very torn, he still would've fallen for anything. It was the best moment of the entire series, and if we hadn't just given up and told him who we were, there's a good chance we'd still be there now, singing karaoke and living with John Fashanu.*

And no one wants that, do they?

# Chapter 34

The third series of *I'm a Celebrity . . .* had been so successful that, by the time we came to do the fourth one, interest in the whole show had increased dramatically. As well as the celebs, that interest, bizarrely, extended to us two. There were more paparazzi skulking around the town we stayed in, and our biggest worry was that, after a day's sunbathing, people would take pictures of us lying around with sliced tomato on our backs.

To deal with the increased press presence, the show hired a security guard (who also doubled as our driver) to stop us being bothered. His name was Junior, and he was a huge ex-rugby player from New Zealand. To give you an idea of his size, I'd say that one of his legs is bigger, stronger and more powerful than me and Ant put together. He was incredibly professional and couldn't have been more vigilant if he'd been looking after Barack Obama – although Barack is unlikely to host *I'm a Celebrity . . .* any time soon. Not unless him and us two did some sort of job swap - and I'm not sure that would work. We'd be fine running America, but I'm not sure how he'd cope with the Bushtucker Trials.

After a few days of being under Junior's surveillance, we noticed that, every time we came out of our hotel rooms, he would magically appear from his room, which was at the other end of the corridor. We couldn't work out how he did it. At first we thought he just had good hearing, so the next time we left our rooms, we agreed to be super quiet, but the moment we opened the doors, he was there.

*Finally, detectives Donnelly and McPartlin got to the bottom of it. We came back from dinner one night, a little bit tipsy, and spotted something:*

*the corridor where our rooms were had always been completely bare except for a massive plant pot outside Dec's room and on this particular night, we noticed that plant pot had a flashing red light in it. Junior had hidden a small camera there, and he had a monitor in his room. Straight away, I thought, 'How dare he?'*

Yeah, he was looking after us, keeping an eye on us, doing his job – it was nothing short of a disgrace . . .

*We decided to have a bit of fun so, one night when we got in from dinner, we tiptoed towards the plant, carefully picked it up and, laughing our heads off, bolted into Dec's room with it. We pointed the camera at the telly so it was filming a boxing match on the sports channel, and thought we were so clever we must have laughed for ten minutes solid – when us two do something we think is funny, boy, do we think it's funny. When our laughter had finally died down, there was a knock at the door, and it was Junior. 'Gimme the plant,' he growled – and we did as we were told. He put it back where it had come from, and we said no more about it.*

We should say that we see Junior every year now and he's really opened up – he's a lovely bloke and we can really have a laugh with him these days.

*Yeah, we should say that – he's absolutely massive.*

When it came to the show itself, topping Peter, Jordan and the rest of them was always going to be tough, but series four delivered one of the finest Bushtucker Trials of all time. The eventual winner was Joe Pasquale. We'd seen him at a wedding the previous summer, got talking and he said, 'They've asked me to do *I'm a Celebrity* . . .' We told him he'd be great, but he revealed, 'I've told them they can stick it up their arse.' It was obvious from talking to Joe that he was a man of principal – he wasn't going to do the show and that was the end of it.

*Cut to the following November; and me, Dec and Joe Pasquale at the Bushtucker clearing. In the three weeks leading up to the show, Joe had only eaten two meals a day – he knew that hunger would be the hardest thing and decided to train himself. It worked a treat, because he went on to be crowned king of the jungle, partly thanks to keeping himself to himself, saying some very funny stuff in the Bush Telegraph, and walking around camp with a couple of emus that had been sent in. I should point out they were real live emus, not the kind Rod Hull used to attack people with, and Joe spent hours on end with those birds. They were small, annoying and went everywhere together. Joe christened them Ant and Dec – I never did find out why.*

That was also the series where we almost had to change the name of Bushtucker Trials to 'The Part of the Show Where Natalie Appleton Cries'. Former All Saint Natalie was chosen to do a record five trials in a row, breaking the previous record set by Fash. The great British public really had it in for her, although I don't think Natalie did herself any favours when, on the trek into camp, she touched a tree with her hand and uttered the immortal words, 'Ah! I touched a tree!' If I didn't know better, I'd say the more squeamish the celeb, the more likely they were to be voted for to do the trial.

The worst thing for us was that the more hesitant, or scared, someone is, the longer it takes to record the trial and, let me tell you, with Natalie, those trials took for ever. She would spend ages trying to decide whether or not to give them a go, in between regular bouts of freaking out. It was also very difficult for the team who create the Bushtucker Trials – they spend a lot of time and effort making sure everything is well designed, properly thought through and, of course, absolutely terrifying, and when one of the celebrities refuses to give them a go, their hard work is wasted.

Occasionally, though, someone other than Natalie would have a chance, and one of those people was Paul Burrell. Paul faced a trial called Hell Holes and, straight off the bat, just so there isn't any doubt, I'm going to admit it, I laughed my head off pretty much from start to finish. He had to put his hand into holes in a piece of rock and retrieve the stars he needed to win food for camp, but, as always, the stars had company. And Paul gave the performance of his life, squealing, screaming, sweating, crying, saying, 'Come to Daddy,' and 'Move over, darling,' to the snakes, rats, spiders and whatever else was in there. Initially, me and Ant tried to bite our lips and not laugh, in the interests of trying to be vaguely professional. Then we looked round at the cameramen and the sound department, and they had tears rolling down their faces. The camera was literally shaking because the cameraman was laughing so much. After I saw that, the floodgates opened and I fell apart.

*History has taught us that Dec is much worse than me at keeping a straight face in these situations. I suppose being grumpy does have its advantages.*

I'm a terrible giggler at the best of times and, once I started, I couldn't stop. Paul's trial became one of the TV moments of the year, and he gave us all sore faces from laughing so much. We never thought we'd get anything funnier than Fash, but this was Fash to the power of ten.

*We eventually got the chance to catch up with Paul at the wrap party. He and the rest of the celebs arrived and, the moment he clapped eyes on me, he came straight over and said, 'I want a word with you.'*

*'Hi, Paul, how are you?' I said.*

*'I've got a bone to pick with you. You were laughing at me during those trials. You and Dec were laughing at me.'*

*'Yes, Paul, we were.' I couldn't disagree, so I thought my best bet was to come clean. 'What you've got to realize, though, is that the way you did those trials won you a lot of fans. My girlfriend, for instance, had been voting for Joe to win, but when she saw you in those trials, she started voting for you.'*

*I looked at him, confident I'd stated my case well, and that this would calm him down. He stared at me, took in what I'd said and then, after a few seconds' consideration, said, 'You've got a girlfriend? I always thought you were gay.'*

**You can't blame him – you can be quite camp sometimes.**

*How very dare you.*

# Chapter 35

*The business of show can teach you some pretty harsh lessons and, on the next series of* Takeaway, *thanks to Little Ant and Dec, we learnt a new one: Bruce Willis isn't exactly a bundle of laughs. In the dozens of interviews the boys did, from David Beckham to Diana Ross to Robert De Niro, there was only one person who ever refused to 'play ball' with the Littles – and that was Mr Willis. And* Die Hard's *one of my favourite films.*

*Bruce was over in the UK to promote his new film,* Hostage, *and he was booked in for the usual Little Ant and Dec treatment – some very silly questions and possibly a bit of dressing up at the end. It never got that far. Despite being a well-known Hollywood hardman who can put up with hijacked planes and exploding buildings, Bruce Willis wasn't too keen on spending ten minutes with a couple of kids from Newcastle.*

The boys' interview included questions like:

'My mum said you made a film about a ghost – were you frightened?' and 'My dad has a T-shirt that says "Baldies Do It Better". You're a baldie, what does that mean?'

Bruce spent the interview giving very brief answers and looking distinctly unamused. At the end of what was a short and very excruciating chat, Georgie Hurford-Jones, who was directing, and the boys left the room in a hurry, while Mr Willis left the room with a frown, keen to have a word or two with his publicist. His name may be Bruce but, when it came to Little Ant and Dec, he didn't think it was nice to see them to see them nice.

*One person who did play their cards right when it came to Little Ant and Dec was a man by the name of Tony Blair. Yes, that Tony Blair. In the same series, the call came through that the Prime Minister wanted to do an interview with the boys at Downing Street.*

*The whole thing happened in the run-up to the 2005 general election, and it actually became a genuine political story. Broadsheet newspapers were up in arms that, while the PM was avoiding interviews with the likes of Jeremy Paxman, he was happy to talk to a couple of kids for a Saturday-night TV show. Regardless of all the criticism and flak that was flying around, it was a really proud moment for us, and for everyone involved in the show. It was a particularly momentous occasion for Dylan and James, who had not only succeeded in scooping the TV interview of the year, but had also got special permission to miss PE and double maths.*

The prime minister was fantastic with them but, after half an hour of being asked silly questions, he turned to Georgie, gave her a look that said, 'How the hell did I get into this?', then asked, 'Is this over yet?', to which she replied, 'No, Prime Minister, it isn't.' After they'd finished talking to Mr Blair, the boys ran around Downing Street pressing buttons and picking up phones they shouldn't have been touching. I think at one point they may have accidentally declared war on a country in South America, but it made for a great piece of television, and that's the most important thing, isn't it?

After that interview, we brought the curtain down on Little Ant and Dec. Not only were they actually getting taller than us, we just felt that we couldn't take the concept any further. Once the boys had interviewed Tony Blair, it couldn't really get any bigger. Plus, we always try and retire strands on *Takeaway* while people are still enjoying them; that way there's no chance of them getting stale and tired. That's the beauty of that kind of programme: you can keep changing the component parts of it, but it's still the same show.

*At the same time, we decided we'd replace Undercover. It felt like that had reached the end of its time too. We'd dressed up as pretty much every character imaginable, and it was getting to the stage where the celebs we were pranking were getting wise to it. Probably the best example had come in the previous series, when we'd posed as a pair of American rappers. One of our 'victims' was Jill Halfpenny, my ex-girlfriend from the Byker Grove*

*nt: Loaded Double Act of the Year 1999.*

ec: But who will get to keep the award?

*nt: I will.*

Dec: With Children's BAFTA for
*The Ant and Dec Show.*

*Ant: A boozy night with mates in The Vortex a.k.a. my old kitchen.*

The first *Pop Idol* final – a victory for Will power.

*Ant: Midnight launch of the new Newcastle United strip. And if you're wondering who wo table football . . .*

Dec: Neither of us did – it was a photo opportunit and we left short after the picture was taken.

*Ant: The video shoot for 'We're on the Ball' in 2002.*

Dec: I didn't know Sven Goran Eriksson smoked . . .

Dec: On the set of *Alien Autopsy* in L.A.

Ant: *The budget wasn't what it should've been. Dec had to double as the cameraman.*

ec: On our way to court.

nt: *It's actually the first day of filming Alien Autopsy. I know, we look cited, don't we?*

ec: 'Who are ya?' One of the proudest moments of our little lives.

Dec: 'I thought you'd never ask. Yes, yes, yes, I will!'

Dec: Our first ever 'Undercover' transformation. Who are you on the phone to?

*Ant: My agent – look at the state of us*

*Ant: Patti and Bernice. Our greatest Undercover creations.*

Dec: Riding a motorbike through a wheel of fire for the Ant v Dec challenge – what could possibly go wrong?

*Ant: As you can see, after Dec's accident with the bike, the challenges got much more sensible.*

*Ant: Backstage at* Saturday Night Takeaway, *with Ronni the dog.*

*Ant: Lisa cleans up after Ronni while I help out by taking pictures.*

ec: Drumming up support for the toon on our Comic Relief trip to Kibera.

*Ant: With Lisa. It was a fancy dress party, honest.*

*Ant: On holiday with Lisa – not in fancy dress, honest.*

Dec: Me and Clare in a tender moment.

*Ant: Ooh, you've got chest hair!*

*Ant: There's that fringe again.*

Dec: On the way to winning our first ever National Television Award.

Dec: Ant and Lisa didn't get the beige/white ensemble memo.

*Ant: Two very special ladies – our mams. Mine is on the right, Dec's is on the left.*

*Ant: Courtenay, Sarha, Lisa and Emma.*

Dec: The Donnelly clan.

*Ant: 'She said yes!' Seconds after I'd popped the question in Dubai.*

Dec: What do you mean I'm 'not coming on the honeymoon'?

Dec: 'Oh, they grow up so quick . .

*Ant: The new Mr and Mrs McPartlin. Doesn't she look beautiful?*

*Ant:* I'm a Celebrity . . . *series one – it's a hard life, isn't it?*

Dec: Australia, series two. 'When are the celebrities getting here? We've been here for seven weeks . . .'

Dec: Being treated for sunburn. With tomatoes!

*Ant:* The obligatory koala shot.

Dec: Our *I'm a Celebrity* . . . entourage
– Toni, Claude and Ali.

Dec: 'And I'll tell you another
thing . . . if I could remember wha
I was talking about.'

*Ant: A birthday in Australia – it's not big,
and it's not clever, but it's great fun.*

Dec: With Ali, our Girl Friday.

# A Day in the Life of *I'm a Celebrity . . . Get Me out of Here!*

...a.m. Get up. Knackered. Leave hotel.

...a.m. Arrive on site and record our
...iceovers for the VT packages that will
...ake up the night's show

...30 a.m. Script meeting with the producers
...d the scriptwriters, then it's time for one
...our favourite parts of the day – watching
...e footage, which happens at around . . .

4.15 a.m. We squeeze into a little portacabin
with the scriptwriters, an editor and a cup of
tea, and watch what's been going on during
the last twenty-four hours. We try and think
of new jokes and stuff we can add to the
script and get to know what's happening in
camp – who's fallen out with who? Who
had to go to the bog in the night? You get
the drift.

5.15 a.m. Make our final changes to the script,
and then head to make-up and wardrobe.

5.30 a.m. Put on show clothes and get made
up. We do this with the help of Toni Porter
(wardrobe) and Claudine Taylor (make-up).
Toni and Claudine have been working with
us since *sm:tv* – they're brilliant at their
jobs, and they're also great friends. It's up to
them to make us look less knackered and
half presentable. Some people would say
they've got the hardest job in television.

6.15 a.m. Grab a script and get driven down to the set.

6.30 a.m. Rehearse our links.

7 a.m. Hello, we're on the telly!

8 a.m. The show finishes – we're not on the telly any more. We drive back to our office, where we have some food and start looking at the script for the Bushtucker Trial. Depending on who you've chosen to do the trial, we can have a long wait, but we usually head down to the trial clearing around . . .

10 a.m. Record the Bushtucker Trial. The celebrities are often terrified, humiliated and scared stiff. It's great.

12.30 p.m. Head back to our hotel and have some lunch, maybe go to the beach or if it's raining watch a DVD.

6 p.m. Have dinner then go to bed. And we repeat that for nineteen days in a row. Yes, nineteen – I'm yawning at the thought of it. But if we're ever off sick and you have to fill in, now you know what to do.

Dec: *Britain's Got Talent* – sadly none of it is featured in this photo.

Ant: *How rock 'n' roll are we?*

Dec: Not very – we're all dressed in pink.

Ant: *With my nephew Ethan at Mam's caravan.*

Dec: I like that jumper.

Ant: *Thanks.*

Dec: Not yours, Ethan's.

*Ant: Me and the Queen . . . meet Her Majesty.*
Dec: That's not even funny.

Dec: The All★Star Cup, 2006.

*t: Celebrating the success of the first All★Star Cup.*

c: **Look at the size of my glass of champagne.**

'All right, own up — were any of you sick in my toilet in the late 90s?'

*Ant: Jonny Wilkes agreed to give us all a song — we didn't have to ask him twice.*

c: **Pop stars' paddling pools are always better.**

*Ant: The lads – Boppa, me, Athey and Goody.*

Dec: Our friend Alan –
he spells crazy with a K!

Dec: Rhumbling on a golf trip to Portugal – ou
groupies weren't what they used to be.

*Ant: Rhumbli*
*at Phil Mount*
*wedding. It wa*
*'Beautiful Day*

*days and, looking back, she probably wasn't the smartest choice. Anyway, Dec was alone in a room with her, in full make-up, pretending to be a twenty-stone black American rapper, when she uttered the immortal words, 'Are you Dec?'*

Call it a hunch, but that was one of the moments when we thought it was probably time for something new. And, besides, we wouldn't have to lose any more sleep over how an Undercover mission would go and how much the whole thing cost. Oh, and we could stop spending seven hours in make-up every week. The new feature we substituted for it would be, we thought, less intense and less time-consuming.

*It turned out to be much more intense and extremely time-consuming.*

The item was called Ant versus Dec and, in case the title doesn't give it away, it involved me and Ant competing in a different challenge every week. The first thing we should say about it is that we get very, very competitive. And I mean *very* competitive. Fortunately, I've managed to win all of them – I just wanted to remind Ant and you lovely readers of that before we go any further.

*Now, now, let's not get competitive in the book, shall we? Every week, we get given a challenge, then we have one day – usually Tuesday – for training. After that, we spend the rest of the week practising our skills (or the lack of them) before we compete in the challenge, which usually happens live, in the studio, with the lovely Kirsty Gallacher in charge. The first challenge we ever did was Gladiators – in the spandex-wearing-TV-stars sense of the word, not the Roman amphitheatre blokes. When we came out into the studio in our brightly coloured Lycra suits, we got a huge reaction from the audience. They laughed their heads off. When it came to the second one, we were both walking a bit of a tightrope – that's not a metaphor by the way, that was actually the challenge: we had to walk a tightrope. So far, so good. Then we got to week three, and the challenge was puppy-training. It was a particularly horrendous challenge.*

Horrendous doesn't do it justice. As always, we had the challenge revealed to us on the Saturday night, live on the show, and we didn't give it another thought, and after the credits rolled, we strolled down to the green room as we did after every show to spend several hours relaxing – the kind of relaxing that means you wake up with a very sore head every Sunday. As it happens, that particular weekend, we were both looking forward to the Sunday, because Newcastle United were playing Chelsea in the cup. We hadn't been able to get home for the game, and it was going to be on the telly, so we decided to watch it in style – down our local pub. If there's football and beer involved, dedication is our middle name.

*On the Sunday, I was woken up at the crack of noon by the doorbell. A mum, a dad and their two girls – or a family, as they're otherwise known – arrived with two brown Labrador puppies called Ronni and Pudding. Ronni belonged to the family and was going to spend the week with me, and Dec was going to have Pudding – the dog that is, not the food. The family stayed for a cup of tea and filled me in on how to look after Ronni, as well as leaving toys, food and instructions on when to walk her.*

I didn't get any instructions. Pudding didn't belong to the family, so they just left her at Ant's without so much as a doggy chew. After I collected her and took her back to mine, I clearly remember me and the dog just looking at each other. I'm not sure who was more worried – me or Pudding. Actually, that's not true, it was definitely me.

Imagine the scene: in two different houses at exactly the same time, me and Ant are looking at these cute, energetic and adorable little puppies, thinking exactly the same thing: 'What time does the football kick off?'

*Fortunately, help arrived in the form of my better half. Lisa loves chocolate-brown Labradors and, bless her, she said she'd look after them while we went to the pub. That kind of behaviour is one of the thousands of reasons I love her so much. We'd been assured by the producers that both puppies were house-trained, so we had nothing to worry about on that front. Me and Dec got to the pub in time and had a great time watching the football.*

*Towards the end of the match, Lisa arrived, with the dogs. She wasn't happy and greeted us with the words, 'These are your dogs – you need to take them.' I could tell by the look on her face that it was a good idea to do what I was told (I know that look well). Apparently, they'd been a nightmare. The dogs had spent all their time fighting, and, when they weren't fighting, they were going to the toilet all over the house – the only place they didn't go to the toilet was the toilet. Then, when they'd finished with the house, they went out into the garden together, did the same out there, then rolled around in what polite people call their 'business', came back into the kitchen and skidded around in it.*

You may have worked it out for yourself by now, but these dogs were not, as previously claimed, housetrained. It was like having a baby in the house – and there's only room for one baby in my house – and that's me. You had to walk them, feed them, get up and let them out . . .

*You do realize you're just describing what it's like to have a dog? Millions of people all over the country manage it.*

I know, but we're on the telly, we don't know how to do stuff like that. My dog, Pudding, was never too keen to wait till she got outside to relieve herself. I'd carry her upstairs, then she'd get excited, run down the stairs and pee all over the cream carpet in my living room. By the time we arrived at the office for our final script meeting on the Friday, I was furious and exhausted – and, to make things worse, we had to bring the dogs to work with us. I sat around the table at the script meeting, ranting about how awful the week had been and how little sleep I'd had – all thanks to this puppy. Everyone there – producers, writers, directors – was sniggering, because they thought I was overreacting and being a drama queen.

*They know him very well.*

We were in the middle of a script meeting when Pudding proceeded to have a poo in the corner of the office. We didn't think the script was that bad, but Pudding clearly wasn't impressed. Suddenly, the very people who'd been laughing at my dog dramas started retching and leaving the room. Now they knew how I felt. It was the only good thing that puppy did all week. Anyway, the main thing is that, now, four years later, I've put the whole thing behind me and it doesn't make me incredibly angry to think about it and talk about it.

*Yeah, listening to you, that's pretty obvious.*

*A couple of weeks after the hounds of hell, which Dec won, we faced possibly the most manly challenge of our entire career: riding motorbikes through a ring of fire. On the surface, it was simple, if a bit scary – we would be taught to ride the bikes off a ramp and through a ring of fire, standing up. The person who jumped the furthest would be the winner. Even saying it now, I can't believe they let us do it.*

When we turned up for the training, and because I'm a slightly smaller gentleman, none of the bikes fitted me. The practice we did was frustrating because I just couldn't 'get it'. The thing is, as you go up the ramp, you've got to speed up, so you have enough momentum to land on your back wheel, because otherwise you'll go over the handlebars. I just couldn't get it right – at one point, I would've happily swapped it for another week of dog-training.

*You don't mean that.*

You're right, I don't but, despite my shortcomings, I was determined to make a go of it for one good reason – I couldn't stand the thought of Ant beating me in a single challenge. To make matters worse, we'd never rehearsed with the fire, it was too dangerous, so the plan was they'd only set it alight for the actual challenge.

When they lit the ring, the whole thing felt more terrifying than ever. Despite all your instincts, you've got to go faster as you get nearer the fire and all the practising goes out the window. In the end, I just had to go for it. As I hit the ramp, the time came to go full throttle, and I pulled on the accelerator but, even as I did it, I knew it wasn't enough. I had, in no uncertain terms, bottled it. The bike still hurtled through the ring of fire, smoke momentarily filled my helmet, and I took off through the air. I'd done it. I'd made it through the fire and was preparing to land. Then, at the peak of my jump, the bike slowly turned, the front wheel dropped and, next thing I knew, I was being thrown over the handlebars and the ground was heading towards me very quickly. I decided to let go of the bike, it went behind me, and I hit the ground – hard.

*I had no idea any of this was going on. I'd been taken to an 'isolation booth', where I had to wear a blindfold and earmuffs, so I wouldn't know how Dec had done. And, by the way, when I say booth, I basically mean a balsa-wood box covered in glitter. I was in there for ages . . . and ages . . . and ages. I started to smell smoke. 'Well, the fire's lit,' I thought, and waited some more. Still no one came to get me. Eventually, I ran out of patience, took off my blindfold and my earmuffs and got out of my balsa-wood box, sorry, booth. The first thing I saw was a group of the army display-team experts, stood in full military uniform and headgear, looking sombrely down at Dec, who was in a heap on the floor. I thought he was dead.*

At least that would've meant you won the challenge . . .

*I rode my bike over and was relieved to hear Dec making some nasty noises, because he'd been so severely winded. The reason everyone was standing around him was because there were paparazzi in the trees, and standing that way meant they couldn't get a photo. To me, though, the circle made it look like they were paying their last respects . . .*

I was taken to hospital with concussion and a fractured elbow. You won't be surprised to hear that the challenges for the rest of the series weren't too physical – we did darts, memory games and anything else that could be done with one arm. But the most important thing was that I still won the series. As I've mentioned before, I've won them all, but the ones that are the most satisfying are the ones I did with one arm and still I beat him.

*All right, that's enough; you'll end up with another broken arm if you keep gloating like that.*

# Chapter 36

*Right, time for Dec to shut up for a while, because I want to tell the readers how my beautiful girlfriend Lisa became my lovely wife Lisa.*

**Sounds like my cue to go and put the kettle on.**

*Thanks, and remember, I have one sugar in coffee but no sugar in tea, and I'd like a . . . tea. Oh, and also there are some Blue Ribands in the bottom cupboard next to the sink.*

**This stuff isn't really meant for the book is it? I'm sure someone'll take it out.**

*So, by the time I actually proposed to Lisa, she and I had been together for eleven years — you can probably tell that I don't like to rush things. As anyone who's been in a long-term relationship will know, when you've been together for ages, people start asking you one question: 'When are you going to propose?' Well, in 2005, I did it. In April, Lisa and I went on holiday to Dubai. What Lisa didn't know is that, before we left, I bought a ring and made a few arrangements for when we would be out there.*

*Once we got there and I'd finished worrying about losing the ring, we went on a trek over the sand dunes. It's one of those expeditions you do as part of a convoy consisting of twenty or so 4x4 dune buggies that drive across the desert together. We'd been to Dubai together once before and had done a similar trip, so when I told Lisa, her response was, understandably, 'What, again? That's such a boysy thing to do.' She wasn't hugely keen, to be honest. But I had a few tricks up my sleeve. So there we were in our dune buggy, and when suddenly all the other buggies went right and I turned left towards a couple of camels waiting for us with a guide, Lisa was very surprised.*

*After a bit of a camel trek, we arrived at a huge Bedouin tent I'd* booked. There was a big rug that had been laid out on the dunes for us and, while dinner was being cooked, we lay down on it and looked up at the moon and the stars. By this point, Lisa definitely thought this excursion was a good idea. So, right there and then, in the moonlight, I asked her to be my wife. She couldn't believe it, which I suppose, considering I'd made her wait eleven years, was fair enough. After she'd finished saying, 'Really? Really? Really?', I said, 'Is that a yes, then?' She told me it was, and I went to get some champagne that had been kept chilled in a cool bag inside the tent. We were engaged – and we were both over the moon, as well as being under the moon, if you know what I mean. Lisa was so happy that she couldn't resist ringing everyone she knew at home.

I was chuffed that everything had turned out so perfectly, especially considering that, twenty-four hours earlier, the whole thing was almost ruined. Because we were on holiday, I had turned my phone off and was just switching it on once a day to check my messages. The previous evening, I'd turned it on, and there was a message from Ali. It said, 'I hate to have to ask you this, but have you bought Lisa an engagement ring from Tiffany's? I've had a call from the Sun, and they're going to publish a story saying you've proposed.' Someone had seen me in the jeweller's shop, and had sold the story.

I was really annoyed – we've never courted publicity as a couple, and this was a personal moment that was in danger of being hijacked by a newspaper. The worst thing was that, because of the time difference between London and Dubai, they were going to run the story before I'd actually popped the question. I knew that, if that happened, then all Lisa's friends would call and text to congratulate us and I wouldn't even have proposed yet. Plus, one of Lisa's mates was expecting a baby any day, so she was constantly checking her phone for news. In the end, the Sun agreed to do the honourable thing and wait a day, but it was a close shave.

Not only did we have a wedding to look forward to, but we were also about to make another big commitment – to star in our first feature film. For the previous few years, Paul, our manager had been sent various film scripts but, when we read them, we felt like none of them was quite right. We had a thing called the twenty-page test, which, as the title suggests, meant that, if it didn't grab us after twenty pages, it went in the bin. Incidentally, the fact that you've got this far in the book means we've passed your twenty-page test, so thank God for that.

*Just before Christmas, Paul teased us by saying, 'I've got something you'll really like, but go away, have your holiday and then I'll show it to you when you get back.' I thought he was going to give me a late Christmas present, maybe a nice jumper, but it turned out to be a film script which he'd been sent and enjoyed which, in hindsight, was better than a nice jumper.*

At the beginning of the year he gave us the script for *Alien Autopsy* and, while we were filming some new opening titles for *Saturday Night Takeaway*, I started reading it between takes. Before I knew it, I was on page forty-five – the equivalent of passing not one but two twenty-page tests. When I'd finished it, I went and told Ant I loved it and that he had to read it. He did and, similarly, loved it straight away. It was a true story about Ray Santilli and Gary Schofield, two blokes from London who, in 1994, had filmed a fake alien autopsy and fooled the world into believing it was genuine footage from the so-called 'alien' spotted in Roswell, New Mexico, in 1947.

*It looked like the right script had finally come along. It had two great parts which, for a double act, is important, and we were really keen to do it. We met up with Will Davies, the writer, Barnaby Thompson, the producer, and Jonny Campbell, the director. Apparently, Jonny had been watching I'm a Celebrity . . . with his wife after reading it, and she'd said, 'What about those two for your film?' His response had been, 'Great idea – but can they act?' If I'd been there in their living room and heard that question, I would've said three words to him: 'Blinded.' 'By.' 'Paintball.'*

*At the meeting with Jonny, Will and Barnaby, we read through a few scenes for them. They seemed pretty happy and then said, 'Great, now can you come and audition?' The last thing we'd auditioned for was Byker Grove – and that was over fifteen years ago. Plus, we'd been messing about on telly for over ten years by this point. Did this sort of thing happen to Robert De Niro?*

I doubt it, but then I'm not sure he would've been any good at Wonkey Donkey either, so I suppose it's swings and roundabouts.

*Preparing for the audition was strange — nerve-wracking, but incredibly exciting too. We had to learn some big scenes, and going back to acting was quite a challenge. It was completely different from* The Likely Lads, *which we'd done a couple of years earlier; it was a 'proper film' that would be shown in cinemas and everything. I remember being filled with some of the same fear and nerves I'd had at the auditions back at the Mitre.*

Despite our fears, the audition went well and we both got the parts — but then I don't suppose they were ever going to hire just one of us. We were very excited when we got the news. It was a brand-new challenge, and the next thing to do was start rehearsals. Jonny, the director, pushed us hard. One of the first things we worked on was the pitch of our performance and the delivery. Because we were so used to entertainment shows, we were inclined to play everything for laughs — when there was a funny line, our voice would naturally go up at the end of the sentence, to draw the audience's attention to the gag. Jonny wanted us to play the whole thing much straighter and more subtly and, at first, we found it difficult to know what he thought of our performances. He wasn't the kind of bloke who'd say, 'Yeah, that's it — well done,' so we were constantly questioning ourselves about how it was going and if we were pitching it right. It might have been a comedy film, but we took it very, very seriously.

*It wasn't until we got on to set and started filming that we got to know Jonny better and struck up a bit of a rapport with him, and it was great to be there, working with other actors. The buzz you got after doing a good scene was amazing — and totally different from the buzz you get from a live TV show, because it wasn't so instant. On a film set, there's no audience laughing and cheering at you — we'd asked for one, but were told it wasn't the done thing. When you're acting, it's more of a slow-burn process, but just as satisfying.*

278

*We had to learn to pace ourselves in more ways than one. Normally, our week builds up to one intense hour of live TV, but with acting you're off and on and, particularly with films, there's a lot of waiting around – although you do at least get a trailer to wait around in, which makes you feel like a film star, even when in our case, you're clearly not one.*

After eight weeks filming in London, it was time to get even more showbiz and fly to Hollywood. It was another one of those experiences when you pinch yourself: we got to film on the Sunset Strip, driving a Cadillac in the middle of the LA sunshine. People were looking at us from the pavement – sorry, sidewalk – and, once they'd clocked the cameras, you could see them straining their necks, thinking, 'Who is it? Who is it?' I wanted to shout, 'It's me! It's me!' I didn't though – they would've thought I was mad, as they didn't have a clue who I was.

*One of the other big thrills about filming in the States was working with Harry Dean Stanton, a craggy-faced American character actor who was in* Paris, Texas, Fear and Loathing in Las Vegas *and played Molly Ringwald's dad in* Pretty in Pink. *Every line on his face seems to tell a different story – at least it would, if he was in the habit of telling any stories: we quickly learnt that Harry likes to keep himself to himself.*

I had one very long scene with Harry, just me and him, on our own, in a car, on a night shoot. We sat in a pick-up truck together for hours, while he gave an incredibly convincing performance as a chain-smoking actor on a night shoot. No matter how much I coughed – which was a lot – he didn't stop. He didn't give a toss and, although I wasn't keen on inhaling his smoke, I admired him for his dedication to cigarettes.

*Because he was such a private guy, not really the sort of man who enjoyed small talk, we were never sure what Harry thought of us. One night, he invited us to go for a drink with him, which was a real thrill. We immediately accepted, and he took us to a place called Dan Tana's on Santa Monica Boulevard. It was one of his regular haunts and was like something out of Goodfellas – all empty wine bottles with candles in, red-and-white-checked tablecloths and a clientele perched at the bar who looked like they could be close business associates of Tony Soprano. Although, if they're reading this, I'm sure they weren't – I don't want to end up sleeping with the fishes.*

*One by one, Harry's friends joined us, and each one was scarier and weirder than the last. There was a detective from the LAPD homicide department, a black guy who ran an after-hours drinking den and, finally, an ex-boxer who'd only ever had one professional fight, which he insisted on telling everyone about in great detail. It was one of the most terrifying meals of my life.*

About six months later, we were back in LA for some meetings about TV shows, and we went out for dinner in a restaurant and, who should be in there, but the world's most dedicated smoker, our old friend Harry Dean. He was deep in conversation with some of his mates, and we didn't want to disturb him, so we waited till we were leaving. I went over (seeing as I'd had the most scenes with him), and opened with, 'Hi Harry, good to see you.' He looked back at me, smiled and said it was good to see me too. I knew it wasn't, and I can confidently say, even though we'd only been filming with him a few months earlier, he didn't have a clue who I was.

They say you know you've made it in Hollywood when your fellow actors start recognizing you in restaurants so, for us two, that was when we knew for definite we *hadn't* made it in Hollywood. We went back to doing what we do best – British telly.

*A year or so earlier, we'd come up with an idea for an innovative, multi-layered high-concept TV show that was all about . . . playing golf. We started playing golf ourselves in 2004, when, with a load of our mates, we formed the Chiswick Royal and Ancient Golf Society. The society includes, among others, Jonny Wilkes, Paul and Darren, Alan Conley (our floor manager), David Staite, Andy Collins (our warm-up man for Takeaway), and Si Hargreaves. Every year, we play four tournaments, and they often mean going abroad for a weekend of committed drinking with a little bit of golf thrown in. I love those weekends, because you can just be yourself, and it doesn't matter who you are, or what you normally do, this is just a chance to be one of the lads.*

One of our first golfing trips was to Portugal and, unsurprisingly, it ended up with all of us in a bar. One member of our society happens to bear more than a passing resemblance to the jockey, Frankie Dettori. His name is Ian McLeish, and he went into this karaoke bar to buy a packet of cigarettes. The karaoke MC immediately started ribbing him with plenty of 'Look everyone, it's Frankie Dettori! Have you lost your horse, Frankie?' comments. Ian came out and told us, and we all went back in mob-handed to put this bloke in his place.

Immediately, the man on the mic looks up and says, 'Look everyone, Frankie's back, with his mates . . . Ant and Dec?' He was a bit lost for words after that. It was just a small bar in a holiday resort in Portugal and, even though we'd gone in there intending to give him a piece of our mind, we ended up staying in there, having a great night and all doing karaoke.

*Jonny Wilkes, who's never shy when it comes to singing in public, got up and did a bit of Frank Sinatra. He was doing his version of 'My Way', and there were a few old couples in tears although, personally, I don't think Jonny's singing is that bad. Someone was looking through the song book, and said, 'Look, they've got "Let's Get Ready to Rhumble".' Me and Dec both looked up and barked, 'No chance.' Two hours later, we were on stage belting it out. There were so many camera phones in that bar that I'm amazed – and very relieved – that performance never turned up on youtube, although the fact that we bought a round for the whole bar might have had something to do with it – bribery never fails.*

*Golf isn't just about drinking and singing 'Rhumble', though, sometimes we actually make it to the course, and it was during a game one day that we had an idea. The Ryder Cup is golf's biggest event, where teams from Europe and the United States compete against each other. We thought we could do a celebrity version – with American and European celebrities, plus some professional golfers. Originally, we pitched the show to ITV, who wanted to make it but decided they couldn't afford it. In the end, it went to Sky. We called it* The All\*Star Cup, *and all we had to do then was book a load of famous people who loved playing golf.*

There were two signings that made *The All\*Star Cup* a success. First of all, Scottish professional superstar golfer Colin Montgomery agreed to captain the European team. To get Monty, as his good friends call him (he asked us to call him Mr Montgomery), was a real coup. He is actually the captain of the European Ryder Cup team in 2010, that's how big he is. The second jaw-dropping booking was Catherine Zeta Jones and Michael Douglas. They're both keen golfers and, with the event being held at Celtic Manor in Wales, Catherine could visit her family and, as for Michael, well, apparently he'd always been a big PJ and Duncan fan, so it was a dream come true. Once we had those three, there were plenty of people who couldn't wait to sign up. Chris Evans, Ronan Keating, James Nesbitt and Ian Wright all played.

We also had the legendary Terry Wogan commentating, and he was the perfect person to talk over hours and hours of live golf coverage. That man could talk over hours of live washing-up coverage and it would be entertaining. We were dying to take part in the game too but, because of our contract with ITV, we couldn't appear on screen and had to settle for a role behind the cameras. We worked closely with the presenters, Kirsty Gallacher and Jamie Theakston, and it was a great success and a proper event, with a massive crowd and great weather. Sometimes, you have ideas for TV shows and they come to nothing, so to sit back and see what we'd created with *The All\*Star Cup* was a huge buzz.

*The game itself couldn't have been better either. It came down to the eighteenth hole on the final and Ronan Keating sunk the winning putt for Europe to beat America. That evening, we had one of the most bizarre after-show parties we've ever been to. It was quite emotional, everyone was hugging us and thanking us, while we were saying, 'We should be thanking you, all we did was watch.' Chris Evans had tears in his eyes: he told us we'd given him the chance to feel like a professional golfer and that it was the best weekend of his life – and, if you believe everything you read, that man has had some pretty decent weekends in his time (including one that ended with Dec chucking up in his downstairs toilet). In the bar afterwards there was a three-piece band, and everyone got up and did a song – Ronan, James Nesbitt (who, by the way, has got a lovely voice if the acting work ever dries up), Chris Evans – and yes, we had a go too, I'm afraid to say. The last thing I remember is Charlotte Church, who'd accompanied Gavin Henson, one of the European team, murdering 'Summertime' while Michael Douglas, wearing his dressing gown, dragged a tipsy Catherine Zeta Jones to bed. Actually, that may have been while we were singing . . .*

A year later, *The All★Star Cup* transferred to ITV, and this time it was hosted by me and Ant. Being producers and presenters at the same time was hard work, and it also meant we didn't have as much time to get drunk with the teams in the bar, which is of course the most important part of any weekend like that. On the plus side, it meant we didn't sing at the after-show party.

*We went from summer on the golfcourse to winter in the rainforest and* I'm a Celebrity . . . Get Me out of Here! *As you'll know from our 'Day in the Life' plate section, we usually arrive on site around 3 a.m., and the first show of the series is always manic: producers and editors are running round with worried looks on their faces, vehicles are coming and going . . . Our car pulled up to the production office, we clambered out – bleary-eyed, half asleep and not quite sure what day it was, when suddenly, Natalka, the executive producer, came skipping up to us.*

*'Great news – the series has started with a bang!'*

*'Wow, what's happened?' we asked. 'A fight already? A budding romance? Someone's not walked out, have they?' If we were still stood there now, we could never have predicted what she was about to say.*

*'Carol Thatcher's had a piss in the middle of camp and we've got it on camera!'*

*Carol was what's technically known as a 'game old bird'. She was even-*
*tually crowned Queen of the Jungle, but was lucky to make it to the end*
*after one of the trials. It involved driving a Mini Moke, which is a kind of*
*miniature jeep, across a huge ravine. She would be harnessed in, so that,*
*when the Moke inevitably came off its tracks, she would be suspended*
*hundreds of feet up in the air. The problem was that Carol got into the*
*Moke and wanted to start it up before she'd even put the harness on and*
*was seconds away from driving across a ravine with no harness and frankly*
*no chance of surviving. Fortunately, Health and Safety got there in the nick*
*of time. Game old bird, or mad posh lady? You decide.*

*I can clearly remember the moment I started to think Carol was going to*
*do well. My mam works at Marks & Spencer's in Newcastle, and she tells*
*me what everyone thinks of all the contestants. Fairly early in the series, I*
*rang home and spoke to her and she told me that her and all the girls at work*
*really liked Carol – she was a bit batty but prepared to give anything a go.*
*It's always great to get feedback from home, although Dec takes it a bit far,*
*and keeps his mobile switched on while we're doing the live show.*

It might sound unprofessional, and that's because it is, but I
like getting texts during the show, because you get an instant
response to what we're doing. Someone who sends them quite
regularly is David Walliams. One show, he complained that me
and Ant were starting to look a bit lacklustre with our opening
cry of 'I'm a Celebrity . . . Get Me out of Heeeerrrreeeee!' on
the bridge, so we did it with extra enthusiasm the following
day, jumping up and down and looking as excited as possible.
Another one was just to tell me that a jacket I was wearing
looked 'a little bit gay'. He's nice like that, David.

*Cannon and Ball were also in camp that year. It was the first time we'd*
*really had a double act in there, which was great for our links, but a scary*
*glimpse into what the future might hold. The last time we'd seen Tommy*
*and Bobby was about ten years earlier, when the four of us were all on the*
*same episode of Noel's House Party – they were the star guests and we*
*. . . weren't. We were still PJ and Duncan and were playing the Crinkly*
*Bottom paperboys. Now, all these years later, they were down in the jungle,*

*while we were the hosts of the show. The saddest moment was when Tommy was voted out first – him and Bobby seemed a bit lost without each other. You know what double acts are like, they can be pathetically inseparable – some of them even write their autobiographies together.*

We got back home just in time for Christmas, which we celebrated in the only way we knew how – by making a TV show. It was the first and only Christmas special of *Saturday Night Takeaway*, and the guest list was fantastic – Little Ant and Dec came back to interview Matt Lucas and David Walliams, we did a sketch with Ricky Gervais, and a massive musical number with Robbie Williams.

I still think the number with Robbie is one of the best things we've ever done – it involved him singing 'White Christmas', while we, and a huge male choir, kept interrupting him with vocals that were actually more fronting than backing. It was quite a complicated little piece. In fact, we were a bit worried at first that it was a little too complicated for Robbie. When you rehearse with him, he can seem like he isn't listening or paying any attention, but the reality is that he's taking it all in, and on the night, he was, of course, brilliant. He's a complete all-rounder – he can sing, he can dance, he can do sketches and he can act.

*He makes me sick.*

# Chapter 37

*Talking of all-rounders like Robbie Williams, 2006 was the year we approached our career as if it were a tapas menu: we tried a little bit of everything. And first on our list was the nationwide release of* Alien Autopsy. *One of the best things about your own feature film coming out is that you get to go to your own premiere. After all, we'd have looked pretty stupid if we'd paid to go and see* Alien Autopsy *at our local Odeon.*

Unless, I dunno, one of us went in disguise, so they could listen to what people were saying about it . . .

*You didn't?*

Let's just get on with the premieres, shall we? Being greedy, we were given not one, not two, but three premieres. Over three nights, we had one in Leicester Square, one in Dublin and one in Newcastle – and, incredibly, Warner Brothers gave us a private jet to travel around in. Yes, really, they gave us a private jet. To think that the first vehicle we ever travelled around in was my MG Metro Turbo and now we were in a private jet. Nothing makes you feel more like a film star – not even being in a film – than travelling in a private jet.

The Leicester Square premiere was amazing, and Warners' even put us up at the very posh Claridges Hotel for the night. Chiswick is only eight miles away from central London, so don't ask me why we got a hotel, but I certainly wasn't complaining. I told them they could've saved their money and just had the jet fly me back home and land in my back garden, but apparently that's 'against aviation laws' or something – spoilsports. When we were ready to leave Claridges, we said to our publicist, 'We just can't wait to get out on the red carpet' and our publicist said, 'Er, actually, it's not a red carpet, it's a green carpet – you know, 'cos of the aliens?' We were both a bit disappointed – we might only ever have one film premiere in our lives and we'd hoped for a red carpet. Still, you can't have everything, can you?

*The whole evening was unforgettable. Tom Cruise may be famous for spending hours with the crowds and talking to everyone, but we out-Cruised Tom that night. We spent about two and a half hours with the crowds – we spoke to people's mams on their phones, we posed for pictures, signed autographs, we did the lot. In fact, they had to delay the start of the screening, because we were still doing radio interviews in the foyer of the cinema.*

All our friends came to see the film and, afterwards, a lot of them had the same reaction, which was 'It's a proper film, isn't it?' I don't know if they were expecting something with sock puppets filmed in Ant's kitchen, but they seemed genuinely surprised by it.

*The last time we'd been to a premiere in Newcastle was in 1993, to see our last series of Byker Grove at the Civic Centre and, now, thirteen years later, we were at the premiere of our own film in our hometown. We couldn't resist going to Top Shop to buy a new shirt and then covering ourselves in aftershave, just for old times' sake.*

The whole Donnelly clan came that night. My sisters spent months wondering what to wear, skipping dessert so they would fit into their new dresses and planning every last detail. The whole thing was perfect – apart from one moment during the film. I was sat in the front row in between my mam and dad when it suddenly dawned on me: I had completely forgotten that, halfway through *Alien Autopsy*, there's a bit of a racy scene with me and Amber Fuentes, the sexy TV reporter played by Nicole Hiltz. And to make matters worse, you don't see any of the 'raciness', you just hear it. And it's loud. I couldn't believe I hadn't thought about this before, but it would be fine, I tried to tell myself, you're a fully grown man, it's nothing to be ashamed of, it's only acting after all. I failed to convince myself. Just before it came on, I felt myself getting hotter and hotter, and I slunk down into my seat. It was the same feeling you get when you're twelve years old, sat in the front room with your parents, and a sex scene comes on the telly. I blushed like I've never blushed before. I'm glad the lights were dimmed.

*My mam, Davey, Sarha, Robbie and Emma were all there and, of course Boppa, Athey and Goody – although Boppa left about halfway through. When I asked him why, he just looked at me and said, 'It's not really my kind of thing.' You can always rely on your mates to keep you grounded, can't you?*

*It might not have been Boppa's 'kind of thing', but he still came to the party and drank the free beer afterwards, which was good of him. Me and Dec used to co-own a bar in Newcastle, the Lodge, so we had the party there. Even though it was less than a mile away, we tried to get the private jet to take us there from the cinema to our bar, but the pilot refused – 'aviation laws' again. Unbelievable.*

*As for the Dublin premiere, it was amazing, emotional and we were very proud. At least that's what we've been told, I can't remember anything about it – three days of partying had taken its toll by then.*

Once the premieres were over and the film was being shown in cinemas, one of the most exciting moments was when the trailers for it started running on telly – seeing your name and your film advertised on TV for the first time is a really special thrill.

*Speak for yourself. I was at home one day and the trailer came on TV for the very first time. I was out of the room, and Lisa screamed, 'It's on! It's on!' I ran in, sat next to her on the settee and cranked the volume right up. It looked brilliant – it had that gravel-voiced American bloke doing the voiceover, it was edited really well and me and Lisa just looked at each*

*other and smiled. Our smiles froze when, at the end of the trailer, the*
*gravel-voiced American man said, 'Alien Autopsy – starring Declan*
*Donnelly and Anthony McFarland'. I rewound it on Sky Plus two or*
*three times to check, but my ears weren't playing tricks on me, he'd said*
*McFarland, not McPartlin. They'd got my name wrong, and if there's one*
*thing I know, it's that my surname is definitely McPartlin. I was stunned*
*– the first trailer for my first film and they'd got my name wrong.*

*We got in touch with Warner Brothers, and they changed it immedi-*
*ately, but not before it had caused me plenty of embarrassment. Call me*
*old-fashioned, but I thought they should get my name right. You don't see*
*trailers saying, 'Starring Brad Pott' or 'Featuring Julia Rabbits', do you?*

The reaction to *Alien Autopsy* was what people in the industry
called 'mixed'. There were a few critics who didn't like it, but
most people we spoke to thought it was a decent film. We
actually got a bigger response from the public when it was
shown on Sky Movies a year or so later. Although we had our
ups and downs making it, it's still something we're both very
proud of and, if the right script came along, we'd definitely do
a film again.

One thing I will never, ever do again, though, is try and help
out with a baby shower. In 2006, Jonny Wilkes and his wife
Nikki were expecting their first child, and Lisa was hosting a
baby shower at her and Ant's house for Nikki and a load of her
friends. They'd made a 'No Men Allowed' rule, which was perfect, 'cos me, Ant and Jonny could go to the pub but, before
we did, we tried to prove we weren't totally useless by giving
Lisa a hand with the food. Despite my dodgy record with sandwiches and knives, Lisa asked me to cut the crusts off the sandwiches and then take the crusts out to the garden and break
them into pieces for the birds. I managed to finish the first bit
– cutting off the crusts – without any problem, and then I took
the plate out into the garden. While I was out there, I got distracted, went back in and got chatting to Ant and Lisa.

Half an hour or so later, the boys headed to the pub and left
the girls to their baby shower. We had a nice long session and

then headed back to Ant's to feast on what was left of the sausage rolls and bowls of Wotsits, but the moment we set foot in the house, we knew we were in trouble – Lisa had a face like thunder. It transpired that, just at the climax of the baby shower, when all the girls had gathered in the conservatory and Nikki was being given all her presents, one of them happened to glance out of the window and let out a massive scream. They all looked at her, shocked, and she shouted at the top of her voice,

'A rat! There's a rat on the table!'

All the girls spun round to look out of the window, and there was the biggest, fattest rat you've ever seen, happily tucking into the plate of sandwich crusts. Lisa was mortified, and Ant and me were thrown out of the house for the second time that day.

*It wasn't just because we were in the doghouse or, more accurately, the rat-house with Lisa, but shortly after that rodent left my garden, we went up to Newcastle, because we'd been invited to Alan Shearer's testimonial. Ever since we started going to the match together on Boxing Day 1990, we've had quite a history with Newcastle United fans. When we were on Byker Grove, we used to go to the match, and we'd often get stick although, to be fair, it did vary. Some days you'd be surrounded by people who gave you a bit of abuse, and then other times, you'd have people pat you on the back and say, 'Well done, son, good for you,' with that sense of Geordie pride that makes us so, well, proud. As we've had a bit more success, the ridicule has decreased and the pride has increased, which has made going to the match a much nicer experience.*

*In the summer of 2001, we went to a testimonial for Robert Lee, one of the best players ever to pull on a black and white shirt, and we were lucky enough to be sat in the director's box. The game was a bit quiet and, one by one, people on the terraces spotted us. Before we knew it, the whole stand was singing 'Let's Get Ready to Rhumble' followed by a chorus of 'Wonkey Donkey, Wonkey Donkey'. It was genuinely one of the proudest moments of my life. Plus, it was much better than 'What are you doing messing about on Byker Grove, you little poof?'*

Alan Shearer is a god in Newcastle. We'd been asked to go on and interview the great man in the centre circle after the game had finished and, of course, we accepted straight away, because it felt like such an honour for us. It was a huge night for the city – the stadium was packed and, with Celtic as the opposition, the decibel levels in the ground couldn't have been higher. It was being televised, and anyone who's anyone in Newcastle was there, including Jimmy Nail, Sir Bobby Robson, Gazza and Brian Johnson, the lead singer of AC/DC. After the final whistle, we stood at the side of the pitch, ready to walk on to the hallowed turf of the best football stadium in the world. To a standing ovation, Alan did a lap of honour with his kids, finished at the dug-out, took his seat, and then it was over to us.

*This was it, our big moment. We started walking towards the centre circle, and the sound of an announcement on the Tannoy echoed round the stadium:*

*'Ladies and gentlemen, please welcome Ant and Dec!'*

*The hairs on the back of my neck were standing up as we arrived at the centre circle to warm applause. I lifted up my microphone, ready to speak but, before I could say a word, a chant directed at us began to swell from the Gallowgate end – the very end we'd stood together in back in 1990. It quickly gathered momentum and made its way round the ground. We tried to work out exactly what they were saying, it didn't sound like 'There's only one Ant and Dec' or 'Stand up if you love Ant and Dec', or 'Walking in an Ant and Dec wonderland', and then, finally, their words were clearly audible to everybody there and the TV audience at home:*

*'Who are ya? Who are ya? Who are ya?'*

*It was brilliant – it was proper terrace wit, and there was no clever response to it: we just had to stand there and take it. Alan Shearer was sat in the dug-out laughing his head off, and it was a uniquely Geordie way of making sure we kept our feet on the ground. Even though there were 52,000 people ridiculing us, I felt strangely proud.*

*It's not often we can say that our work is seen by people all over the world, but that happened the very same month as Alan Shearer's testimonial match, on a lovely spring day at a little place called Highgrove. We'd been invited back to do a second interview with Prince Charles, and we were joined by two other people – you may have heard of them: William and Harry, they're quite well known on the Prince scene. Five years had passed since we'd interviewed Prince Charles to commemorate twenty-five years of the Prince's Trust and now it was the Trust's thirtieth anniversary. I'll let you into a secret – 2011 will be their thirty-fifth anniversary. Don't ask me how I know this stuff, I'm just connected.*

*When the call came through to our management to ask if we would be interested in doing the first ever interview with all three princes together, we didn't even need to talk about it – you don't say no to royalty, do you? And, besides, we've always thought 'Ant and Dec MBE' has got a nice ring to it. Just like five years earlier, they wanted a more informal interview, and one that would be guaranteed to cover all the work the Trust does, rather than anything too political or heavyweight. Let's face it, being political and heavyweight are two things you could never accuse us two of being, well, not unless we're carrying a bit of holiday fat, which happens from time to time. It would be very easy for us to sit here and say we were honoured, flattered and proud, so we will: we were honoured, flattered and proud. Plus, it was one in the eye for Little Ant and Dec – they'd got Tony Blair, but we'd got one better and got the three princes.*

When we arrived at Highgrove, we were shown into a private room in the main house. The plan was for the five of us to have a cup of tea, a little chat and break the ice before the cameras started rolling. We were being shown into the room by an actual real-life butler when William came down the stairs, and Harry appeared from a room nearby. We all introduced ourselves and, observing royal etiquette, asked the young princes how they would like to be addressed. The immediate answer was 'William' and 'Harry', which seemed easy enough to remember – and obviously we told them we were happy with 'Ant' and 'Dec'.

Just then, William, who was wearing a blue jumper, shirt and chinos, noticed that his younger brother was also sporting a blue jumper, shirt and chino combo. They both eyed each other up, and we could tell they were thinking the same thing:

'Oh no, we can't go on TV wearing identical outfits.' Someone would have to get changed. 'How do these things work themselves out in royal circles?' we thought. 'Does it come down to who's first in line to the throne? Do they get their father, the future king, to adjudicate? Or is everyone just relieved that Harry's picked an appropriate outfit for the occasion for once?' In the end, it came down to one of the oldest laws known to man: William looked at Harry and, with a gesture of the head, said, 'Well, go and get changed then.' After a quick sigh, Harry obediently went off to change his jumper. Big brothers always win. I should know, being the youngest of seven.

After the royal-wardrobe malfunction had been resolved, we made our way into the ice-breaking room (I don't think that was its official title . . .), and that was when Prince Charles came in. We sat opposite the three of them for ten to fifteen minutes of dedicated ice-breaking. Before long, we'd turned to the subject that men fall back on when they don't know what else to talk about – football. William is an Aston Villa fan, while Harry is an Arsenal supporter, and he took great pleasure in ribbing us about Newcastle United. He stopped short of chanting, 'Who are ya? Who are ya? Who are ya?' though. It immediately put us at ease – if there's one thing us two are experienced at, it's being teased about how bad Newcastle are.

*The ice was well and truly broken and we were getting on famously when the tea arrived on a tray in a massive king-sized teapot – although it might have been a future-king-sized pot, I couldn't be sure. The butler put the tray down and backed away from the table. The conversation carried on, and nobody seemed to have any intention of pouring any tea. Then, suddenly, me and Dec had exactly the same thought: 'What's the protocol? Are we supposed to pour? Are they expecting me to pour? If I do pour, am I being presumptuous? What if I pour and spill it?' Being clumsy in front of royalty is not something I was keen to do. One thing was certain: none of the princes had any intention of pouring – they probably have someone to put their socks on for them, they're not likely to bother making tea for a couple of blokes from the west end of Newcastle. It had become very clear – we were locked in a tea stand-off.*

After what seemed like forever, the butler reappeared and made his way towards the tray. He picked up the future-king-sized pot and poured the tea. Oh, the relief. But our problems didn't end there: we quickly realized, now it was poured, it would have to be drunk, and that meant picking up the cup and saucer. I knew my hands would shake because I was so nervous and so, in turn, I became very nervous about showing my nerves, and causing my cup and saucer to rattle in front of the future kings of England. My mouth was so dry by this point that this tea seemed like the most appealing, thirst-quenching beverage in history. I tried to pick it up a couple of times but, after a quick wobble, quickly put it down again.

*Neither of us ever managed a single sip of that tea. It just sat there and went stone-cold. I've never been so thirsty in all my life.*

Finally, and despite the fact that our throats were almost too parched to speak, we went to the main room and did the interview. All three princes were articulate about the Trust, and the interview was going so well that we quickly started straying into other subjects, like music. Before we knew what was happening, William was ribbing us two about our previous life as PJ and Duncan. He explained to his dad that we'd been pop stars – for some reason, PJ and Duncan had passed Prince Charles by, but I suppose he can't make time for everything – and we all had a good laugh about it, or they laughed at us, to be more precise. We asked them if they ever got starstruck meeting any celebrities and Charles answered that he was starstruck by us two. Sitting in front of Prince Charles saying he was starstruck was one of the most surreal things that's ever happened to me, although I don't think he actually was starstruck – he certainly didn't have any problem drinking *his* tea.

*Charles gave most of the answers while William chipped in, and Harry was the classic younger brother – teasing everyone and not taking things too seriously. Walking round the gardens afterwards and admiring the topiary, I asked William and Harry if they had anything to do with how the grounds looked. Had they perhaps chosen any of the – flora and fauna? Harry gave a very short, simple and honest answer: 'No – if it was up to me, the whole thing would be concreted over.' This made me laugh out loud but, fortunately, I don't think Prince Charles heard, although if he's reading this, I've just shot myself in the foot, not to mention put that MBE in serious jeopardy.*

*William explained that tours of the grounds were often given as prizes in charity auctions, which meant that he would regularly wake up, draw open the curtains and see a load of strangers walking around admiring the garden. Which, I suppose, gives strength to Harry's argument. If he had his way, that wouldn't happen – after all, no one wants to go on a tour of a concrete garden, do they?*

Just as with the first Prince Charles interview, there was a big part of us that was thrilled when it was over – it had gone really well and, even better, Conor McAnally hadn't been there to ask about jam. And it's a real privilege to have spent some time with Prince Charles. Whenever we bump into Tara Palmer-Tomkinson, she always tells us that 'Sir says hello' – I'm not sure if he really does, but it's nice of her to say it. We've also seen him at various functions since, and he's always very polite. So, even if Harry Dean Stanton doesn't recognize us, at least Prince Charles does. I'm not sure he would've been any good in *Alien Autopsy*, but Prince Charles gets my vote every time.

*This may be the only book in history to feature Prince Charles and Jonny Wilkes on the same page, but we can't help the people we hang around with, can we? We got to know Jonny and Robbie Williams when we were doing sm:tv, and what cemented our friendship was our weekly West London kickabout together, which also featured, at various stages, Ralf Little, Dane Bowers, Craig David, Brian McFadden and Michael Greco.*

*Before kick-off, opponents, on seeing our squad, would often ask, 'Is the Met Bar shut tonight?'*

*For as long as we've been friends with Jonny and Robbie, those two have been coming up with hare-brained schemes – like the four of us racing across America in the Gumball Rally (for charity), flying to Argentina to challenge Diego Maradona to a game of football (for charity), or putting together an enormous international football event featuring celebrities and legends from around the world (for charity). The last one, Soccer Aid, actually came off – twice.*

By far the most hare-brained of the lot, though, was when they asked us to join them on stage in front of a stadium full of people. At the time, Robbie was in the middle of his world tour and, every night, he'd do a little set with Jonny where they'd perform 'Me and My Shadow'. They decided it would be a laugh if me and Ant joined them for Robbie's concert in Milton Keynes. In front of 65,000 people. Like the Gumball Rally, we didn't think it would ever happen; the next thing we knew we were getting measured up for jackets to match Jonny's and Robbie's.

Every night, at the start of the show, Robbie would make his entrance by coming up through a trap door and on to the stage, and it was decided Ant and me would be introduced in the same way. The plan was that Jonny and Robbie would say they thought they were the best double act in Britain, at which point, we would pop up through the same trap door and put them right.

*Using Robbie's trap door, the pair of us shot up on to the stage, much to the surprise of the 65,000 watching the concert, and proceeded to take the two of them to task over their claims.*

*'Who do you two think you are?' Robbie said with mock incredulity.*

*We both looked at him. 'Who do we think we are? Who do we think we are? We used to be PJ and Duncan.'*

*Immediately, 'Let's Get Ready to Rhumble' began booming out of the PA system. The whole place went absolutely bananas. It was amazing. As*

*they screamed, I looked out at the crowd, shook my head and just smiled*
*– no matter where Dec and me go, no matter what we do, that song will*
*follow us for the rest of our lives. As the crowd sang along to our number-nine*
*smash, we laughed our heads off. But it was a great feeling, and we felt*
*strangely proud. Then, as planned, Robbie asked for the music to be cut.*
*What wasn't planned, though, was the crowd's reaction. They let out an*
*almighty chorus of boos. Robbie and Jonny looked shocked and even slightly*
*hurt. 'Hang on,' pleaded Rob. 'You can't boo me – it's my name on the*
*ticket.' The four of us performed his hit 'Strong' together and had a really*
*great time doing it. We were messing around like mates do, except on a*
*stage in front of a packed-out stadium.*

Those ten fateful minutes on stage in Milton Keynes had
whetted our appetite, and we realized what we'd been missing. Me and Ant immediately hatched a plan to hit the road
with our own tour. We instructed our management to make
all the necessary arrangements and start selling tickets. We
began to work on new material for what would be our fourth
album and put in a call to Truck Fest 2006: 'Keep those cows
where they are, the boys are coming back.'

*No, we didn't – we went back to the hotel and got drunk.*

Oh yeah, thank God for that.

# Chapter 38

Marriage is a sacred and special thing but, before a man takes his vows, it's very important he experiences humiliation and embarrassment in front of his closest friends or, as it's otherwise known, a stag do. As Ant's best man, my first big decision was that he should have not one but two stag dos – I know, I spoil him, don't I? One was in London and one was in Latvia, which, believe it or not, is a very popular destination for people who want to humiliate their friends.

The London one was first, and it featured all the usual suspects – Boppa, Athey, Goody, and most of our golf posse. We were also joined by Robbie and Jonny later in the evening.

The theme was the Monopoly Board. Don't worry, we didn't spend the day playing board games – especially not after the trouble we had with the *Who Wants to be a Millionaire?* one. The Monopoly approach to stag dos is fairly common and it involves a pub crawl round the monopoly board. You start at a pub on the Old Kent Road at eleven o'clock in the morning and finish up in Mayfair at eleven in the evening.

*That's not quite the whole story, is it?*

Oh yeah, I almost forgot, the stag gets either Community Chest or a Chance card in each pub, just like the board game. The card will typically say something like 'Congratulations, you've won a beauty contest,' and then the stag will get made up and dressed as a beauty queen. Looking back, it's hard to know which one of the costumes Ant was forced to wear I enjoyed most – the gay biker, the chav, and Wolf from *Gladiators* all spring to mind.

*I'll never forget, as the full-time whistle went in England's World Cup warm-up game against Jamaica, leaving the pub to head to McDonald's for some much-needed sustenance. And the reason I'll never forget it is because I was dressed as a French maid – thanks a lot, Dec.*

You're welcome. I'd also like to point out that, as the best man, I took precautions to make sure things ran smoothly. Normally, you'd travel around London on the tube as part of the Monopoly-board stag do, but I decided the easiest – not to mention safest – thing to do was hire a minibus – and, out of my own pocket, a security guard to keep an eye on the groom.

*That's supposed to be the best man's job – to be sensible and keep an eye on the groom.*

I know – and that's exactly why I had to pay a responsible adult to do it. Despite the precautions I took, there was still the odd hitch. We got snapped by the paparazzi pretty early on, and whoever took those pictures obviously sent them back to the newsdesk of one of the tabloids and, from that, some bloodhound of a journalist worked out we were doing the Monopoly-board route, and knew exactly where we'd be for the rest of the day.

Later that night, we were in a pub when a bunch of girls came over, had a bit of a chat and had their picture taken with me and Ant. We didn't think anything much of it – well, apart from the fact that Ant was dressed as a gay biker, but that was par for the course that day. The next day, the *Sunday People* ran a story by a journalist called Alice Walker who was 'the only journalist to be invited on Ant's stag do'. She was one of the girls in the pub – she turned the chat she'd had with us into an interview and used the snap she'd taken on her camera phone to make it look like she'd been there the whole time. They're crafty types, those journalists.

*If I thought that, after a day of parading around London dressed up in various outfits, things couldn't get any more embarrassing, I was wrong because, at the end of the night, we managed to leave Lisa's dad, Derek, behind. Not a wise move. We'd all gone back to Chiswick in the minibus, and I was staying at Dec's, so when we pulled up and all fell out of the bus, Lisa came out of the front door. Straight away, I was full of drunken bravado: 'You can't say anything to me, no matter how drunk I am, I'm the stag and I'm staying at Dec's tonight.' She smiled sweetly and, after a short pause, replied, 'Where's my dad?' I went white as a sheet: somehow we'd managed to leave him all alone in Central London. Fortunately for him and, more importantly, for me, one of the other lads on the stag had picked him up in a cab and brought him back to ours later, but it was a very close shave.*

The Latvian leg of the stag do was even more hardcore than the London one although, on the plus side, Ant did at least get to wear his own clothes. And I should point out that, while we were away, we didn't just drink solidly for the whole three days. We enjoyed two other activities – go-karting and shooting guns although, fortunately, not at the same time. We went to a shooting range and, although we were assured it was all official and licensed, it did seem to be mainly based around a bloke's shed and a table of guns and ammo in his garden.

The guy running it could only speak three words of English, which were 'Hello', 'Shoot' and 'Goodbye'. He had a couple of targets at the bottom of the garden which we all took shots at. The other thing that made me suspect it wasn't 100 per cent safe was that we had to avoid his washing when we aimed at the target. Still, that and an hour's go-karting kept us from spending seventy-two hours drinking – I think it was about sixty-eight hours in the end. The important thing is that Ant had a good time on both stag dos, and he survived the whole thing. Plus, if we ever fall out, I can always blackmail him with pictures of him dressed in that French maid's outfit.

*I got married on the 22 July 2006 at St Nicholas Church in the beautiful Berkshire village of Taplow. Me and Lisa were offered lots of money to sell our wedding to various magazines. You can probably guess which ones but, just in case, I'll give you a clue — it wasn't* Auto Trader. *It was never about money to us, though, this was a personal day to share with our friends and families and not something we wanted to see on the shelves of W. H. Smith. We looked at quite a few venues, and settled for Cliveden House in Berkshire. Cliveden is set in 376 acres of National Trust parkland and overlooks the River Thames and was built in 1666 as a hunting lodge for the second duke of Buckingham. In later years, it was regularly visited by Queen Victoria and, now, me, a lad from Fenham, was getting married there.*

*I asked my old mates Boppa, Athey and Goody, plus Lisa's brother, Stephen, my step-brother Robbie and my brother-in-law, John, to be ushers, and kitted them out with tailor-made suits from Tom Baker, the master tailor who makes most of our suits for our TV shows. And, of course, as best man, Dec got a suit too.*

Took you long enough to book me as best man though, didn't it? The only reason you actually asked me was because Lisa made you.

*That's not strictly true.*

It strictly is true. Let me fill you in, readers. When Ant and Lisa came back from Dubai, we held a little engagement drinks party for them, and then they got on with organizing their wedding. To be fair, I did assume I would get the best-man gig, but he'd never actually asked me outright. A month or two after the engagement, I was round at his one day, and he made a joke about something to do with the wedding, then he said, 'Well, you'd better know that you're my best man.' 'Am I?' I replied, then Lisa pitched in with, 'Well, have you actually asked him?', to which Ant said, 'No, I just assumed . . . so, will you . . . be my best man?', and of course I said yes — it was never one of those dramatic, blood-brothers moments, although we did go round the corner for a pint to celebrate.

22 July was an incredibly hot day, and getting hitched went off without any hitches. Dec didn't even forget the rings – in fact, he didn't even pretend to forget the rings.

It was amazing. Lisa looked beautiful. She was wearing an incredible ivory satin dress with a lace bolero jacket and a tiara. She looked absolutely stunning as she walked down the aisle. As well as being the happiest day of my life, it was also the hottest day of my life. Everyone in the church was fanning themselves with their order-of-service sheets; it was like getting married in Louisiana. As Lisa approached, I realized I was pouring with sweat: it was literally running down my face. Fortunately, she grabbed a hanky from her dad, who was walking her up the aisle, and when she arrived at the altar, passed it to me. I can still see that hanky now: it was embroidered with a picture of one of my favourite men in the world, some-one who's been an inspiration to me for years – Homer Simpson. I grate-fully mopped my brow but didn't notice that the embroidery on the hanky had left scratches all over my face. I looked like I'd been dragged through a bramble bush. Luckily, the scratch marks had disappeared by the time we got our photos taken.

After the ceremony, we made our way back to Cliveden for the cham-pagne reception and wedding breakfast. As part of the day, we'd booked a magician, who was going to work the tables doing close-up, sleight-of-hand magic, although he almost didn't make it into the venue. When Lisa and me first arrived, we were waiting outside, ready to be called in for that bit where the bride and groom arrive and everyone claps. I looked over and there was this guy sitting there in a black suit hanging around, and neither me nor Lisa recognized him, I thought he was a photographer or a journal-ist, and we were about to have him thrown out. One of the security guys went up and asked who he was, and he told us he was the magician and he was waiting for everyone to arrive before he came in – he'd nearly man-aged to make himself disappear before he'd even started work.

We had two rooms for the meal – there were so many people there that we couldn't fit them all into one. Before the food arrived, I quickly went round all the tables to thank everyone for coming. One of the last tables I spoke to had Ed, who executive produces Takeaway, and Andy, our scriptwriter, on it, and I chatted away for a couple of minutes and then ended by saying something funny. The whole table laughed, and I walked *off at the perfect moment, slick as you like, and opened the door that would take me back to the next room. There was only one problem – it wasn't the door to the next room, it was the door to the cleaning cupboard. I'd had a tableful of people in stitches, and opened a door that revealed an ironing board and a couple of bottles of bleach. It got a bigger laugh than anything I said at the ceremony.*

*Before the wedding, we were both given one piece of advice: make sure you spend some time together on the day; everyone will be wanting a word with you both, but make sure you spend time together, which we did. After an incredible afternoon at Cliveden House, it was speeches time. We headed to the grand staircase, Lisa took her seat on a throne that looked like it might actually have been used by Queen Victoria and was flanked by me and Dec.*

Ant had told me he was just going to do a really quick speech and that would be it – he said he wasn't going to do loads of gags, he'd keep it simple and say his thank-yous. The liar. He did a brilliant speech that went down an absolute storm. It was almost as if he'd spent half his life performing to big groups of people. Lisa's dad went next and did the same – everyone loved it. By the time it got to me, I was in a right panic. I might be a natural show-off, but being your best mate's best man is a different kettle of fish. I've never been so nervous – my mouth was too dry to even swallow the glass of wine in front of me, and the paper was shaking in my hand. Forget drinking tea in front of Prince Charles, making a film, hosting TV shows or performing at Truck Fest, this was the toughest gig of my life.

I'd put off writing my speech until a week before and, even then, I didn't know where to start. In the end, I decided to start at the beginning – I'm clever like that. I sat down in front of my laptop with a blank page looking back at me and just started to write. Ant was born two months premature, so I started there and pretty much cracked jokes at his expense from that point on. I finished it in an afternoon, printed it off and just hoped it was good. The night before the wedding, I got the opportunity to have a practice run. All the lads got together for dinner after a day's golf, including Jonny Wilkes, who unfortunately wouldn't be staying for the wedding, as he had a prior engagement that he reckoned he couldn't wriggle out of – it was performing to 80,000 people at the San Siro stadium in Milan with Robbie which, when you think about it, is a pretty decent excuse. Jonny really wanted to hear my speech, and I realized I'd only ever practised it out loud to myself on the sofa, so this would give me an audience – and a welcome rehearsal.

I read it from start to finish, putting in all the pauses, hitting the punchlines bang on, and finished the whole thing by telling Ant and Lisa how proud and happy I was to be part of their big day. I finally got to the end, looked up and saw Jonny sitting there with tears running down his face. He looked at me and said, 'It's beautiful,' then I started crying too. I thought, 'How the hell am I going to do this to a full room?'

Of course, the following day I found out when the big moment arrived – I stepped up to a round of applause, took the mic from Lisa's dad, looked down at the sheet of words in front of me, up to the expectant faces in the room and began to talk and talk and talk. For five pages. Somehow I got through it, and it seemed to go down okay . . .

*'Okay?' Don't be so modest, it was fantastic. The speech was perfect – it was emotional, touching, moving but, most of all, it stitched me up an absolute treat. I've got your speech written out here. It included gems like:*

*Most of the stories I wanted to tell about Ant would have got him strung up by his mam; a lot of the others would have got me strung up by my mam; and the rest of them involved Ant stringing himself up in a pair of fishnet tights.*

*And also:*

*He's been a brilliant friend to me over the years, he was there when I broke my nose playing football. In fact, he broke it. He was there when I split up with my girlfriend, he was there when I fell off a motorbike while filming and broke my arm. In fact, come to think of it, you've been a bloody jinx!*

*After the speech, Dec moved on to the telegrams, and the first three were:*

*To Ant and Lisa, congratulations! To our no. 1 customers, from everyone at the Crown and Anchor.*

*To Ant and Lisa, our best customers! Hope you have a wonderful day, from everyone at Thresher.*

*To Lisa and Ant, wishing our best customers lots of luck, from Hounslow Council Bottle-Recycling Team.*

*It was hilarious. He'd really taken a lot of time on it, and that's not something you can always say with Dec: he usually loses interest in things pretty quickly. After the speeches, me and Lisa went back to our room to freshen up and, when we re-entered the main hall, it was time for our first dance.*

*The band played Burt Bacharach's 'This Guy's in Love with You'. Years earlier, when Lisa and me first met, I had that song on an old Telstar CD in mine and Dec's flat, and it became 'our song' – that's mine and Lisa's, by the way; me and Dec don't have a song, that would just be weird. When we were in the studio with Ray 'Mad Man' Hedges working on the second album, I actually recorded a version of it, with me singing, and gave it to Lisa. Incidentally, the best version of it ever is the Sacha Distel one, which I've still never been able to find, so if anyone out there can find it, give me a shout, eh?*

*After our first dance, it was time to party, and the next song the band played was the Kaiser Chiefs' 'I Predict a Riot'. And, let me tell you, the Kaiser Chiefs' lyrics proved to be very accurate.*

**There wasn't actually a riot, I'd like to make that clear, we just had a great time.**

*Me and the new Mrs McPartlin left the wedding reception at 2 a.m. in a carriage that took us down to the cottage in the grounds of Cliveden. When we arrived, the staff there had laid out all our presents and cards and a lovely spread of food, all of which was surrounded by candles. It was beautiful and, two days later, we went off on honeymoon to the Maldives, where we spent an idyllic two weeks together.*

I was absolutely lost without him – I even considered flying out there, but when I texted Ant to find out the name of his hotel, he never replied.

# Chapter 39

As officially the busiest year of our lives, both privately and professionally, 2006 was also when we devised, hosted and sold our first gameshow, *Poker Face*, which, I should say right from the off, was nothing to do with hitting people in the face with a poker. It was 'the question-and-answer quiz with an element of bluff'. The idea was basically to play poker with questions instead of cards, so the contestants had to bluff about whether they knew any of the answers.

We tried it out with a few friends in the upstairs room of our local pub, and it seemed to work, so we went and pitched it to ITV. We met with Nigel Pickard, who was now the Director of Programmes, and Claudia Rosencrantz, who was still the Controller of Entertainment, at Soho House, a private members' bar and restaurant in the middle of London.

At the dinner, we'd talked about *Takeaway* and *I'm a Celebrity . . .*, as planned, and then we told them about our idea for a gameshow. 'Great,' Nigel said, 'as long as it's not another bloody question-and-answer quiz – I'm sick of them; all I ever get is question-and-answer quizzes.' Never easily put off, we thought on our feet and asked him if he'd had a question-and-answer quiz where you don't have to understand any of the questions or know any of the answers to win. He and Claudia both looked intrigued and, after a glass of wine, agreed to a pilot.

We did two series of Poker Face, with the winner of each final taking away £1 million – I know, £1 million. It was an incredible feeling to know that a show we'd invented would change people's lives for ever. The format has since been sold to, at the last count, fifteen countries, including India, Columbia and Norway – apparently, it's also very big in Portugal. A couple of years after we'd made the British version, we were in Australia *after finishing a series of* I'm a Celebrity . . . *and we went to Sydney to see Robbie Williams, who was playing a gig at the Telstra Stadium. There was a TV on backstage; and a trailer for the Australian version of* Poker Face *came on. It was a bizarre moment. I think it was just after* Neighbours *and right before* Home and Away.

We might have had an international TV hit on our hands, but we weren't ready to rest on our laurels. We'd told the new production team on *Takeaway* that we wanted the latest series to really hit the heights, but what they came up with wasn't really what we'd had in mind. The first Ant versus Dec challenge of that series was one of the scariest things we've ever done – and that includes an interview with John Lydon. We had to abseil down the side of the London Studios – on live TV. I still can't quite believe we did it, but it was sprung on us during the live show and we didn't have any time to really think about it. If we'd had a week of rehearsals, like we do with a lot of things, I'm not sure we would have gone through with it but, live, on the night, we just went for it.

*As usual, the challenge was revealed to us just before an ad break. During that break, we got changed, and went up to the roof. Some Royal Marines talked us through what was about to happen. Their first tip was that we shouldn't, on any account, look over the edge. I listened to what they said very carefully, took it all in and then looked over the edge. It was terrifying, and I immediately regretted it. I'd been relatively calm up till then.*

*Next thing I remember was a marine strapping me in and saying, 'There you go, Dec.' He was about to send me down the side of a twenty-four-floor building and he didn't even know which one was Ant and which one was Dec. He told me to go down slowly, because if you hit the ground too fast you can injure yourself and, after Dec's trouble with the motorbike, the last thing we needed was more casualties. Once we were harnessed in, a Klaxon sounded and off we went. Just like I'd been told, I went slowly, then I looked over at Dec, who was ahead of me and going much faster, which was really annoying, because no matter how scared you are, you still get into the competitive spirit.*

I'll be honest with you, once I'd gone off the roof, I just couldn't wait to get to the bottom – partly because we're both so competitive and partly because any sane person would. I remember going past all the floors of the building, looking through the windows and thinking, 'I can't believe how dirty those windows are . . . that's a very messy desk, how can anyone work in such a mess?'

*That's what it takes to get you domesticated? Live abseiling?*

I think so, yeah. It was incredible, exhilarating and terrifying all at the same time. As soon as I got to the bottom, I had a moment where I had an important realization.

*That we'd completed an incredible stunt?*

No – that I'd won.

*It was only in the pub the next day that the madness of what we'd done really dawned on us. A few people came up to us, saying how crazy they thought it was – some of them even bought us a drink, which, odd as it might sound, isn't unusual when we're in a pub together. Because we're matey and laid-back on telly, people think they can just come up and say anything to us. It's not uncommon for us to be sat in the pub having a drink with friends and for someone to pull up a chair and say, 'All right, lads?', join in our conversation and start trying to take the Mickey out of us. After a couple of minutes, they're telling me how big my forehead is, or trying to crack jokes about Dec's height. You can always spot those kind of people when you walk into a pub: they clock you early on and then, by the time they've had a couple of pints, well, it's anyone's game.*

I suppose if we really wanted to avoid it, we shouldn't stay longer than a couple of pints, but where's the fun in that? We'd be home by 9.30 every night.

*I was in a pub once and there was an old guy sat on his own, nursing a half of bitter. I felt a bit sorry for him, we got chatting at the bar and I bought him a pint.*

**You got a round in – did they put a plaque up?**

*Later, as I was leaving, he looks at me and says, 'Hey, you're getting fat, mind.' I couldn't believe it.*

**You *were* carrying a little bit of holiday weight back then.**

*That's not the point. I don't go to people's work place and tell them I don't like what they're doing, so it's hard when they come up to you and say, 'Your haircut's s\*\*\* and you're fatter than you look on the telly.'*

**You're absolutely right.**
    **That *is* funny about you getting fat though.**

*In November of 2006, we flew out for the sixth series of* I'm a Celebrity . . . *and, two days before the show started, I got some terrible news from home. My Nanna Kitty had passed away. Getting the news while I was on the other side of the world was really tough and, of course, I immediately wanted to fly back for the funeral, but my mam wouldn't have it. My mam was furious when I suggested it, she said that Nanna wouldn't have wanted me to come home. I thought about it long and hard, spoke to Sarha about it on the phone and had a long conversation with Dec, and I decided to stay in Australia. The first show of that series was dedicated to Nanna. Of all the shows we do,* I'm a Celebrity . . . *was her favourite, so I like to think that dedication would have meant a lot to her. You couldn't hope to meet a prouder grandma than my nanna – when she was in hospital, she insisted on telling every single person who her grandson was, whether they liked it or not. Of course I still miss her terribly, and I know she'd love the fact that she's in this book.*

**Although Ant had a very difficult start to that series, things gradually got back to normal, and that trip ended up providing**

one of our most memorable TV moments. Wherever we are and whatever we're doing, there are four words that are guaranteed to put a smile on our faces: 'Dean', 'Gaffney', 'live', 'trial'. Live Bushtucker Trials are, to put it mildly, a bit of an unknown quantity, and little did we know we were about to be involved in the greatest one ever.

*It was also the most unprofessional you've ever been on telly.*

*If you didn't see it, well, get on youtube and have a look and, if you did see it, then allow me to refresh your memory. Former EastEnder Dean Gaffney arrived in Australia halfway through the series and was thrust into the limelight with a live Bushtucker Trial called Bush Spa. It involved Dean sticking his head, feet and pretty much anything else you can imagine into sinks, buckets and containers full of a wide variety of critters and creepy crawlies. To say Dean went for it would be the understatement of the century.*

Just thinking about it, I'm laughing already. Dean was already slightly in shock because he knew he was about to go straight into the camp, but when he was told he'd immediately be facing a live trial, he went into a kind of weird heightened state that was part shock, part excitement and part madness.

We were standing in the clearing, waiting for the live show to start, and Dean was already all over the place. Before the opening titles had even been played, he'd been sick in a bush and, after that, things just got worse. He couldn't stop dry retching, and I thought he was going to faint. Ant had to hold on to him so he could keep his balance – I must say that, throughout the whole trial, Ant was brilliant.

*Well, someone had to be – you were no use. While I was holding up a vomiting soap star, Dec was laughing. And I'm not just talking a little giggle or a snigger, I'm talking full-on hysterics.*

I lost it – I completely and utterly lost it – my face was hurting with laughter even before we started.

*Dean was terrified of everything. He spent the whole trial screaming and yelping and retching, and it was hilarious. We had to try and calm him down, but it was pretty pointless. And, by the way, he swore like an absolute trooper. There's a slight delay on the TV, so it was dipped as much as possible but, being right there, we got pure, 100 per cent uncensored Gaffney. Halfway through the trial, we threw in a break, which gave us all the chance to have a bit of a breather – quite literally, in Dean's case, as Medic Bob came in and clamped an oxygen mask to his face.*

Well, that just set me off again.

*No one has ever, ever responded to a Bushtucker Trial like that – not even Paul Burrell – and I'll be astounded if anyone ever does again.*

Afterwards, it was impossible to know if it had been great entertainment, or a slightly disturbing piece of television. It was either one of the best bits of telly we'd ever done, or a career-ending mistake. I actually felt a bit guilty. I'd spent half an hour laughing solidly at someone else's misfortune.

We went back up to our office on site and both turned our phones on. We had over one hundred text messages between us. We often get texts about the show, but this was off the scale – and people loved it, absolutely loved it. I was so relieved.

*In eight series of* I'm a Celebrity . . ., *it's by far my favourite moment. It just goes to show that you can never predict what will happen on that show. Who'd have thought the bloke who used to walk Wellard round Albert Square would provide such TV gold?*

Apart from Dean, the big star of that series was David Gest, who was another great example of how the show can change the public's opinion of someone. Before he was voted out, he formed a very sweet friendship with Jason Donovan and Matt Willis. It was the most open series we've ever done – no one had a clue who was going to win. The last three were Matt,

Jason and Myleene Klass, who'd also succeeded in changing what the public thought of her. And she did that by showing the viewers every single side of her. Literally – that white bikini was a masterstroke.

*There was a reason Matt won it. It wasn't the fact he's a nice guy, which he is, or that he got on with everyone, which he did, it was the fact that he ate a kangaroo's anus on national television. If that doesn't make people pick up the phone, I don't know what will. It's amazing how immune we've got to the horrible things that are eaten in those trials. In the early days, when Uri Geller chowed down on a wichety grub, it turned our stomachs, but these days we think nothing of watching the celebrities munch their way through eyes, tongues, penises and testicles. And while we're here, I should just say that what you see on your telly is a very edited-down version of what happens. Trust me, it takes a long, long time to chew a testicle before it pops. And, as for chewing a penis, well, it's three times longer than it looks at home.*

You might want to rephrase that.

*Right, yeah, I meant the length of the chewing, not the length of the actual penis. Anyway, hats off to Matt Willis – he ate that kangaroo's anus and he won the show.*

That's what I love about writing this book – it shows that we're not just performers, we're intellectuals too.

If we thought that, after watching the bass player from Busted chew a kangaroo's anus, our job couldn't get any stranger, we were wrong. For most of the previous year, we'd been talking on and off to Simon Cowell's production company, Syco TV, about a new show called *Britain's Got Talent*. We'd been sent tapes of the US version, which we both really enjoyed, but we thought the host's role wasn't as clearly defined as it could be. After much to-ing and fro-ing, we agreed to host the show on two conditions: (1) there was a clear role for us two and (2) Simon Cowell was one of the judges. We thought that, five years after *Pop Idol* had finished, people would be interested in seeing the three of us on screen together again. Even though we love poking fun at him, we respect Simon a lot and enjoy working with him enormously.

After a while, we all came to an agreement and, before we knew it, we were back on the road, and ready for the most important part of any talent show – the auditions.

*Piers Morgan had signed up to join Simon on the judging panel, and the third judge, a female, was still to be confirmed. The producers were confident it would be Cheryl Cole but, for one reason or another, Cheryl never became a* Britain's Got Talent *judge and the job instead went to Amanda Holden. Initially, what really appealed to us about the show was the fact that anybody of any age and any talent could enter, and the uniqueness of the prize – a spot on the bill at the Royal Variety Performance.*

When it came to the auditions, we were very conscious of making sure our own role on the show was clear. As well as doing links and interviewing the acts, our most important role was, again, to stand at the side of the stage, watching the auditions. As with *I'm a Celebrity* . . ., our job was to be the voice of the audience – and, of course, to laugh at people when they did stupid things. What can I say? We have a gift. We found that, as we travelled round the country, the audience reactions differed a lot. The further north you go, the more vicious the crowds get. Cardiff can be quite sedate, London's not too bad but, by the time you get to Glasgow, the acts have got about ten seconds to impress before the crowds starts chanting 'Cheerio, cheerio, cheerio' in a thick Scottish accent. Forget Cowell and Morgan – the nastiest judges are always the ones sitting in the audience.

I dread to think how us two would have fared as teenagers auditioning for the show. If I'd come out with a cabbage on a dog lead while Dec was reciting 'There's a one-eyed yellow idol to the north of Kathmandu' it would have been three buzzes in quick succession, a series of no's from the judges and all sorts of abuse from the audience. I take my hat off to each and every single act who has the bottle to give it a go, or at least I would do, if I wore hats.

It's not always easy to look at an act and tell if they're any good or not. The winner of the first series was mobile-phone salesman turned opera singer Paul Potts, and he didn't exactly scream star quality. When he went on stage, there was an audible groan from the audience. And, I must confess, from the wings.

*We'd interviewed Paul before he went on, and he didn't give us much – it was mainly yes or no answers, and he wasn't exactly overflowing with funny anecdotes about the Carphone Warehouse. So when he shuffled apologetically on to the stage and said he was going to sing opera, we both had exactly the same thought: 'Let's go and grab a sandwich.' We weaved our way through the dark and dusty corridors of the theatre, got to our dressing room, sat down, tucked in, and then heard this sound coming over the Tannoy: it was Paul, and he had the most incredible voice you've ever heard. Being as professional as ever, we did the sensible thing – stuffed down the rest of the tuna baguette and legged it back to the side of the stage. We caught Paul on the way off and, that day, we realized two things: it was going to be a great series and, after missing Paul, we'd now have to interview every single act in the competition, just as we had with series two of* Pop Idol *after we'd missed Will Young in the first one. Hmm, there's a pattern emerging here . . .*

During *BGT*, we're filmed non-stop in the wings. Somewhere in the bowels of ITV, there are hundreds of hours of unused footage of us two talking absolute gibberish.

I have to admit, there *are* days when we get slightly delirious and just try to make each other laugh – mainly with things that we know will never make it on to the telly. I'm afraid I can't give you any examples, for the same reason they're not broadcast. In fact, there's one sure-fire way you can tell that we think what we're saying won't be used. If Ant is drinking a latte, then we're pretty sure we're in the clear.

*After the auditions were over, we had to give the most important autograph of our entire career, when we signed our latest contract with ITV. By this point, we'd been exclusive to them for seven years and with three returning shows that we loved doing for different reasons, we weren't interested in going anywhere else. The new contract would take us up to the end of 2009 and it was reported to be the biggest deal in UK TV history. There's a very good reason we're telling you that fact – not because we're a couple of show-offs, but because of the effect it had on one man – Simon Cowell. The previous December, Simon had signed his new ITV deal, which, at the time, was reported to be the biggest ever – at least it was, until we signed our new contract. Simon later told us that he heard about our deal over breakfast one morning, and he swears that the news curdled his porridge and turned his milk sour. Turning that man's milk sour ranks as one of our greatest achievements.*

Aside from ruining the Prince Of Darkness's breakfast, it was also an incredibly proud moment for both of us. After our first exclusive deal, that we signed in the car next to the news-agents in between rehearsals for *sm:tv*, we'd come a long way – we'd worked incredibly hard behind the scenes to get shows like *Takeaway*, *I'm a Celebrity* . . . and *Britain's Got Talent* right, and this was recognition of that. The ink was hardly dry on the contract when we headed straight for the studios to host the first live shows of *Britain's Got Talent* – where we'd watch dozens of acts, find the country's best undiscovered performer and, best of all, really tease Simon Cowell about our new contract.

# Chapter 40

*The next project we embarked on couldn't have been more different - or more heartbreaking - because we made an appeal film for Comic Relief. We've done stuff in the studio in the past, but this time we wanted to do something different, and we ended up going to visit some of the projects they fund in Kibera in Kenya. We both remember buying red noses when we were at school, and going to Kibera would give us the opportunity to see some of the projects first hand and try to raise as much money as possible for a very worthwhile cause.*

No matter how many films you've watched and how much footage you've seen of the terrible conditions people live in, nothing can prepare you for what you see when you go there. One of the most striking things about our trip was just how close poverty and luxury coexisted – they were virtually side by side, and we stayed in a hotel very close to areas that are brutally affected by poverty.

*On our first morning in Kibera, we got into a car with the director and the cameraman. The way they work is very clever – they hardly tell you anything, because the best way is to discover everything for yourself so they get a genuine reaction on camera. The journey to the slums, incredibly, took hardly any time at all. Bizarre as it sounds, we turned left at PC World, then down a dirt track and, suddenly, we were there – in the middle of the biggest slum in Africa. There are one and a half million people there, all living and eating and washing in what is essentially a giant rubbish tip. There were kids going through bins, and people would empty their toilets into a stream that, fifty metres further away, children were washing in.*
*It seems obvious to say it, but it was heartbreaking. We were in shock. We spent the first day looking around the place and talking to*

*some of the project managers, but by far the toughest part of it was the second day.*

That was when we met children and families who lived there. You just can't comprehend how people can live like that – day in, day out. A big part of the film was about the living conditions, and we spent some time in a tiny shack that thirteen people lived in together. Thirteen people. They showed us how they slept at night – lying top to toe with nothing but plastic covering on the floor. The room must have been eight foot by eight foot and, because it was so small, the few belongings they did have were hanging from the ceiling on pieces of string. I just kept thinking, 'How the hell do they keep going?' Every night, they just lie together in this cold, filthy environment, starving hungry. I was overcome by the enormity of the situation. They were a large, loving family unit, exactly like the one that I had come from, and yet they had less than the basic requirements for human survival. I had to walk away and try to pull myself together, but I could feel the emotion swelling inside me, and I burst into tears.

*It was a complete tragedy, but the positive thing was that, by going there, we hoped it would make people donate and realize how terrible things are. I think we were both very proud that, in some small way, with that visit, we could draw attention to those people's problems and try to change their lives for the better.*

There's no easy way to follow a section about *Comic Relief*, so I'm just going to take you on a trip to America.

After a failed attempt to get *Saturday Night Takeaway* made in America a few years earlier, in 2007 we finally got to make a series there – and we didn't even have to listen to a vertically challenged bloke playing 'Don't Let the Sun Go Down on Me' to make it happen. In January, we'd had a meeting with Andrea Wong, the President of Entertainment at ABC. On the day of the meeting, we'd just had typhoid and yellow-fever injections for our *Comic Relief* trip to Kenya, so we weren't on the greatest form. That, and the fact that we'd already had our fingers burnt with the American version of *Takeaway*, meant that we were fairly indifferent to the idea of cracking America.

Although it wasn't a deliberate ploy, it seemed our indifference worked a treat because, a few weeks later, Andrea rang up and told us she had a show she wanted us to host. It was called *Wanna Bet?*, and it was going to be an American version of a show we knew in Britain as *You Bet*, which had been hosted by Bruce Forsyth, Matthew Kelly and Darren Day – not together, by the way, at different times.

*Working out there, we quickly discovered there were lots of differences between making a TV series in England and making one in America – and not all of them were good. For a start, there were the floor managers. Most of the shows we do in the UK are floor-managed by our good friend Alan Conley. He's brilliant at his job, totally reliable and now owes us another £50 for bigging him up in this book. In LA, we had two floor managers, Donny and Steve, two old West Coast hippies in their fifties, and to say they were slightly laid-back is like saying Simon Cowell is slightly critical.*

*When it came to do the first show, we were both very nervous – this was our American network television debut and we were working in a country where no one really knew who we were. Phil Gurin, the producer, had prepared what's called a 'sizzle tape', which was basically designed to introduce us to the audience – it featured us interviewing the three princes, working with Simon Cowell, shooting our film, and basically anything that would make an American audience think we were kind of a big deal.*

*On the day of the first show, they played the tape in the studio. It went down a storm. We came out on to the stage to a standing ovation, the audience were clapping and cheering, they laughed at our jokes and the whole show went like a dream. We came off stage on such a high. We couldn't believe how well it had gone. This was it, we were going to crack America – mansions, limos and our own swimming pools were surely around the corner.*

'I like to live in America! OK by me in America!'

*Shush. We turned to one of the American producers and said, 'Wow, what a brilliant audience.' Without missing a beat, he replied, 'Yeah, it's amazing what you can get for $15 an hour.' Seeing the puzzled looks on our faces, he patiently explained that studio audiences in America actually get paid.*

And we thought it was because we were hilariously funny and brilliantly entertaining. The alarm bells should have been ringing the moment we made that assumption. We enjoyed making the show, though, and spending time in LA – it's a crazy place, but there's no better city in the world to be working in showbusiness. It's a show-off's paradise, but I'm not sure I could live there full time . . .

*Good, 'cos nobody's asked us to . . .*
    *After we'd finished filming the series, and to celebrate our first American show, our management company, James Grant, treated us to a trip to Vegas.*

We started the day in LA with a hearty breakfast and headed off with Paul, Darren and Ali to the gambling capital of the world. They'd arranged some fantastic stuff – we had rooms at the Bellagio, one of the best hotels in Vegas, they'd booked us a limo to ferry us around and show us the sights and told us the only thing we'd have to pay for was drinks and our chips. Incidentally, I mean gambling chips; we weren't going to the local Vegas chippie for dinner. The five of us went to a fantastic steak restaurant in the Hotel Wynn, and it was shaping up to be one of the best nights of our lives. Ant and me had just ordered our steaks when disaster struck.

*I think it was me who went to the toilet first. I'd suddenly come over very queasy and, once I was in the restroom, which is American for toilet, I started throwing up. A lot. After about ten minutes of continuous vomiting,*

*I pulled myself together and went back to the table, trying to convince myself I'd feel better soon.*

That was when I got up and ran to the toilet. I won't go into graphic detail in case you're reading this while you're having your dinner, but I had a very upset stomach. After about ten minutes of continuous . . . well, I'm sure you can guess, I got back to the table, and everyone told me I'd gone white as a sheet. Well, everyone except Ant, who was on his way back to the toilet to throw up again.

The two of us spent the next hour playing tag-team toilet. We were the only two who'd eaten eggs that morning, so we worked out we had food poisoning. Ali suggested we get back in the limo and go back to our hotel. All the hotels in Vegas have everything you can think of inside them, including chemists, so on the way to the car, Ali popped in and got us some Alka-Seltzer and a packet of chewable Pepto-Bismol.

We were both feeling more sick with every passing minute. I popped the tablets into my mouth and began to chew. We made our way towards the exit, through the casino, past all the gaming tables. The sound of fruit machines filled the air, and it was like a monkey banging a pair of cymbals in my head. We quickened our pace, as the tablets hadn't yet had the desired effect and were only succeeding in making me feel even more queasy.

*I got in the limo first, and was busy turning a lighter shade of green when I looked round to see Dec, bent over a bush, vomiting everywhere.*

And, of course, being Vegas, the bushes were plastic. Everything out there is fake, and I still hate to think of some poor sod having to wipe clean the shrubbery the next day. What made it worse was that because of the Pepto-Bismol tablets, my vomit was bright pink.

*Meanwhile, I'm in the limo with Ali, who started shouting, 'Dec's being sick! Dec's being sick!' All I could say was, 'What do you expect me to do?*

*I feel bad enough myself.' The limo took us back to the Bellagio, which it managed without Dec turning the inside of it bright pink, and we both went to our rooms, determined to pull ourselves together and get back to our Vegas night-of-a-lifetime. We were in our rooms for the next twelve hours. The whole night, the only time I spent that wasn't in the toilet or in bed was when I got up to read a text someone had sent. I crawled over to where my phone was and opened the message, which was from Darren. 'Oh, that's nice,' I thought, 'he's texting to see how I feel.' He wasn't. His text simply read, 'Can you believe it? I've just won $500 on roulette – whoopee!' I think I threw up immediately.*

We got up the next morning, ready to fly back to LA. We were both on the mend by this point and whatever it was that had given us food poisoning was obviously well and truly out of our system and safely in a fake bush at the Hotel Wynn. As we came out of the lift, we met Paul, Darren and Ali in reception, which leads straight on to the hotel casino floor. Paul and Darren said, 'You can't come to Vegas and not gamble once.' They gave us each a one-hundred-dollar chip and told us to stick it on the roulette table. We headed to the nearest table, where the croupier told us to place our bets. I put mine on red and Ant went for black – that way, we thought, we were bound to come away with something between us. The croupier spun the wheel, released the ball and, after what seemed like for ever, the ball hopped, skipped and jumped and finally came to rest.

'Zero!' the croupier shouted. We looked at the table – zero was neither red nor black. It was green. We both lost our one-hundred-dollar chips.

*It summed up the whole trip to Vegas – disastrous.*

We arrived back in LA, at the hotel where we'd stayed while filming *Wanna Bet?* We were determined to rest, recuperate and, most of all, avoid having eggs for breakfast. This hotel had the best maître d' in Hollywood and, once he found out we were English and in TV, he always had some celebrity gossip to share with us. He would come up to us and say things like, 'Michael Caine will be dining with us tonight, do you know him?' 'No, we don't,' we'd reply, much to his disappointment. 'David and Victoria Beckham will be dining here this evening, do you know them?' And, for once, we could say yes. They're not our best friends or anything, we'd met them on a handful of occasions, but we weren't going to hang around the restaurant hoping to catch a glimpse of them. Plus, we had dinner plans ourselves, so we went off for some food and, by the time we came back to the hotel, well, let's just say we were a little the worse for wear. I decided to go to bed – I'm always sensible like that: I know when I've had my fill.

*He's never sensible like that and he never knows when he's had his fill but, for some reason, on this particular night, he retired early. I was in the bar with Ali, and on the way back from the toilet, I get accosted by our friend the maître d'. He tells me that David isn't there, but Victoria is and 'Would you like to come and say hello?' I tried to tell him I didn't want to disturb her, but he took me by the arm and walked me towards the restaurant. On the way, he says, 'Eva is there – do you know Eva?' Before I know what's going on, I'm standing in front of Victoria Beckham, Eva Longoria and about four other stunning women, clearly on a girls' night out. Suddenly, matey boy peels away and leaves me on my own. They all look up at me expectantly and I look back at them, drunkenly. In a flash, I decide the only way out of this potentially embarrassing situation is to be as loud and brash as I can.*

*'Alreet?' I say to Victoria. 'Thish town issssn't big enough for the both of ush!'*

I'm embarrassed just listening to this.

*To be fair to Victoria, she was lovely. She got up and was very nice and asked what I was doing there and how things were going, and we had a quick chat. I'd held it together, so I decided to get out of there and said my goodbyes. As I turned to leave, my foot struck something hard and metal, which clattered across the dining-room floor and came to rest in full view of everyone.*

*'Hey, that's her crutch,' cried Victoria.*

*I couldn't believe it. One of Victoria's friends had had a crutch leaning against her chair, and I'd sent it flying halfway across the restaurant. Embarrassed, I went over, picked it up and tried to re-balance it on the back of the chair. I don't know if anyone reading this book has ever tried to balance a crutch on the back of a chair in front of Victoria Beckham and Eva Longoria after a few beers, but if you haven't, then trust me, it's not easy. Eventually I managed it, said my goodbyes – again – and left Victoria, Eva and the girls to it. I got back to the table where Ali and the rest of our little posse were sitting and told them about the whole incident. Straight away Ali pointed out that Dec was going to be devastated at missing an encounter like that – Eva Longoria is his ideal woman.*

**I love that Desperate Housewife.**

*Just then I got a text from Dec. 'Has he heard Eva's in the hotel?, I wondered. 'Shall I go up and tell him the woman of his dreams is just a few floors away?' All these thoughts instantly vanished from my head the moment I read the text, which simply said:*

*'Ring home and tell Lisa to Sky-Plus* Match of the Day.'

**Well, Newcastle had just beaten Bolton – and they don't win very often these days.**

We enjoyed a lot of things about that trip to LA, but when the show finally went out, about a year later, it didn't do as well as we'd hoped. It wasn't in a great time slot and it got hardly any promotion on the channel. We went out there and promoted it ourselves but, without the channel behind it, it was always going to be fighting with one arm behind its back.

*On the plus side, I'll be dining out on that Victoria Beckham and Eva Longoria story for the next five years.*

**I still can't believe I missed it.**

*Don't worry, I'm sure yours and Eva's paths will cross one day.*

No, *Match of the Day*, I meant – you forgot to tell Lisa to Sky-Plus it. I still haven't seen those goals.

# Chapter 41

After we got back from LA, I laid the foundations for one of the biggest projects of my whole life – literally. I began to build a new house. The previous year, after their wedding, Ant and Lisa had moved to a bigger place, and not long afterwards, I decided the time had come for me to start looking for somewhere new. I wanted to stay in Chiswick and I found what I thought was the perfect spot. There was only one problem – it was three doors away from Ant and Lisa's new house. People thought it was weird enough when we lived next to each other before, so for the two of them to move, and then for me to follow, well, I was convinced everyone would think it was doubly weird.

*My attitude was 'Sod what everyone else thinks, I think it's a great idea, but there's one person we should ask first – Lisa.' So Dec came round to mine to have a word with her. Once we were all sat in the front room, she looked at us both and, having seen that look on our faces a million times before, immediately enquired, 'What? What have you two done now?'*

*Silence.*

*Finally I broke that silence. 'Dec's got something to ask you.'*

'Thanks,' I thought. 'Leave it to me then.'

'I've found a spot for my new house,' I said, not quite telling the whole story.

'Great!' Lisa seemed to be genuinely happy for me.

'Erm . . . It's three doors away from your new house . . .'

'You are kidding . . .'

'Don't worry,' I piped up immediately, 'I'm not going to buy it, people will think it's weird.'

'That's a shame; I think it's a great idea.'

'Great! In that case I'll buy it then! Can I borrow your tin opener?'

The last bit isn't true, but Lisa was completely fine about having a new neighbour – well new-ish – and it was exciting to think I'd be living close to my best friends again. When they moved the first time I had no one whose house I could just drop in to, and have a chat with, and more importantly, no one to remind me which night to put the bins out. Lisa really does look after me – and always has done. When Clare and me split up she was a great help and has been ever since, which has meant a lot. She's brilliant with the little things too. For example, if one of our friends has a birthday, the two of us always have the same conversation:

'Have you got a birthday card?'
    'Oh no, I've completely forgotten.'
    'Well, it's a good job I've bought one for you then.'

By the way, apologies to any of my friends who've just realized I don't buy their birthday cards. It's also quite common for Ant and me to be in the car, on the way home from work, and I'll get a phone call. Ant hears me saying, 'Pork chops? . . . Sounds great . . . Lovely – see you about six.' I'll then turn to Ant and let him know we're having pork chops for tea. Lisa's brilliant and I love her dearly and, if you don't believe me, ask yourself this, if she wasn't, would I let her off with calling me 'Deccy Doolittle' all the time? Exactly.

Whilst we're on the subject of embarrassing revelations, you'd think after Ant's crutch-kicking antics in Los Angeles he might have learnt his lesson about being clumsy, but you'd be wrong. It almost ruined the next series of *Saturday Night Take-away*. We were filming a pre-recorded feature called *Beat the Boys*, where we raced against other famous double acts – strangely Victoria Beckham and Eva Longoria didn't respond to our invitation to appear – and, thanks to a self-inflicted injury, Ant put the whole shoot in jeopardy.

*I'll pick up the story from here, shall I?*

**Okay, but be careful you don't drop it.**

*We'd both been out playing five-a-side football and, when I got home, Lisa was in the middle of one of her cleaning sprees. I recognized the symptoms the moment I opened the front door – a strong smell of Mr Sheen, air freshener and Febreze and the sound of Lisa singing. It was about ten o'clock at night and I just wanted to have a long soak and sort myself out for the following day's filming. Lisa was in the study, all dusters and deter-mination, so I popped in to say hello and give her a kiss. Fatal mistake. The moment I walked in, she asked – by which I mean told – me to give her a hand. She was eyeing a cabinet that's home to – and there's no easy way to say this without sounding like an egomaniac – my awards. Within seconds, Lisa had devised her strategy: I had to hold on to the awards while she dusted the cabinet. Even though I like to think of myself as a fairly decent goalkeeper, I made a schoolboy error and dropped one. On my bare foot. I was in agony and, when I looked down, I noticed there was blood pouring uncontrollably from my left foot. Lisa wanted to call the hospital, but I refused, it was only a silly little cut. I bandaged it up in what can only be described as a haphazard fashion – wrapping about ten Elasto-plasts round it – and insisted I was fine. I was NOT, under any circum-stances, going to the hospital.*

*Five minutes later, after a futile attempt to stop the bleeding and all the Elastoplasts had fallen off, Lisa was driving me to the hospital.*

*We arrived in A&E to find that it was, as you'd probably expect, packed. Is there ever a time when any A&E department anywhere isn't packed? There was a stream of doctors and nurses passing by and people with a variety of injuries waiting to be seen. There was some bloke with a head wound, a kid who appeared to have swallowed a small toy and, my personal favourite, a drunk in the corner who kept slapping himself in the face. 'Great,' I thought, 'first I maim my own foot and now I'm at the back of the queue behind slappy-face guy – could things get any worse?' My early night before the next day's big shoot was out the window and I still hadn't had that bath. Eventually, my name was called and I hobbled up the corridor to see the doctor, Lisa by my side. The doctor drew the curtain, sat me on the edge of the bed and looked at his clipboard. 'So, Mr McPart-lin, what have we here? What exactly did you drop on your foot?' Me and Lisa both answered his question at once:*

| ANT | LISA |
|-----|------|
| *A bookend.* | *A National Television Award for Best Presenter.* |

*I couldn't believe it. In the space of two hours, I'd played an exhausting game of football, gashed my foot, spent goodness knows how long in the waiting room and now I was coming across like a vain egomaniac. The clearly overworked doctor looked at me with an understandable air of dis-gust – his eyes were saying, 'Is that all you do with your life, dress up in football kits and play with your awards? You make me sick.' I had three stitches, and they sent me home, but I could've sworn I heard the doctor call me 'Awards Boy' under his breath as I was leaving. I hobbled out into the waiting room and, after being stopped for several camera-phone photos (three of which were with slappy-face guy), I was off home to finally have that soak. The next day I managed to go on the shoot, much to the relief of our new producer, Anna Blue. On the plus side, I've been excused from dusting ever since.*

It's the most showbiz injury in history.

Another series of *Takeaway* meant another pilgrimage of visitors to come and stay with us in London and, as with every series, our families made up some of those visitors. My mam and dad came down from Newcastle to see the show and have a weekend in the capital. Whenever they visit, it only takes about five minutes before I feel like *I'm* in *their* house. During the series on a show day I would probably get out of bed around eight thirty, but by eight, without fail, my mam's knocking on the door telling me it's time to get up. I lie there thinking, 'I know, I manage to do this every week!' My dad has a potter round the garden, as most dads do. He'll be up at eight and down the paper shop before he pops in to see Ken the butcher to get some 'nice' sausages – he knows more about my local shops than I do. My mam won't go back to Newcastle until the laundry basket is empty and the house is tidy. I don't ask them to do any of this stuff, I think they actually like it. Over the years, I've stopped fighting it and, besides, there's a lot to be said for leaving the house having already read the paper and enjoyed a sausage sandwich.

As well as my mam and dad, I'll have other members of the family to stay too. My sisters, Moyra and Camalia, always venture down at some point with their families, as do some of my brothers – incidentally, at the last count, I noticed eleven nieces and nephews have been conjured up from somewhere. There's Ainé, Colm, Sarah, Thomas, James, Matthew, Eleanor, Dominick, Oliver, Clodagh and Daniel. Although that number may well have increased by the time you read this book.

One of the lovely things about having so many nieces and nephews in the family is how confused they get about me being on the telly. Until they're three or four years old, it's very simple – they just think everyone's uncle is on TV. The next stage is bewilderment – they don't quite understand how it's possible for me to be on TV and in the room with them at the same time. They point at the telly and shout 'Dec', then point at me and shout 'Dec'. That lasts for a little while and then, finally, it all makes sense and they ask me to come and pick them up from school, to prove to their mates that they aren't making it up.

Newspapers can freak them out a bit too. A few weeks ago, Camalia's three-year-old son Daniel ran in holding the paper, which had a picture of me and Ant on the front page.

'That's you!' he informed me. 'You're in the paper!'

'Is it?' I said. Don't get me wrong – I could clearly see it was me, but I played along anyway.

'Why's that?' I asked. 'What am I doing in the paper?'

'I don't know,' he said incredulously, 'I cannot read!'

After a quick trip to Australia for a night shift or nineteen and a series that was won by Christopher Biggins, we came back to England for Christmas. Just before Santa came down the chimney, I remember bumping into Biggins, who told me that, since being in the jungle, he'd never signed so many autographs in his life.

*That is one of the strange things about fame – people asking you for auto-graphs. I can understand it with kids, but otherwise I've always thought the idea of getting someone to write their name on a piece of paper is weird. If it's a football team who've all signed a shirt or something then I can under-stand it, but getting me to sign a Burger King napkin somehow doesn't seem quite so exciting.*

*The other thing people do is walk up to me and say, 'Are you Ant?' You tell them you are and then they'll go, 'You're not,' and you're think-ing, 'Do I have to prove it somehow?'*

**My favourite is 'Are you who I think you are?' – I always think of answering, 'I don't know – who do you think I am?'**

*Along with the enquiries about our identity and requests to sign napkins, the other big part of our life in the public eye is the camera phone. If you're on telly, it comes with the territory that people might want to take pictures of you, but here's a little piece of advice for anyone who wants to take a photo of someone famous with their phone. Don't pretend you're sending a text – we can hear the phone click and we can see it pointed up in the air – no one holds their phone like that to send a text.*

**And at least switch it to camera function before you raise it – because we can tell when you're holding that phone up and you can't find the camera function. Don't get me wrong, we understand that it's par for the course but, take my word for it, it's easier to just come up and ask.**

*And while we're on the subject, if you do come and ask, make sure you know how your phone works. I've lost count of the number of times I've been stood somewhere thinking, 'Hurry up, mate, I've had my arm round your sister for ten minutes and it's just getting embarrassing now.' Before you know what's happening, they've taken three pictures of their own face by mistake and when they finally work out how to use it, the memory's full.*

331

*I've been stood in pubs or shops or restaurants on numerous occasions with my arm around someone I don't know while some bloke decides which photos of his family he can delete and replace with 'one of Ant and Dec'. I can hear them now: 'No, not that one – that's Christmas with the kids.'*

On the subject of the great British public, we hit the road again in early 2008 for the auditions of the second series of *Britain's Got Talent*. During the auditions, it was very clear that most of the acts had watched series one very, very carefully – we had a load of opera singers. And none of them was as good as Paul Potts.

*One of the stand-out auditions from that series came from a double act that consisted of a clever and dedicated professional and a simple creature who did as he was told.*

Sounds familiar . . .

*Kate and Gin the Dog turned out to be the first decent dog act we'd had on the show, and Simon Cowell in particular was ecstatic about that. You might not think it, but he loves dogs . . .*

It's just humans he's got a problem with . . .
    Other highlights on this series were a double act called Signature, which consisted of a Michael Jackson impersonator and an Indian sidekick posing as a cleaner with a broom. And of course the fourteen-year-old breakdancer George Sampson.

*George went on to win the second series. He had originally auditioned for series one, but didn't make the cut, so winning the show at the second time of asking made him a bona fide comeback kid.*

I like to think that, in many ways, he was influenced by the finest child breakdancer in history – Declan Donnelly at the Tyneside Irish Club in the mid-eighties. I like to think that, even though it's not true.

*It's easy to sound wise after the event, but we both genuinely thought George should have made the semi-finals the year before. It's true! But in series two he came back better than ever and it was a real rags-to-riches story We were both really pleased when he won it — he provided a really positive image for young kids in Britain: so many get labelled hoodies and thugs and George was and is a great role model.*

## Just like me in the eighties.

*Yeah, just like you in the eighties — except he's successful, talented and he doesn't collect coins in ashtrays.*

After we'd finished our whistlestop tour of theatres for the auditions, we went straight to a new series of *Saturday Night Takeaway*. The Ant versus Dec feature, where we're challenged not to break our arms, let dogs poo in our houses and not die abseiling down twenty-four-storey buildings, became a battle of the teams, which led to the clever title, Ant versus Dec – The Teams. As you'd expect, there were some challenges that involved danger for the teams, like bobsleighing in Austria, and some challenges that involved danger for the audience's eardrums – like singing in barber-shop quartets. The first challenge we faced was a military field-gun challenge, and it almost ended with me coming to blows with Paul Daniels. He was on my team, by the way, I don't just pick fights with TV magicians for the sake of it.

*It was a classic case of little-man syndrome — it's bad enough when you have one bloke with it, but put two of them together and you're bound to get fireworks.*

The first show of any series on *Takeaway* is hectic – me and Ant have been working so hard on every last detail of the show all week, and when it comes to Saturday, there are so many different elements to remember that the last thing we need is to get sidetracked by a row with Debbie McGee's other half, but that's what happened. We were rehearsing the challenge, which is essentially an army assault course that involves dragging a huge cannon under, over and through obstacles, when the trouble started.

*As competitive as ever, I looked over at Dec's team during rehearsal and it seemed like they were, well, breaking the rules! As part of the challenge, the whole team had to get over one obstacle before any of them could start on the next one – if they failed to do that on the night, it was instant disqualification, and much as I desperately want to win Ant versus Dec – not least because I've never won a single series – I didn't want to win by a disqualification, so I told Dec about his team's mistake.*

I thanked Ant and reminded my team of the rules. They were all fine with it, except for one person – Paul Daniels. Paul started to debate it, saying the rules had changed, why had no one told him? I tried to calmly say to him that the rules hadn't changed, they had always been that way – the next thing I know me and Paul are standing toe to toe, jabbing our fingers in each other's faces, having a full-on argument. Ex-Manchester United winger Lee Sharpe was looking on open-mouthed as me and Paul bawled at each other, and then, just as things were about to get really heated, former *X-Factor* contestant Chico came in and broke it up.

*I just remember looking over, thinking, 'Yep, that's* Takeaway . . .'

We both calmed down, and I apologized to Paul. I was feeling the pressure of the first show and took it out on him. Even as I was shouting I was thinking to myself, 'Shut up, you tit, you really shouldn't be shouting at Paul Daniels!' Incidentally, my team won the challenge, and as a certain someone might say, 'Now *that's* magic.'

*I can't believe you're still gloating over that – now* that's *tragic.*

# Chapter 42

As you've read over the last few chapters, life in 2007 and 2008 included arguing with magicians and making American TV shows, but those years also included some of the toughest and most horrible times of our entire career. In 2007, ITV began investigating irregularities with phone-in competitions and voting on a number of TV shows. At first, even though *Saturday Night Takeaway* and another programme we'd hosted, *Gameshow Marathon* were two of the shows being investigated, we weren't worried – we didn't for a moment expect there to be any wrongdoing on any of our shows. We were shocked when, in October 2007, a report was published by the company undertaking the investigation, Deloitte, which said it had found there were irregularities with both shows. People had spent money entering competitions they had no chance of winning, which is, of course, indefensible. We were given the news by Paul and Darren in a meeting at James Grant Management. We both instantly felt physically sick.

*A couple of days earlier, I'd had a journalist call at my house and ask me if I wanted to comment on allegations of TV fakery, so even then I had started to worry. Because two of our shows were investigated, and we were two of the highest profile performers supposedly involved in the scandal, we were savaged by the press. We were credited as being executive producers of* Takeaway, *so people said we must have known these irregularities were occurring, but our role as executive producers was purely a creative one. Our overall concern was the content of the show, and we oversaw that side of things. We had no idea how the phone lines worked, or about health and safety procedures or risk assessments or how any of the legalities worked – we dealt with the ideas, the words and scripts and what the viewers saw on screen. And I can guarantee that's pretty much how it works with any performer with an EP credit.*

*When the first report was published, our first concern was for the audience. Innocent people had spent hard-earned money entering competitions they would never win. That wasn't right. We then became worried that the viewers who had been affected would think we had known all about it, and sanctioned these actions. That would have led to our audience not being able to trust us and, once that happens, it's all over. It was an awful thought. Huge mistakes had been made – the fact that people lost money was inexcusable, and we'd come so far and done so much, the thought of something like this ending our career was heartbreaking.*

*We've always thought of our career as being a three-way relationship – between me, Dec and the audience. Ever since we've been on telly, we've prided ourselves on trying to understand our audience, and for something like this to happen was upsetting and maddening. We released statements apologizing, but that didn't stop there being a feeding frenzy by the media – people were saying we should've been arrested and even gone to prison, they implied we'd lied in our statements when we attempted to reassure viewers that we had no knowledge of what had happened. 'No smoke without fire' was the phrase they most enjoyed trotting out but, worst of all, some people claimed we knew about the phone-line procedure but didn't care and helped maximize the profit so we could take a cut of the phone revenue, which is just a downright lie.*

In the autumn of 2007, on the way to Australia for *I'm a Celebrity . . .*, we stopped off in LA for some meetings. While we were out there, the National Television Awards were taking place back in London. We've always regarded the NTAs very highly – they're voted for by the public so you're able to get a real sense of what the audience is enjoying. Because of the timing, it was impossible not to see the NTAs as a big test – if the public had lost faith in us it would be made very clear; they just wouldn't vote for us. Even our publicist, Simon Jones, was being told by the newspapers behind the scenes that the result would be an indication of whether or not the public thought we were guilty. The *Mirror* even ran a piece the very day of the awards saying we feared 'a backlash from viewers'.

We told the NTAs that, unfortunately, we wouldn't be able to attend the awards because of our American commitments, but that if we did win anything we would be available to do a live satellite link. They said they wouldn't know anything for certain until four o'clock in the afternoon British time on the day, which was 8 a.m. in LA. Paul, our manager, promised he'd ring us from London as soon as he had any news. I set my alarm for seven thirty just to be sure I didn't miss the call, but I needn't have bothered, I was awake long before that – in fact I barely slept. Eight o'clock came and went, and the phone didn't ring. I lay in bed and stared at the ceiling, minutes felt like hours and I was feeling increasingly anxious. Then, just before quarter past, the phone rang; it was Paul. I couldn't really deal with small talk, so I just asked him outright, 'Have you heard anything?' My heart was beating and my stomach was in knots.

'You'd better get dressed,' he said. 'You've got a satellite link to do.'

The joy and the relief were indescribable. The minute I put the phone down, I lay on my bed and sobbed my heart out. I've never been so thankful.

*I was in the hotel restaurant having breakfast and Paul rang me straight away. I felt the same as Dec – relief, joy, gratitude, just so many emotions at once. It was nothing to do with winning an award, it was about what it signified, the audience knew we hadn't betrayed them, we hadn't been part of the phone-line 'fixing' and they still had faith in us. They still wanted to be part of that relationship which meant – and means – everything to both of us. We went to Australia, determined to put in the performance of our lives – after everything that had happened, it was the least we could do as a thank-you to our audience.*

*In May 2008, ITV's fine was announced and the whole story was dragged up again. The press and media were full of the same stories. It was the lead story on all TV news bulletins, they used images from Takeaway and we went through the whole thing all over again.*

337

*Despite how horrible it all was, however, there were some positives to come out of it. PRTS – which stands for Premium Rate Telephone Service – is still a relatively new thing in television. As we said a few chapters ago, Pop Idol was the first talent show to let viewers choose the winner by phone voting, which means that this kind of viewer interactivity and accessibility is really less than ten years old. That makes it very hard to police. People were still learning about how the whole thing worked and, although that in no way excuses what happened, it means that nothing like that should ever happen again. Now, there's no danger of viewers spending any money without a fair and honest chance of winning a competition.*

At the same time as the fine, in May 2008, a report was also published into a mistake that had been made at the 2005 *British Comedy Awards*.

Through a 'voting error', we were given the People's Choice Award, which was actually won by, and should have gone to, Catherine Tate. We were just guests at the ceremony, so obviously had no idea what was happening with the votes, but that didn't stop the press lumping it in with the phone-line problems on our shows. 'No smoke without fire,' they lazily regurgitated. We issued a statement saying we were appalled and immediately returned the award to ITV, who sent it to Catherine.

A few weeks after the Comedy Awards incident, I was in my local branch of Marks & Spencer's buying some apples and I heard this voice behind me say, 'Put them down, they're my apples.' I looked round and it was Catherine Tate. Even though we hadn't personally done anything wrong, I couldn't help blushing and I heard myself apologizing in the middle of Marks's fruit aisle. Catherine told me not to be silly and that she was fine with it, which was good of her, we chatted a little and she accepted my apology. We went our separate ways and I went back to shopping for my five-a-day.

*The investigation is still going on, and hopefully once it's closed we might find out what happened. The whole thing – the reports, the fine, the mix-*

*up — was a terrible time, and it reminded us how incredibly lucky we are to have the career we have — we would never, ever take anything for granted and we're very fortunate to enjoy the support of the public, so sorry if this sounds cheesy, but thank you.*

# Chapter 43

*The Pride of Britain Awards* reward British people who've committed remarkable acts of bravery. It's produced in association with the *Mirror* and televised on ITV. We've been involved on a regular basis and have done various things for them down the years and, in 2008, we told them we wanted to do something a bit different. 'Fine,' came the reply. 'How would you like to go to Afghanistan?' They wanted us to present an award out there to a unit called MERT (Medical Emergency Response Team). The MERT unit is basically a flying A&E department that goes to the front line of battle in a helicopter with a doctor, a nurse, paramedics and a surgeon, picks up casualties and takes them back to the hospitals at the base. Even though it wasn't quite the answer we were expecting, after talking it through (a lot), we eventually agreed.

*We flew out with Ali from RAF Brize Norton on an old Tristar jet, which is exactly like a normal plane, except that it has three beds at the front for casualties. Before we left, we were all fitted for body armour and given a helmet – you think to yourself, 'I'll never need this,' but once you get there, you're told to keep them with you at all times. Twenty minutes before we landed, we were told to put on our body armour and helmet, and they turned off all the lights so as to land in the cover of darkness. It was one of the most surreal and scary things I've ever experienced. Nobody talks, so we all silently zipped up our body armour and put our helmets on and waited to hear the plane's wheels touch down. We got off the plane at Kandahar Airport, and boarded a Hercules jet, which took us to Camp Bastion, a big UK army base that MERT operates from. Looking out into the Afghan desert night, we could see small, glowing lights everywhere, which the pilots told us were Taliban campfires. When we arrived at Camp Bastion, we grabbed a few hours' sleep on a campbed in a tent and, the next day, started filming.*

The following morning, we were being briefed on the work the MERT does, when the unit got a call through – there were casualties on the front line and they had to go and collect them. Our filming schedule went out of the window, and instead we just captured what was happening as the situation unfolded. They took two helicopters and, when they returned, the walking wounded came off the helicopter, followed by the more seriously injured. There was a young soldier who had been shot in the leg and an Afghan National Army soldier who had been shot in the head.

We asked if we could talk to the walking wounded once they'd been cleaned up – the corporal in charge went in to ask them and was away for ages – when he came out he explained that it had taken a while to convince them it wasn't a wind-up. I suppose that's understandable. You've just been wounded in action, flown back to the base and, while you're getting treated, someone comes in and says, 'Ant and Dec are here and they'd like to have a chat with you' – you could be forgiven for thinking your medication had kicked in early.

*After a day's filming at the base with the wounded and recovering, we stayed the night there. The following day we did some more filming and handed over the award to the members of the MERT team on the airstrip where their helicopters land. Being there was very moving, we had young soldiers coming up to us and saying, 'Thanks for coming' – they told us it meant a lot to them. Those guys are away from their homes and families for months on end risking their lives. They know some people are opposed to the war so they felt encouraged to have some support, even if it was from a couple of daft blokes off the telly.*

*After we presented the award we went back to Kandahar Airport to check in for our flight home. We were waiting for our turn and had started to watch a giant plasma screen that was on in the corner of the check-in area, which was basically a big marquee tent. They have what they call BFBS, which is British Forces Broadcasting Services, and* This Morning *was on – it was strange watching Phil and Fern in Afghanistan. Just as they were finishing an item with Dr Chris, a piercingly loud siren started going off – it was like a fire alarm, or an old air-raid siren. I turned from the TV and noticed that the whole room had cleared except for me, Dec and Ali. A soldier came in wearing full body armour, helmet and gun and shouted at us, 'Hit the deck. Incoming, incoming.' I looked down and saw the room hadn't cleared at all – they were all on the floor with their hands over their heads. We followed suit and got down too. After a minute or two, the siren ceased. Everyone lay incredibly still, and explosions went off which didn't sound too far away. The only sound in the room was Philip Schofield and Fern Britton on* This Morning *in the middle of one of their legendary giggling fits. I looked up at the screen and saw them laughing away, and all I could think was 'How can you two laugh at a time like this? We're being bombed!' It was bizarre – lying there, we'd worked out by now that the base was under attack and our lives were in danger, but I was strangely calm. There was no fear or panic, just a weird realization of what the situation was. I looked around to see what everyone else was doing, and they were all still face down, some with eyes closed, some with eyes open staring at the floor. Then I saw Ali was looking around, too, but she was in fits of laughter – the whole situation was so strange it had brought on the giggles, and she couldn't stop.*

*Another officer came into the room and ordered us all outside, so we went and lay face down in the dirt under a table, still with no idea what was going on. I was getting rather uncomfortable lying there so at one point I decided to sit up and stretch out a little. Immediately the soldier next to me said, 'Every time I've seen anyone sit up during one of these attacks they've never sat up again – if you know what I mean?' I knew exactly what he meant and immediately wriggled back down into the dirt.*

*Eventually, after around forty minutes under the table, it was deemed safe to go back inside. Word got to us of exactly what had just happened. We'd been under mortar attack from the Taliban, and the explosions were just 200 metres away. We'd been told to leave the tent because that was probably the first target they'd try and hit.*

When we finally checked in and boarded, some of the casualties we'd seen at Camp Bastion the previous day were on the plane home with us, and it was fascinating to see first hand how efficiently the whole process worked. It was incredibly quick – they were wounded and arrived back at camp on Tuesday, flown to Kandahar on Wednesday and got home to the UK the same day. The whole experience was inspirational – you watch the news and read the papers, but the only way to truly understand what life is like out there is to see the place. The day after we got back, we were in the gym and the fire alarm went off – I nearly jumped out of my skin.

The next time we left the country, it was for a much more trivial and shallow reason. By the time it came round to *I'm a Celebrity . . .* in November, we hadn't been in your front rooms for about six months, so we couldn't wait to get back on the telly. The cast was as brilliant as ever, and it included a man we'd spent some time with in LA the previous year. No, not the maître d', although he would have been good. It was George Takei, aka Mr Sulu from *Star Trek*. George had been one of the celebrity panellists on our American show, *Wanna Bet?*, and as well as being one of the few people we'd actually heard of, he was a real charmer, with the most amazingly theatrical voice. When we got back from the States, we told the producers all about him. Despite being seventy-two years old, George passed the medical and, incredibly, agreed to go on the show. You could say he was ready 'to *oldly* go where no man has gone before'.

*You could, but I wish you hadn't.*

*Once we got to Australia, the producers went to meet all of the cast individually. They do that every year, as they feel it's important the contestants are prepared for how to deal with the whole jungle experience and, trust me, if they're not scared witless when the producers arrive, they certainly are by the time they've left. The three executive producers, Richard Cowles, Beth Hart and Chris Brogden, came to fill us in after they'd seen the celebs and they were all struck by how nice George was. One of the things they'd asked him was exactly how to pronounce his surname – Tak-eye or Tak-ay. To make sure they got it right, George told them a little story, which went like this:*

*'On Star Trek, William Shatner always used to call me George Tak-eye. He would constantly refer to me as George Tak-eye, no matter how many*

343

*times I told him it was George Tak-ay. Then one day I said to him, "It's Tak-ay – Tak-ay. It rhymes with toupee, you should know!" He never got it wrong after that!'*

*We knew there and then George would be great fun – and also that we'd never get his name wrong.*

The series was won by Joe Swash, who was a worthy King of the Jungle – he was true to himself from day one and stood up for people he thought were being unfairly treated, plus he struck up an unlikely but close friendship with George, who he christened 'Gorgeous George'. The big stars of the series, though, were a hilarious double act.

*We were good, weren't we?*

I meant David Van Day and Timmy Mallet. They were annoying, funny, confrontational and divisive – in other words, perfect *I'm a Celebrity . . .* contestants. When it came to David Van Day – well, how can you fail to love a man who walks around camp in red hot-pants, holding a fly swat and talking to himself?

This was our eighth year of *I'm a Celebrity . . .* with, by and large, the same people every year, which has made for a great atmosphere on the show. There are, among others, our regular make-up and wardrobe team of Claude and Toni; Andy and Mark the scriptwriters; Chris the director; and Richard and Natalka, the executive producers. The whole thing feels like one big family – if you think of a family as a group of people who spend three weeks filming, editing and Bushtucker-trialling a load of famous people, anyway.

*And, of course, another upside is the air miles. Me and Lisa used up a few thousand of them on a trip to New York to see in the New Year. Lisa is always complaining that, when we're in America, she never spots anyone famous – the best she's managed in LA is the back of Mike Tyson's head, and Fabio, a male model from the nineties. You know, Fabio? No, me neither. Dec and me always seem to spot our fair share of celebs out there, including Matthew Perry in a restaurant and Harrison Ford at the baseball (thanks for asking), but poor Lisa never seems to do too well. Whilst waiting for our flight we treated ourselves to a glass of champagne in the Concorde lounge at a jam-packed Heathrow. Lisa complemented the bubbles with a packet of Frazzles, a copy of Closer and a bit of music on her iPod, and I was reeling from the football I'd just watched — Newcastle United 1–Liverpool 5. I'd already had a few 'comments' about my team from football fans and check-in staff at the airport when I saw a huge black guy smiling and heading towards me in a Liverpool cap. 'Oh no, here we go again,' I thought — yet another Scouser who's going to rub my nose in it. I slid deeper into my chair and got ready to take some stick over the result and then, hopefully, get rid of him.*

*I took a deep breath and steeled myself for another bout of ridicule, but the ridicule didn't come. He didn't even mention the football; he just delivered an enthusiastic 'Happy Holiday!' in an American accent. 'Who the hell is this guy?' I thought. I stood up, reluctantly about to shake his hand, when I noticed who the hell he was: Samuel L. Jackson! Yes, that Samuel L. Jackson. And he'd come over to say hello to me. Yes, that mè. Before I knew what was happening, I heard myself saying 'Happy Holiday' back to him. I was standing at Heathrow, gleefully shaking hands with one of the most iconic men in film: it was brilliant — and he still hadn't even mentioned the football.*

*As we stood there in the middle of a very busy lounge chit-chatting about golf, how we spent our Christmas holidays, golf and more golf, one thought was rushing through my head: 'How the hell does he know who I am?' He started asking how me and my 'buddy' were doing and I said, 'Fine, thanks,' as if this was the most natural thing in the world. I knew he'd been interviewed by Little Ant and Dec but I was sure we'd never met — but who cares? I was chewing the fat with Samuel L. Jackson.*

*After a few more rounds of fat-chewing, our chat finally moved round to the one subject I was dreading — football. Samuel had spent some time in Liverpool making a film a few years ago, and as a result had adopted them as his team. He teased me about the game, but even then I didn't seem to mind — he could have slapped me round the face with a wet fish and I would have thanked him for it.*

*I looked round at Lisa, who was in her own little world, thanks to the distractions of her iPod and* Closer, *so I tapped her on the shoulder to reveal my new best friend. She looked up and nearly dropped her Frazzles. She whipped out her earphones and shook hands with him – although she later told me she was worried she'd smeared crisp dust on his palms – and the three of us had a little chat before he went off to do whatever it is film stars do in airports. To celebrate her best ever celeb spot, I bought Lisa another bag of Frazzles.*

There aren't many gentlemen left in the world but, Ant McPartlin, you are one of them.

# Chapter 44

*Apart from taking Lisa to New York, there's one other way I like to celebrate the start of a new year, and that's with a round of Britain's Got Talent auditions. This year, for the third series, we were due to start in Manchester, and we couldn't wait to get going. The previous year's series had been huge, and we were looking forward to getting back to what we laughingly call 'work'.*

*We arrived at our hotel and went down to the bar for a meeting with Nigel Hall and Andrew Llinares, two of the executive producers, Ben Thursby, the series producer and Clair Breen, the producer. We sat down and they told us they had some news – Simon Cowell had decided there was going to be a fourth judge and it was Kelly Brook. It came completely out of the blue to both of us, and for twenty seconds we sat there in complete silence.*

We had two questions: 'Why is there a fourth judge?' and 'Why is it Kelly Brook?' None of them could answer us. Obviously, as hosts of the show, we have to justify that kind of thing to the audience, and no one could give us a good reason why Kelly was on board. The simple answer was that Simon, without talking to anyone, had decided it was a good idea. We didn't agree. Three judges on the show works, it means someone always has the casting vote, and our reaction was 'If it ain't broke, don't fix it.' We were also annoyed we hadn't been consulted – we've always had a good relationship with Simon and there's a mutual respect between the three of us, so this was disappointing. Plus it had all happened so fast and it had a negative effect on the morale of the crew – everyone seemed a bit confused by the whole thing, and most people didn't find out about it till the next day, when the auditions started. We might not have been happy, but we were stuck

347

with it, so we went to the theatre to start the auditions, not knowing what to expect.

When we arrived, we got a call asking us if we wanted to go up to the judges' room and meet Kelly, which we thought was a good idea. We went in there, said hello to Piers, Simon and Amanda, and then welcomed Kelly. She looked nervous, so I told her it was going to be great fun and to just relax and enjoy it. She nodded, then looked at me and said, 'And what do you do on the show?' I looked at Simon, who was sat next to me, he turned to Kelly and said, 'Kelly, you have seen the show, haven't you?' To which she replied, 'Yeah . . . well, bits.' I don't want to sound like an egomaniac, but the last person who said, 'And what do you do?' was the Queen when I met her at the party for ITV's fiftieth anniversary, and that was excusable for two reasons – she's the Queen and I'm still chasing that MBE.

*Once the auditions started, it became clear how confusing it was to have four judges. When two of them said yes to an act and two of them said no, no one knew what to do and it just didn't work. It also made the days much longer: the judges speak for two minutes after each act, which takes enough time when there's three of them, so a fourth judge meant adding two minutes to every audition, and there's usually about forty of them in a day, which means each day was longer by . . . a lot, let's not get bogged down with figures. At the end of the first day, Simon rang me and asked us if we wanted to go up to his hotel room. There was nothing funny going on, he just wanted to talk about the fourth-judge situation. When we got there, the first thing he did was apologize – he said he knew he should have consulted us and was sorry that he hadn't. He was already reconsidering his decision, and it was a good, honest chat and that cleared the air, which was just as well – Simon's such a heavy smoker that it's always good to clear the air when you're anywhere near him.*

We got through the three days in Manchester, still unsure what was going to happen and then, the following week, Ant and me were away for a weekend playing golf between auditions and we got a call from Richard Holloway, one of the executive producers. Richard told us that Kelly wouldn't be coming back. It wasn't that it was anything personal with Kelly; it was just that four judges didn't work. We both felt sorry for her, because she'd been thrown into this whole thing, and it hadn't worked out.

*After a rocky start to the audition tour, things settled down into their usual pattern – boozy nights in the hotel bar and long days by the side of the stage. One of the things people don't know about* Britain's Got Talent *is that, when you see us in the wings, there's usually another curtain and behind it are a few chairs, where we occasionally grab a seat between auditions – sometimes you just need a breather from the talent madness. In an average day by the side of that stage, you're surrounded by dogs, fire breathers, dance troupes and sword swallowers and, after a while, there's only so much 'entertainment' you can take.*

*Initially, that area just had those few chairs and a packet of biscuits, in case we fancied one with a cup of tea or one of my lattes. Over the three series, though, the amount of food in that area has grown and grown and, on the latest tour, there was a huge plastic box containing every kind of snack imaginable – fruit, crisps, sweets, chocolate and biscuits. The box has a sign on it that says, 'Ant and Dec's – keep off', but the last people who actually eat any of that food are us two. There's so much of it round there now that we've christened it the picnic area. There are more chairs too, and people come and sit there at various points in the day. There's Georgie, one of the executive producers, Andy, our writer, Claude who does our make-up – they're the regulars – and then there are various other visitors: Ali will sit there if she's come to the auditions, my missus, who does Stephen Mulhern's make-up on the ITV2 show pops in, and Ali Barker, Simon's assistant, will sometimes put in an appearance. You can hear the rustle of crisps and sweet packets being opened on stage and it has been known for us, in the middle of talking to an act, to have to put our head round the curtain and tell the picnic area to keep the noise down.*

During the auditions, there's usually someone showing round foreign TV producers, who are hoping to make the show in their country and have come to see how it works. On this series, there was a group of Scandinavians being given a guided tour of the backstage area and while we were taking one of our breathers, they came over for a quick chat. They were keen to know about our role, and were scribbling things on a notepad as we answered their questions:

'So you interview all the acts, yess?'
   'Just about, yeah.'
   'And you are always watching all the performances, yess?'
   'Yeah.'
   'I have one final question about ze job you do – why isss there always so much chocolate next to you?'

Every single person in the picnic area looked at the floor, sniggering and embarrassed at the same time.

*There really is food everywhere on* Britain's Got Talent. *We were doing auditions in Birmingham this year, and we'd had a late one in the hotel bar the night before. I'll be honest: I had a stinking hangover and a real craving for a packet of smoky bacon crisps.*

Very wise – salt and vinegar just won't cut it when you've got a hangover; you need a specialist flavour like smoky bacon.

*I'd seen a bag in the picnic area the day before and that had put the idea in my head. Needless to say, it wasn't there the next day – one of the picnickers had no doubt wolfed it down. I asked Georgie because, obviously, as executive producer, one of her main roles is to make sure we have the right flavour crisps, if I'd be able to get a bag, and she went off to speak to someone. Ten minutes later, a runner appeared. 'I'm really sorry,' she said, 'there's none in the building . . . but I'm going out to get coffees anyway, so I can get you a packet?' I told her if she was going out anyway and it was no trouble that would be great.*

   *Half an hour later, the runner came back with a bag of smoky bacon. Not a single bag but a carrier bag with eight individual packets in it. I had one, which did wonders for the hangover, and was as happy as Larry. Ten minutes later, we were in the middle of yet another fascinating interview with a couple of knife throwers who worked at Kwik Fit, when I heard a rustling come from the picnic area. I quickly worked out what was going on – the picnickers had started tucking into the rest of my crisps. I pulled back the curtain, ready to shush them, only to find another lot of smoky bacon crisps being delivered.*

*Little did I know that, when the word got out about the smoky-bacon emergency, a second runner had overheard the request and had gone and bought a load too – another seven packs.*

*It was starting to get embarrassing – I'd only wanted one bag and now most of the city's supply had arrived. We got back to work and got talking to another contestant. In the middle of the interview, I cracked a joke about Simon Cowell's teeth and there was a ripple of laughter from the picnic area. We finished the chat and I turned to the picnickers, ready to revel in the glory of my Cowell's teeth gag. I pulled back the curtain and was struck with déjà vu – there was a third runner emptying another half a dozen packs of smoky bacon into the giant Ant and Dec snack box.*

*I looked like the biggest crisp diva in showbusiness.*

**As you can see, Ant is a very powerful man – when he says he wants something, people everywhere run out and get it.**

*They certainly do. Although, if I knew the response was going to be that good, I would have asked for something a bit more exciting.*

**What? A tube of Pringles?**

*Exactly. Anyway, I felt really guilty – although I did take them home, and I've still got at least six bags in my crisp cupboard. By the time you read this, that may be down to two, or even, depending on my hangover quotient, one.*

*We went straight from auditioning talent to trying to use our own, with a brand-new series of* Saturday Night Takeaway, *and the latest instalment of Ant versus Dec – The Teams. I had a lovely team this year – Jonny Wilkes, Yvette Fielding, Liz McLarnon, Lembit Opik and Brian*

Conley. Jonny is obviously an old friend of ours, and Brian Conley is Alan Conley, the floor manager's brother (the name's a dead giveaway) and we had a great time.

I had a great team too – Nicky Clarke, Edwina Currie, Bobby Davro, Antony Costa and Sinitta – and in case you were wondering: we won the series.

*Don't remind me.*

I think my favourite member of Team Dec was Nicky Clarke – he was a real team player, always prepared to muck in, and great fun. Who am I kidding? He used to cut my hair. For free.

*We were in the O2 arena, where both teams were supposed to be practising for a truck-pull challenge, I was having a chat with Jonny about team tactics and I looked over at Dec to see Nicky Clarke cutting his hair. In the middle of the O2.*

You know what they say – 'It's not what you know, it's who you know.'

*You did have a very good haircut that series, I have to say.*

*Ant versus Dec is a massive part of* Takeaway, *and both teams quickly learnt how much it really does take over your life for the duration of the series. Whether it's learning donkey's names, an* Oliver *or* Grease *medley, or writing and recording a charity single, we take every challenge very seriously and, as we've said before, we get very, very competitive. Even our families get in on the act, and they take it personally when we lose. If I've lost a challenge, I've had lots of consoling chats with my mam on the phone after the show. And considering I still haven't won a series, you'll start to understand how big my phone bill is during a run of* Takeaway.

*Even my nieces and nephew get into it, although not necessarily in the way I'd like them to. The daughters of Lisa's brother Stephen – Courtenay, who is eleven, Morgan, who is six and Bonnie, who is two – leave voice-*

mail messages on my phone after I've lost a challenge in which they shout, 'Loser!'. When it first started, my nephew, Ethan, used to cheer for Team Dec – because they wear blue and my team wear red, which, in his three-year-old mind, is a girl's colour. I made sure I got lots of Team Ant memorabilia and gave it to him, so he knows exactly who to support. I'm glad to say he's now firmly behind my team, so much so that the last time he came down, he spent the whole train journey back up to Newcastle running up and down the carriage shouting, 'Team Ant! Team Ant!' I was very proud of him, even if we did still lose the series.

One other thing I'm very proud of is that, like Dec with his mam and dad, last year, I bought Sarha a house. Unfortunately, her marriage broke up, but the house we got is next door to my mam and Davey and, these days, I have a room at Sarha's when I go home. As we've both said before, the best thing about the success we've enjoyed is that we can help out our families, and that's really important to both of us. It's a one-in-a-million opportunity to get to where we have, and you've got to share with the people who really matter to you.

They didn't run up and down the train carriage screaming, 'Team Dec', but my mam and dad came down to the latest series of *Takeaway* too. Every single time my dad comes to the show, the same thing happens – he always says he's going to sit in the audience and then, five minutes before the show starts, he pipes up with, 'I'll just watch it from here' – and he stays in the green room with a bottle of beer. The Donnelly men love a bottle of beer and a bit of telly.

*My mam and Davey sit in the audience when they come down, and when they come for a drink after the show, all my mam wants to talk about is Andy Collins, our warm-up man. Our post-show chat is always the same:*

'Hi, mam, what did you think of the show?'
 'Wasn't Andy Collins good – he is brilliant.'
 'Yeah, he is – did you like the show?'
 'He did this bit during the adverts with this bald fella, it was hilarious . . .'

*'Did you like Ant versus Dec?'*
*'I think Andy should have his own show, you know.'*
*'Right.'*

The other visitors we had down to that series were Little Ant and Dec. They were about fifteen or sixteen by this point, and I didn't even recognize Little Dec at first. I was standing in the corridor talking to someone after the show and, out of the corner of my eye, I could see a teenage lad standing there listening in. After a couple of glances I worked out it was Dylan, or the artist formerly known as Little Dec. We had a really nice chat and he told me he's trying to get into acting – and even though his first job was to play a miniature version of me, I'm sure he'll make it.

*I had a chat with Little Ant, who couldn't have been more different – he's got no interest in getting into showbusiness, and told me he'd like to be a mechanic. Doing Little Ant and Dec had put him off performing for life. Personally, I blame Bruce Willis.*

Incidentally, they *are* both much taller than us two now, and have much deeper voices. We are now officially Little Ant and Dec. And with that ordinary, everyday tale of a reunion with our miniature selves, we come to the final part of this book.

This epic story, which began with *Geordie Racer* and *Why Don't You?* is almost at an end. We'd love to go on, but we've realized it's quite tricky to write an autobiography that's set in the future.

As we sit here, writing the last few pages, you'll be pleased to know that we're in the same place we've spent most of the last twenty years – a TV studio. In a few hours, we'll go on stage and host the first semi-final of *Britain's Got Talent*. By the time you read this, you'll know who won the series, so in a way you already know something we don't – I hope you feel nice and smug about that.

*Before we go, though, there's just time for the big ending – the bit where we tell you what we've learnt about ourselves and how we've grown as human beings during the making of our life story.*

When we agreed to write this book, we thought it would be great fun, and we were absolutely right. In twenty years, this is the first time we've really stopped and looked back. We're already on to our third career – after acting and pop music, we're now TV presenters. I'm sure that over the course of the last 355 pages, we've missed out things that happened and people who helped us, and we're sorry for that but, strangely, we can't remember every day from the last twenty years.

*One thing that surprised us about the whole experience was that, at times, writing this book felt a bit like having therapy, especially our music career, which was one of the toughest parts. We both know that we wouldn't be where we are today without it but looking back was sometimes difficult. We were doing something that, towards the end, we didn't really believe in and we were working so, so hard for very little reward – either creatively or financially. Having said that, it taught us to be more resilient, it made us who we are today and it led to the career we have now. Plus we got to travel the world, perform to sell out crowds and we've still got some precious memories from those days, so I don't think either of us would change a second of it.*

We've been incredibly fortunate to have enjoyed such a remarkable time. We told you at the start that whenever something memorable happens, we look at each other and say, 'One for the book,' and writing this has shown just how many of those moments we've had in the last twenty years. Throughout it all, we've always had one constant that's kept us sane – each other. In two decades, we've never spent more than two weeks apart. Some people might not understand it, but our friendship is a massive, massive part of where we are today.

*I always think back to the two of us, down at the Quayside, sat in Dec's MG Metro Turbo after we'd left Byker Grove. We were eighteen years old and about to start our music career. We didn't have a clue what the future held for us, how our lives were going to pan out, or whether we'd ever be able to make a living doing the things we loved. Despite all that, we made an agreement — whatever happened, we'd be mates for ever, and neither one of us would ever be on our own out there. Sitting here today, that's as true as it's always been. If it all ended tomorrow, we'd still speak every day, we'd still see each other all the time and we'd still be best mates. And that's something we're both very proud of.*

Without a doubt, the best thing to come out of the last twenty years, the greatest thing we've ever achieved, our biggest success, has been our friendship. And nothing will ever, ever change that.

*Right, fancy a pint?*

I thought you'd never ask . . .

# Thank you

We would like to thank everyone we've worked with over the last twenty years. From those early days on *Byker Grove*, right through to the present day, in front of and behind the camera, you've all played a significant part in our story so far.

And to our families, friends and loved ones, for your unconditional love and support, and for allowing us to believe we could do it, thank you.

We wouldn't be where we are today without you all.

Cheers.

# Picture and lyric permissions